# Ethernet Networks

- Design
- Implementation
- Operation
- Management

**Gilbert Held**

**John Wiley & Sons, Inc.**
New York ■ Chichester ■ Brisbane ■ Toronto ■ Singapore

Associate Publisher:  Katherine Schowalter
Editor:  Paul Farrell
Managing Editor:  Elizabeth Austin
Editorial Production & Design:  Electric Ink, Ltd.

This text is printed on acid-free paper.

*Library of Congress Cataloging-in-Publication Data*

Held, Gilbert
      Ethernet networks : design, implementation, operation, and
   management / by Gilbert Held.
            p.     cm.
      Includes index.
      ISBN 0-471-59717-1 (alk. paper)
         1. Ethernet (Local area network system)      I. Title.
   TK5105.8.E83H45   1994
   004.6'8—dc20                                               93-27492
                                                                   CIP


Printed in the United States of America
10  9  8  7  6  5  4  3  2  1

# Contents

iii

**CHAPTER 4**   Frame Operations                       101

**CHAPTER 5**   Internet Hardware and
Networking Software                                    125

**CHAPTER 6**    Bridge Routing Methods
and Network Performance
Issues                                                 167

# Preface

The objective of this book is to incorporate into one reference source the material that readers will need to understand how Ethernet networks operate, the constraints and performance issues that affect their design and implementation, and how their growth and use can be managed both locally and as part of an enterprise network. I assume that readers have varied backgrounds in communications terms and technology. Thus, to maximize the use of material presented in this book, the first two chapters are designed to provide all readers with a common foundation of knowledge. Those chapters cover networking concepts and network standards—two topics on which material in succeeding chapters is based. Succeeding chapters examine Ethernet concepts: frame operations; network construction; the use of bridges, routers, and gateways; and the management and future of Ethernet networks.

Chapter 3 covers Ethernet concepts. This chapter provides a detailed examination of different types of Ethernet networks, their hardware components, and the general methods by which this type of local area network is constructed. The following chapter examines the composition and flow of Ethernet frames that transport data on the network. This chapter provides a foundation for an in-depth examination of the use of bridges, routers, and gateways, and of the tools and techniques you can use to expand and manage your network.

In writing this book, I have attempted to incorporate practical information you can readily use in designing, operating, implementing, and managing an Ethernet network. Although Ethernet had its origins in the 1970s and can be considered a relatively "old" technology, in reality, the technology is anything but old. Only a few years ago, the standardization of what is now known as 10BASE-T (a twisted-wire version of Ethernet) resulted in a considerable expansion in the use of this type of local area network. In 1993, several vendors were developing prototype hardware for a 100-Mbps Ethernet that would provide an operating rate an order of magnitude higher than that of a 10BASE-T network. This technology, then, is still relatively new, and can be expected to continue to evolve to satisfy the communications requirements of business, government, and academia.

For over 20 years I have worked as a network manager responsible for the design, operation, and management of an enterprise network in which local area networks throughout the United States are interconnected through the use of different wide area network transmission facilities. This challenging position has provided me with the opportunity to obtain practical experience in designing, operating, and interconnecting Ethernet networks to Token-Ring, SNA, and other types of networks—experience which I have attempted to share with you. This book will help you consider the practicality of different types of routing protocols and gateway methods. These and other network design issues are crucial to the efficient and effective expansion of a local Ethernet so that users on that network can access resources on other networks.

As a professional author, I very much value readers' comments. Those comments provide me with feedback necessary to revise future editions so that they better reflect the information requirements of readers. I look forward to receiving your comments, as well as suggestions for information you would like to see in a future edition of this book. You can write to me directly or through my publisher, whose address is on the back cover of this book.

Gilbert Held
Macon, GA

# Acknowledgments

This book would not have been possible without the work of two people whose foresight and pioneering efforts were instrumental in the development of the technology upon which Ethernet is based.

One of the key concepts behind Ethernet—that of allocating the use of a shared channel—can be traced to the pioneering efforts of Dr. Norman Abramson and his colleagues at the University of Hawaii during the early 1970s. The actual development of Ethernet is due to the foresight of Dr. Robert Metcalfe. Working at the Xerox Palo Alto Research Center in Palo Alto, CA, Dr. Metcalfe headed a development team that interconnected over 100 computers on a 1-km cable using a carrier sense multiple access collision detection (CSMA/CD) protocol. In addition to pioneering the technical development of Ethernet, Dr. Metcalfe coined its name, after the luminiferous ether through which electromagnetic radiation was once thought to propagate. I would be remiss if I did not thank Dr. Abramson, Dr. Metcalfe, and their colleagues for their visionary efforts in developing the technology through which millions of people now communicate.

Writing and producing a book about technology requires not only the technology itself, but also the efforts of many individuals. First and foremost, I would like to thank my family for their understanding for the nights and weekends I disappeared to write this book. Once again, I am indebted to Mrs. Carol Ferrell for taking my notes and drawings and converting them into a manuscript. Last, but not least, I would like to thank Paul Farrell, Katherine Schowalter, and the many other persons at John Wiley & Sons who were instrumental in backing this project and in facilitating the conversion of my manuscript into the book you are reading.

# CHAPTER 1

# Introduction to Networking Concepts

One of the most logical assumptions an author can make is that readers will have diverse backgrounds of knowledge and experience. Making this book as valuable as possible to persons with different backgrounds requires an introductory chapter that covers basic networking concepts. Unfortunately, basic concepts for one person may not be the same as basic concepts for another person, which presents an interesting challenge for an author.

To meet this challenge, this book takes two courses of action. First, it assumes that some readers will have limited knowledge about the different types of communications systems available for transporting information, the relationship between wide area networks (WANs) and

1

local area networks (LANs), and the relationships among different types of local area networks. Thus, this introductory chapter was written to provide those readers with a basic level of knowledge concerning these important topics. Secondly, readers who are already familiar with these basic concepts may wish to consult individual chapters separately, rather than reading through the entire book. To satisfy those readers, each chapter was written to be as independent as possible from preceding and succeeding chapters. Thus, readers who are familiar with wide and local area networking concepts, as well as the technical characteristics of LANs, may elect to skim or bypass this chapter. For other readers, information contained in this chapter will provide a level of knowledge that will make succeeding chapters more meaningful.

In this introductory chapter, we will first focus our attention on the key concepts behind the construction of wide area networks and local area networks. In doing so, we will examine each type of network to obtain an understanding of its primary design goal. Next, we will compare and contrast their operations and utilizations to obtain an appreciation for the rationale behind the use of different types of local area networks.

Although this book is about Ethernet networks, there are other types of local area networks that provide a viable data transportation highway for millions of users. By reviewing the technological characteristics of different types of LANs, we will obtain an appreciation for the governing characteristics behind the use of different local area networks. In addition, because many local area networks are connected to other LANs and WANs, we will conclude this chapter by focusing on the technological characteristics of local area networks. This will form a foundation for discussing a variety of Ethernet networking issues in succeeding chapters of this book.

# 1.1 Wide Area Networks

The evolution of wide area networks can be considered to have originated in the mid- to late 1950s, commensurate with the development of the first generation of computers. Based on the use of vacuum tube technology, the first generation of computers were large, power-hungry devices whose placement resulted in a focal point for data processing and the coinage of the term *data center*.

## Computer-Communications Evolution

Originally, access to the computational capability of first-generation computers was through the use of punched cards. After an employee of the organization used a keypunch to create a deck of cards, that card deck was submitted to a window in the data center, typically labeled input/output (I/O) control. An employee behind the window would accept the card deck and complete a form that contained instructions for running the submitted job. The card deck and instructions would then be sent to a person in production control, who would schedule the job and turn it over to operations for execution at a predefined time. Once the job was completed, the card deck and any resulting output would be sent back to I/O control, enabling the job originator to return to the window in the data center to retrieve his or her card deck and the resulting output. With a little bit of luck, programmers might see the results of their efforts on the same day that they submitted their jobs.

Since the computer represented a considerable financial investment for most organizations, it was understandable that these organizations would be receptive to the possibility of extending their computers' accessibility. By the mid-1960s, several computer manufacturers had added remote access capabilities to one or more of their computers.

## Remote Batch Transmission

One method of providing remote access was the installation of a batch terminal at a remote location. That terminal was connected via a telephone company–supplied analog leased line and a pair of modems to the computer in the corporate data center.

The first type of batch terminal developed to communicate with a data center computer contained a card reader, a printer, a serial communications adapter, and hard-wired logic in one common housing. The serial communications adapter converted the parallel bits of each internal byte read from the card reader into a serial data stream for transmission. Similarly, the adapter performed a reverse conversion process, converting a sequence of received serial bits into an appropriate number of parallel bits to represent a character internally within the batch terminal. Since the batch terminal was located remotely from the data center, it was often referred to as a *remote batch terminal*, while the process of transmitting data was referred to as *remote batch transmission*. In addition, the use of a remote terminal as a mechanism for grouping card decks of individual jobs, all executed at the remote data center, resulted in the term *remote job entry terminal* being used as a name for this device.

Figure 1.1 illustrates in schematic form the relationships between a batch terminal, transmission line, modems, and the data center computer. Since the transmission line connects a remote batch terminal in one geographic area to a computer located in a different geographic area, Figure 1.1 represents one of the earliest types of wide area data communications networks.

Paralleling the introduction of remote batch terminals was the development of a series of terminal devices, control

**Figure 1.1** Remote batch transmission. The transmission of data from a remote batch terminal represents one of the first examples of wide area data communications networks.

units, and specialized communications equipment, which resulted in the rapid expansion of interactive computer applications. One of the most prominent collections of products was introduced by the IBM Corporation under the trade name *3270 Information Display System*.

## IBM 3270 Information Display System

The IBM 3270 Information Display System was a term originally used to describe a collection of products ranging from interactive terminals that communicate with a computer, referred to as *display stations*, through several types of control units and communications controllers. Later, through the introduction of additional communications products from IBM and numerous third party vendors and the replacement of previously introduced products, the IBM 3270 Information Display System became more of a networking architecture and strategy rather than a simple collection of products.

First introduced in 1971, the IBM 3270 Information Display System was designed to extend the processing power of the data center computer to remote locations. Since the data center computer typically represented the organization's main computer, the term *mainframe* was coined to refer to a computer with a large processing capability. As the mainframe was primarily designed for data processing, its utilization for supporting communications degraded its performance.

## Communications Controller

To offload communications functions from the mainframe, IBM and other computer manufacturers developed hardware to sample communications lines for incoming bits, group bits into bytes, and pass a group of bytes to the mainframe for processing. This hardware also performed a reverse function for data destined from the mainframe to remote devices. When first introduced, such hardware was designed using fixed logic circuitry, and the resulting device was referred to as a *communications controller*. Later, minicomputers were developed to execute communications programs, with the ability to change the functionality of communications support by the modification of software—a considerable enhancement to the capabilities of this series of products. Because both hard-wired communications controllers and programmed minicomputers performing communications offloaded communications processing from the mainframe, the term *front-end processor* evolved to refer to this category of communications equipment. Although most vendors refer to a minicomputer used to offload communications processing from the mainframe as a front-end processor, IBM has retained the term *communications controller*, even though their fixed logic hardware products were replaced over 20 years ago by programmable minicomputers.

## Control Units

To reduce the number of controller ports required to support terminals, as well as the amount of cabling between controller ports and terminals, IBM developed *poll and select* software to support its 3270 Information Display System. This software enabled the communications controller to transmit messages from one port to one or more terminals in a predefined group of devices. To share the communications controller port, IBM developed a product called a *control unit*, which acts as an interface between the communications controller and a group of terminals.

In general terms, the communications controller transmits a message to the control unit. The control unit examines the terminal address and retransmits the message to the appropriate terminal. Thus, control units are devices that reduce the number of lines required to link display stations to mainframe computers. Both local and remote control units are available; the key differences between them are the method of attachment to the mainframe computer and the use of intermediate devices between the control unit and the mainframe.

Local control units are usually attached to a channel on the mainframe, whereas remote control units are connected to the mainframe's front-end processor, which is also known as a communications controller in the IBM environment. Since a local control unit is within a limited distance of the mainframe, no intermediate communications devices, such as modems, are required to connect a local control unit to the mainframe. In comparison, a remote control unit can be located in another building or in a different city; it normally requires the utilization of intermediate communications devices, such as a pair of modems, for communications to occur between the control unit and the communications controller. The relationship of local and remote control units to display stations, mainframes, and a communications controller is illustrated in Figure 1.2.

## Network Construction

To provide batch and interactive access to the corporate mainframe from remote locations, organizations began to

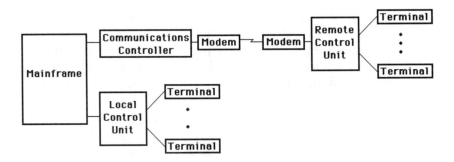

**Figure 1.2**   Relationship of 3270 information display products.

build sophisticated networks. At first, communications equipment such as modems and transmission lines was obtainable only from AT&T and other telephone companies. Beginning in 1974 in the United States with the well-known Carterphone decision, competitive non-telephone company sources for the supply of communications equipment became available. The divestiture of AT&T during the 1980s and the emergence of many local and long-distance communications carriers paved the way for networking personnel to be able to select from among several or even hundreds of vendors for transmission lines and communications equipment.

As organizations began to link additional remote locations to their mainframes, the cost of providing communications began to escalate rapidly. This, in turn, provided the rationale for the development of a series of line-sharing products referred to as *multiplexers* and *concentrators*. Although most organizations operated separate data and voice networks, in the mid-1980s communications carriers began to make available for commercial use high-capacity circuits known as T1 in North America and E1 in Europe. Through the development of T1 and E1 multiplexers, voice, data, and video transmission can share the use of common high-speed circuits. Since the interconnection of corporate offices with communications equipment and facilities normally covers a wide geographical area outside the boundary of one metropolitan area, the resulting network is known as a *wide area network*.

Figure 1.3 shows an example of a wide area network spanning the continental United States. In this example, regional offices in San Francisco and New York are connected with the corporate headquarters, located in Atlanta, via T1 multiplexers and T1 transmission lines operating at 1.544 Mbps. Assuming that each T1 multiplexer is capable of supporting the direct attachment of a *private branch exchange (PBX)*, both voice and data are carried by the T1 circuits between the two regional offices and corporate headquarters. The three T1 circuits can be considered the primary data highway, or *backbone*, of the corporate network.

In addition to the three major corporate sites that require the ability to route voice calls and data between locations, let us assume that the corporation also has three smaller area offices located in Sacramento, CA; Macon, GA; and New Haven, CT. If these locations only require data terminals to access the corporate network for routing to the computers located in San Francisco and New York, one possible mechanism to provide network support is tail circuits. These tail circuits could be used to connect a *statistical time division multiplexer (STDM)* in each area office, each serving a group of data terminals to the nearest T1 multiplexer, using either analog or digital circuits. The T1 multiplexer would then be configured to route data terminal traffic over the corporate backbone portion of the network to its destination.

## Network Characteristics

There are certain characteristics we can associate with wide area networks. First, the WAN is typically designed to con-

**Figure 1.3**   Wide area network example. A wide area network uses telecommunications lines obtained from one or more communications carriers to connect geographically dispersed locations.

nect two or more geographical areas. This connection is accomplished by the lease of transmission facilities from one or more communications vendors. Secondly, most WAN transmission occurs at or under a data rate of 1.544 Mbps or 2.048 Mbps, which are the operating rates of T1 and E1 transmission facilities.

A third characteristic of WANs concerns the regulation of the transmission facilities used for their construction. Most, if not all, transmission facilities marketed by communications carriers are subject to a degree of regulation at the federal, state, and possibly local government levels. Even though we now live in an era of deregulation, carriers must seek approval for many offerings before making new facilities available for use. In addition, although many of the regulatory controls governing the pricing of services were removed, the communications market is still not a truly free market. Thus, regulatory agencies at the federal, state, and local levels still maintain a degree of control over both the offering and pricing of new services and the pricing of existing services.

# 1.2 Local Area Networks

The origin of local area networks can be traced, in part, to IBM terminal equipment introduced in 1974. At that time, IBM introduced a series of terminal devices designed for use in transaction-processing applications for banking and retailing. What was unique about those terminals was their method of connection: a common cable that formed a loop provided a communications path within a localized geographical area. Unfortunately, limitations in the data transfer rate, incompatibility between individual IBM loop systems, and other problems precluded the widespread adoption of this method of networking. The economics of media-sharing and the ability to provide common access to a centralized resource were, however, key advantages, and they resulted in IBM and other vendors investigating the use of different techniques to provide a localized communications capability between different devices. In 1977, Datapoint Corporation began selling its Attached Resource Computer Network (Arcnet), considered by most people to be the first commercial local area networking product. Since then, hundreds of companies have developed local area networking products, and the installed base of terminal devices connected to such networks has increased exponentially. They now number in the tens of millions.

## Comparison to WANs

Local area networks can be distinguished from wide area networks by geographic area of coverage, data transmission and error rates, ownership, government regulation, and data routing—and, in many instances, by the type of information transmitted over the network.

### Geographic Area

The name of each network provides a general indication of the scope of the geographic area in which it can support the interconnection of devices. As its name implies, a LAN is a communications network that covers a relatively small local area. This area can range in scope from a department located on a portion of a floor in an office building, to the corporate staff located on several floors in the building, to several buildings on the campus of a university.

Regardless of the LAN's area of coverage, its geographic boundary will be restricted by the physical transmission limitations of the local area network. These limitations include the cable distance between devices connected to the LAN and the total length of the LAN cable. In comparison, a wide area network can provide communications support to an area ranging in size from a town or city to a state, country, or even a good portion of the entire world. Here, the major factor governing transmission is the availability of communications facilities at different geographic areas that can be interconnected to route data from one location to another.

To better grasp the differences between LANs and WANs, we can view the LAN as being analogous to our local telephone company, while the WAN can be compared to the long-distance communications carrier. Telephone support in different cities is provided by the local telephone company in each city. However, for calls between cities, the local telephone companies must connect to the long distance carrier. Similarly, we can have separate LANs in different cities or within different buildings in the same city; however, to interconnect those LANs we would normally require a wide area network.

## Data Transmission and Error Rates

Two additional areas that differentiate LANs from WANs and explain the physical limitation of the LAN geographic area of coverage are the data transmission rate and error rate for each type of network. LANs normally operate at a low megabit-per-second rate, typically ranging from 4 Mbps to 16 Mbps, with one recently standardized fiber optic–based LAN operating at 100 Mbps. In comparison, the communications facilities used to construct a major portion of most WANs provide a data transmission rate at or under the T1 and E1 data rates of 1.544 Mbps and 2.048 Mbps.

Since LAN cabling is primarily within a building or over a small geographical area, it is relatively safe from natural phenomena, such as thunderstorms and lightning. This safety enables transmission at a relatively high data rate, resulting in a relatively low error rate. In comparison, since wide area networks are based on the use of communications facilities that are much farther apart and always exposed to the elements, they have a much higher probability of being disturbed by changes in the weather, electronic emissions generated by equipment, or such unforeseen problems as construction workers accidentally causing harm to a communications cable. Because of these factors, the error rate on WANs is considerably higher than the rate experienced on LANs. On most WANs you can expect to experience an error rate between 1 in a million and 1 in 10 million ($1 \times 10^6$ to $1 \times 10^7$) bits. In comparison, the error rate on a typical LAN may exceed that range by one or more orders of magnitude, resulting in an error rate from 1 in 10 million to 1 in 100 million bits.

## Ownership

The construction of a wide area network requires the leasing of transmission facilities from one or more communications carriers. Although your organization can elect to purchase or lease communications equipment, the transmission facilities used to connect diverse geographical locations are owned by the communications carrier. In comparison, an organization that installs a local area network normally owns all of the components used to form the network, including the cabling used to form the transmission path between devices.

## Regulation

Since wide area networks require transmission facilities that may cross local, state, and national boundaries, they may be subject to a number of governmental regulations at the local, state, and national levels. Most of those regulations govern the services that communications carriers can provide customers and the rates (*tariff*) they can charge for those services. In comparison, regulations affecting local area networks are primarily in the areas of building codes.

Such codes regulate the type of wiring that can be installed in a building and whether the wiring must run in a conduit.

## Data Routing and Topology

In a local area network, data is routed along a path that defines the network. That path is normally a bus, ring, tree, or star structure, and data always flows on that structure. The topology of a wide area network can be much more complex. In fact, many wide area networks resemble a mesh structure, including equipment to reroute data in the event of communications circuit failure or excessive traffic between two locations. Thus, the data flow on a wide area network can change, while the data flow on a local area network primarily follows a single basic route.

## Type of Information Carried

The last major difference between local and wide area networks is the type of information carried by each network. Many wide area networks support the simultaneous transmission of voice, data, and video information. In comparison, most local area networks are currently limited to carrying data. In addition, although all wide area networks can be expanded to transport voice, data, and video, many local area networks are restricted by design to the transportation of data. Table 1.1 summarizes the similarities and differences between local and wide area networks.

## Utilization Benefits

In its simplest form, a local area network is a cable that provides an electronic highway for the transportation of information to and from different devices connected to the network. Because a LAN provides the capability to route data between devices connected to a common network within a relatively limited distance, numerous benefits can accrue to users of the network. These can include the abil-

**Table 1.1**   Comparing LANs and WANs

| Characteristic | Local Area Network | Wide Area Network |
|---|---|---|
| Geographic area of coverage | Localized to a building, group of buildings, or campus | Can span an area ranging in size from a city to the globe |
| Data transmission rate | Typically 4 Mbps to 16 Mbps, with fiber optic-based networks operating at 100 Mbps | Normally operate at or below T1 and E1 transmission rates of 1.544 Mbps and 2.048 Mbps |
| Error rate | 1 in $10^7$ to 1 in $10^8$ | 1 in $10^6$ to 1 in $10^7$ |
| Ownership | Usually with the implementor | Communications carrier retains ownership of line facilities |
| Data routing | Normally follows fixed route | Switching capability of network allows dynamic alteration of data flow |
| Topology | Usually limited to bus, ring, tree, or star | Virtually unlimited design capability |
| Type of information carried | Primarily data | Voice, data, and video commonly integrated |

ity to share the use of peripheral devices, thus obtaining common access to data files and programs, the ability to communicate with other people on the LAN by electronic mail, and the ability to access the larger processing capability of mainframes or minicomputers through common gateways that link a local area network to larger computer systems. Here, the gateway can be directly cabled to the mainframe or minicomputer if they reside at the same location, or it may be connected remotely via a corporate wide area network.

Peripheral sharing allows network users to access laser printers, CD-ROM systems, and other devices that may be needed only a small portion of the time a workstation is in operation. Thus, users of a LAN can obtain access to resources that would probably be too expensive to justify for each individual workstation user.

The ability to access data files and programs from multiple workstations can substantially reduce the cost of software. In addition, shared access to database information allows network users to obtain access to updated files on a real-time basis.

One popular type of application program used on LANs enables users to transfer messages electronically. Commonly referred to as *electronic mail* or *E-mail*, this type of application program can be used to supplement and, in many cases, eliminate the need for paper memoranda.

For organizations with mainframe or minicomputers, a local area network gateway can provide a common method of access to those computers. Without the use of a LAN gateway, each personal computer requiring access to a mainframe or minicomputer would require a separate method of access. This might increase both the complexity and the cost of providing access.

## Technological Characteristics

Although a local area network is a limited distance transmission system, the variety of options available for constructing such networks is anything but limited. Many of the options available for the construction of local area networks are based on the technological characteristics that govern their operation. These characteristics include different topologies, signaling methods, transmission media, access methods used to transmit data on the network, and the hardware and software required to make the network operate.

## Topology

The *topology* of a local area network is the structure or geometric layout of the cable used to connect stations on the network. Unlike conventional data communications networks, which can be configured in a variety of ways with the addition of hardware and software, most local area networks are designed to operate based upon the interconnection of stations that follow a specific topology. The most common topologies used in LANs include the loop, bus, ring, star, and tree, as illustrated in Figure 1.4.

**Loop**   As previously mentioned in this chapter, IBM introduced a series of transaction-processing terminals in 1974 that communicated through the use of a common controller on a cable formed into a loop. This type of topology is illustrated at the top of Figure 1.4.

Since the controller employed a poll-and-select access method, terminal devices connected to the loop required a minimum of intelligence. Although this reduced the cost of terminals connected to the loop, the controller lacked the intelligence to distribute the data flow evenly among terminals. A lengthy exchange between two terminal devices or between the controller and a terminal would thus tend to bog down this type of network structure. A second problem associated with this network structure was the centralized placement of network control in the con-

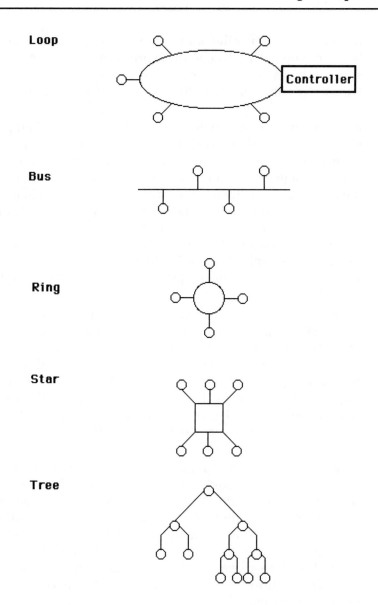

Loop

Bus

Ring

Star

Tree

**Figure 1.4**  LAN topology. The five most common geometric layouts of local area network cabling form a loop, bus, ring, star, or tree structure.

troller. If the controller failed, the entire network would become inoperative. Due to these problems, the use of loop systems is restricted to several niche areas, and they are essentially considered a derivative of a local area network.

**Bus**   In a bus topology structure, a cable is usually laid out as one long branch, onto which other branches are used to connect each station on the network to the main data highway. Although this type of structure permits any station on the network to talk to any other station, rules are required for recovering from such situations as when two stations attempt to communicate at the same time. Later in this chapter, we will examine the relationships among the network topology, the method employed to access the network, and the transmission medium employed in building the network.

**Ring**   In a ring topology, a single cable that forms the main data highway is shaped into a ring. As with the bus topology, branches are used to connect stations to one another via the ring. A ring topology can thus be considered to be a looped bus. Typically, the access method employed in a ring topology requires data to circulate around the ring, with a special set of rules governing when each station connected to the network can transmit data.

**Star**   The fourth major local area network topology is the star structure, illustrated in the lower portion of Figure 1.4. In a star network, each station on the network is connected to a network controller. Then, access from any one station on the network to any other station can be accomplished through the network controller. Here, the network controller functions like a telephone switchboard, since access from one station to another station on the network can occur only through the central device.

**Tree**   A tree network structure represents a complex bus. In this topology, the common point of communications at the top of the structure is known as the *headend*. From the headend, feeder cables radiate outward to nodes, which in turn provide workstations with access to the network. There may also be a feeder cable route to additional nodes, from which workstations gain access to the network.

**Mixed Topologies**　　Some networks are a mixture of topologies. For example, as previously discussed, a tree structure can be viewed as a series of interconnected buses. Another example of the mixture of topologies is a type of Ethernet known as 10BASE-T, which is described in detail in Chapter 3. That network can actually be considered a *star-bus* topology, since up to 16 devices known as *stations* are first connected to a common device known as a *hub*, which in turn can be connected to other hubs to expand the network.

## Comparison of Topologies

Although there are close relationships among the topology of the network, its transmission media, and the method used to access the network, we can examine topology as a separate entity and make several generalized observations. First, in a star network, the failure of the network controller will render the entire network inoperative. This is because all data flow on the network must pass through the network controller. On the positive side, the star topology normally consists of telephone wires routed to a switchboard. A local area network that can use in-place twisted-pair telephone wires in this way is simple to implement and usually very economical.

In a ring network, the failure of any node connected to the ring normally inhibits data flow around the ring. Due to the fact that data travels in a circular path on a ring network, any cable break has the same effect as the failure of the network controller in a star-structured network. Since each network station is connected to the next network station, it is usually easy to install the cable for a ring network. In comparison, a star network may require cabling each section to the network controller if existing telephone wires are not available, and this can result in the installation of very long cable runs.

In a bus-structured network, data is normally transmitted from a single station to all other stations located on the network, with a destination address appended to each transmitted data block. As part of the access protocol, only the station with the destination address in the transmitted data block will respond to the data. This transmission concept means that a break in the bus affects only network stations on one side of the break that wish to communicate with stations on the other side of the break. Thus, unless a network station functioning as the primary network storage device becomes inoperative, a failure in a bus-structured network is usually less serious than a failure in a ring network. However, some local area networks, such as Token-Ring and FDDI, were designed to overcome the effect of certain types of cable failures. Token-Ring networks include a backup path which, when manually placed into operation, may be able to overcome the effect of a cable failure between hubs (referred to as *multistation access units* or *MAUs*). In an FDDI network, a second ring can be activated automatically as part of a self-healing process to overcome the effect of a cable break.

A tree-structured network is similar to a star-structured network in that all signals flow through a common point. In the tree-structured network, the common signal point is the headend. Failure of the headend renders the network inoperative. This network structure requires the transmission of information over relatively long distances. For example, communications between two stations located at opposite ends of the network would require a signal to propagate twice the length of the longest network segment. Due to the propagation delay associated with the transmission of any signal, the use of a tree structure may result in a response time delay for transmissions between the nodes that are most distant from the headend.

Although the first type of Ethernet network was based on a bus-structured topology, other types of Ethernet networks incorporate the use of different topologies. Today you can select bus-based, star-bus, or tree-structured Ethernet networks. Thus, you can select a particular type of Ethernet network to meet a particular topology requirement.

## Signaling Methods

The *signaling method* used by a local area network refers to both the way data is encoded for transmission and the frequency spectrum of the media. To a large degree, the signaling method is related to the use of the frequency spectrum of the media.

## Broadband Versus Baseband

Two signaling methods used by LANs are broadband and baseband. In *broadband signaling*, the bandwidth of the transmission medium is subdivided by frequency to form two or more subchannels, with each subchannel permitting data transfer to occur independently of data transfer on another subchannel. In *baseband signaling*, only one signal is transmitted on the medium at any point in time.

Broadband is more complex than baseband, because it requires information to be transmitted via the modulation of a carrier signal, thus requiring the use of special types of modems, as discussed later in this chapter.

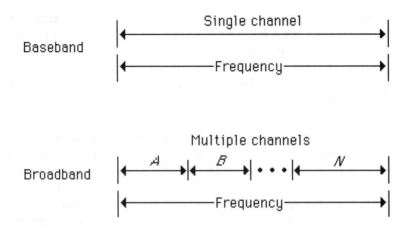

**Figure 1.5**  Baseband versus broadband signaling. In baseband signaling the entire frequency bandwidth is used for one channel. In comparison, in broadband signaling the channel is subdivided by frequency into many subchannels.

Figure 1.5 illustrates the difference between baseband and broadband signaling with respect to channel capacity. It should be noted that although a twisted-pair wire system can be used to transmit both voice and data, the data transmission is baseband, since only one channel is normally used for data. In comparison, a broadband system on coaxial cable can be designed to carry voice and several subchannels of data, as well as fax and video transmission.

**Broadband Signaling**   A broadband local area network uses analog technology, in which high frequency (HF) modems operating at or above 4 KHz place carrier signals onto the transmission medium. The carrier signals are then modified—a process known as *modulation*, which impresses information onto the carrier. Other modems connected to a broadband LAN reconvert the analog signal block into its original digital format—a process known as *demodulation*.

Figure 1.6 illustrates the three primary methods of data encoding used by broadband analog systems: amplitude, frequency, and phase modulation. The most common mod-

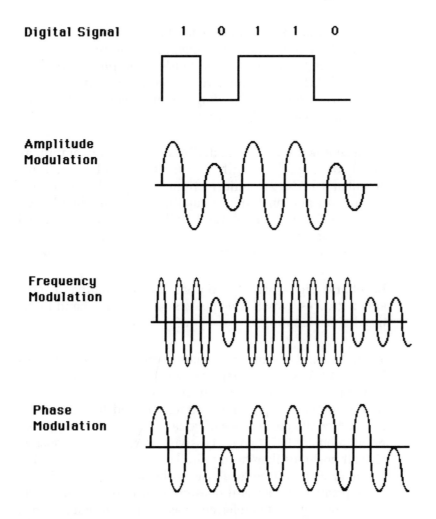

**Figure 1.6**  Modulation methods. Baseband signaling uses amplitude, frequency, or phase modulation, or a combination of modulation techniques to represent digital information.

ulation method used on broadband LANs is *frequency shift keying (FSK)*, in which two different frequencies are used, one to represent a binary 1 and another frequency to represent a binary 0.

Another popular modulation method uses a combination of amplitude and phase shift changes to represent pairs of bits. Referred to as *amplitude modulation phase shift keying (AM PSK)*, this method of analog signaling is also known as *duobinary signaling* because each analog signal represents a pair of digital bits.

Because it is not economically feasible to design amplifiers that boost signal strength to operate in both directions, broadband LANs are unidirectional. To provide a bidirectional information transfer capability, a broadband LAN uses one channel for inbound traffic and another channel for outbound traffic. These channels can be defined by differing frequencies or obtained by the use of a dual cable.

**Baseband Signaling**    In comparison to broadband local area networks, which use analog signaling, baseband LANs use digital signaling to convey information.

To understand the digital signaling methods used by most baseband LANs, let us first review the method of digital signaling used by computers and terminal devices. In that signaling method, a positive voltage is used to represent a binary 1, while the absence of voltage (0 volts) is used to represent a binary 0. If two successive 1 bits occur, two successive bit positions then have a similar positive voltage level or a similar zero voltage level. Since the signal goes from 0 to some positive voltage and does not return to 0 between successive binary 1s, it is referred to as a *unipolar non-return to zero signal (NRZ)*. This signaling technique is illustrated at the top of Figure 1.7.

Unipolar non-return to zero

Manchester coding

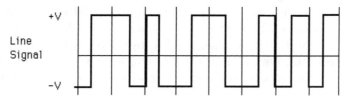

**Figure 1.7**  *Unipolar non-return to zero signaling and Manchester coding. In Manchester coding, a timing transition occurs in the middle of each bit and the line code maintains an equal amount of positive and negative voltage.*

Although unipolar non-return to zero signaling is easy to implement, its use for transmission has several disadvantages. One of the major disadvantages associated with this signaling method involves determining where one bit ends and another begins. Overcoming this problem requires synchronization between a transmitter and receiver by the use of clocking circuitry, which can be relatively expensive.

To overcome the need for clocking, baseband LANs use *Manchester* or *Differential Manchester encoding*. In Manchester encoding, a timing transition always occurs in the middle of each bit, while an equal amount of positive and negative voltage is used to represent each bit. This coding technique provides a good timing signal for clock recovery from received data, due to its timing transitions. In addition, since the Manchester code always maintains an equal amount of positive and negative voltage, it prevents direct current (DC) voltage buildup, enabling repeaters to be spaced farther apart from one another.

The lower portion of Figure 1.7 illustrates an example of Manchester coding. Note that a low to high voltage transition represents a binary 1, while a high to low voltage transition represents a binary 0. Under Differential Manchester encoding, the voltage transition is used only to provide clocking. The encoding of a binary 0 or 1 is represented by the presence or absence of a transition at the beginning of each bit period. Refer to Chapter 4 for specific information concerning Manchester encoding on different types of Ethernet networks.

Along with providing users with a choice of topologies, Ethernet also provides a choice of signaling methods. Although most types of Ethernet networks use baseband signaling, a broadband Ethernet is also available. In fact, you can connect baseband- and broadband-based Ethernet networks to satisfy different organizational requirements. Refer to Chapter 3 for specific information concerning the signaling methods used by different Ethernet networks and the hardware components used to construct and interconnect such networks.

## Transmission Medium

The transmission medium used in a local area network can range in scope from twisted-pair wire, such as is used in conventional telephone lines, to coaxial cable, fiber optic cable, and electromagnetic waves such as those used by FM radio and infrared. Each transmission medium has a number of advantages and disadvantages. The primary differences between media are their cost and ease of installation; the bandwidth of the cable, which may or may not permit several transmission sessions to occur simultaneously; the maximum speed of communications permitted; and the geographic scope of the network that the medium supports.

## Twisted-Pair Wire

In addition to being the most inexpensive medium available for LAN installations, twisted-pair wire is very easy to install. Since this wiring uses the same RJ11 and RJ45 modular connectors as a telephone system, once a wire is cut and a connector fastened, the attachment of the connector to network devices is extremely simple. Normally, a screwdriver and perhaps a pocket knife are the only tools required for the installation of twisted-pair wire. Anyone who has hooked up a pair of speakers to a stereo set has the ability to install this transmission medium.

Although inexpensive and easy to install, unshielded twisted-pair (UTP) wire is very susceptible to noise generated by fluorescent light ballasts and electrical machinery. In addition, a length of twisted-pair wire acts as an antenna. Thus, the longer the wire length, the greater the noise it gathers. At a certain length, the received noise will obliterate the signal, which attenuates or decreases in strength as it propagates along the length of the wire. This noise can affect the error rate of data transmitted on the network, although lead-shielded twisted-pair (STP) cable can be employed to provide the cable with a high degree of immunity to the line noise and enable extended transmission distances.

Since the bandwidth of twisted-pair cable is considerably less than coaxial or fiber optic cable, normally only one signal is transmitted on this cable at a time. As previously explained, this signaling technique is known as baseband signaling and should be compared to the broadband signaling capability of coaxial and fiber optic cable.

Although a twisted-pair wire system can be used to transmit both voice and data, the data transmission is baseband since only one channel is normally used for data. In comparison, a broadband system on coaxial or fiber optic cable can be designed to carry voice and several subchannels of data, as well as fax and video transmission. Other constraints of unshielded twisted-pair wire are the rate at which data can flow on the network and the distance it can flow. Although data rates up to 16 megabits per second (Mbps) can be achieved, normally local area networks employing unshielded twisted-pair wiring operate at a lower data rate. In addition, unshielded twisted-pair systems normally cover a limited distance, measured in terms of several hundred to a few thousand feet, while coaxial and fiber optic cable–based systems may be limited in terms of miles. Extending transmission distances over twisted-pair wire requires both the use of shielded wire and the periodic insertion of repeaters into the cable. A repeater receives a digital signal and then regenerates it, hence it is also known as a *data regenerator*.

### Coaxial Cable

At the center of a coaxial cable is a copper wire, which is covered by an insulator known as a *dielectric*. An overlapping woven copper mesh surrounds the dielectric, and the mesh, in turn, is covered by a protective jacket consisting of polyethylene or aluminum. Figure 1.8 illustrates the composition of a typical coaxial cable; however, it should be noted that over one hundred types of coaxial cable are currently marketed. The key differences between such cables involve the number of conductors contained in the cable, the dielectric employed, and the type of protective

**Figure 1.8**   Coaxial cable.

jacket and material used to provide strength to the cable so it can be pulled through conduits without breaking.

Two basic types of coaxial cable are used in local area networks. The type of cable used is based upon the transmission technique employed: baseband or broadband signaling. Both cable types are much more expensive than twisted-pair wire; however, the greater frequency bandwidth of coaxial cable permits higher data rates than you can obtain over twisted-pair wire.

Normally, 50-ohm coaxial cable is used in baseband networks, while 75-ohm cable is used in broadband networks. The latter coaxial is identical to that used in cable television (CATV) applications, including the coaxial cable used in a home. Data rates on baseband networks using coaxial cable range from 50 to 100 Mbps. With broadband transmissions, data rates up to and including 400 Mbps are obtainable.

A coaxial cable with a polyethylene jacket is normally used for baseband signaling. Data is transmitted from stations on the network to the baseband cable in a digital format, and the connection from each station to the cable is accomplished by the use of a simple coaxial T-connector. Since data on a baseband network travels in a digital form, those signals can be easily regenerated by the use of a device known as a *line driver* or *data regenerator*. The line driver or data regenerator is a low-cost device that is constructed to look for a pulse rise, and upon detecting the occurrence of the rise, it will disregard the entire pulse and regenerate an entirely new pulse. Thus, you can install low-cost line drivers into a baseband coaxial network to extend the distance over which transmission can occur on the cable. Typically, a coaxial cable baseband system can cover an area of several miles, and may contain hundreds to thousands of stations on the network.

Obtaining independent subchannels defined by separate frequencies on coaxial cable broadband transmission requires the translation of the digital signals from workstations into appropriate frequencies. This translation process is accomplished by the use of radio-frequency (RF) modems, which modulate the digital data into analog signals and then convert or demodulate received analog signals into digital signals. Since signals are transmitted at one frequency and received at a different frequency, a headend or frequency translator is also required for broadband transmission on coaxial cable. This device is also known as a *remodulator*, as it simply converts the signals from one subchannel to another subchannel.

The need for modems and frequency translators normally makes broadband transmission more expensive than baseband. Although the ability of broadband to support multiple channels provides it with an aggregate data transmission capacity that exceeds baseband, baseband transmission generally permits a higher per-channel data flow. While this is an important consideration for main-frame-to-mainframe communications when massive amounts of data must be moved, for most personal computer interactive screen sessions and file transfer operations, the speed of either baseband or broadband transmission should be sufficient. This fact may be better understood by comparing the typical transmission rates obtainable on baseband and broadband networks to drive a high-speed dot matrix printer and the differences between the time required to transmit data on the network and the time required to print the data.

Typical transmission speeds on commonly employed baseband and broadband networks range from 2 to 16 Mbps. In comparison, a high-speed dot matrix printer operating at 120 cps would require approximately 200 seconds to print 1 second's worth of data transmitted at 2 Mbps, or 1600 seconds to print 1 second's worth of data transmitted at 16 Mbps.

## Fiber Optic Cable

Fiber optic cable is a transmission medium for light energy, and as such, provides a very high bandwidth, permitting data rates ranging up to billions of bits per second. The fiber optic cable has a thin core of glass or plastic, which is surrounded by a protective shield. Several of these shielded fibers are bundled in a jacket, with a central member of aluminum or steel employed for tensile strength.

Digital data represented by electrical energy must be converted into light energy for transmission on a fiber optic cable. This is normally accomplished by a low-power laser, or through the use of a light-emitting diode and appropriate circuitry. At the receiver, light energy must be reconverted into electrical energy. Normally, a device known as a *photo detector*, as well as appropriate circuitry to regenerate the digital pulses and an amplifier, are used to convert the received light energy into its original digital format.

In addition to their high bandwidth, fiber optic cables offer users several additional advantages over conventional transmission media. Since data travels in the form of light, it is immune to electrical interference and to the building codes that often require expensive conduits for conventional cables. Similarly, fiber optic cable can be installed through areas where the flow of electricity could be dangerous.

Since most fibers provide only a single, unidirectional transmission path, a minimum of two cables is normally required to connect all transmitters to all receivers on a network built using fiber optic cable. Due to the higher cost of fiber optic cable, the dual cable requirement of fiber cables can make them relatively expensive in comparison to other types of cable. In addition, until recently it was very difficult to splice fiber optic cable, and sophisticated equipment and skilled installers were required to implement a fiber optic–based network. Similarly, once this type of network was installed, until recently it was difficult to modify the network.

Currently, the cost of the cable and the degree of difficulty of installation and modification make the utilization of fiber optic–based local area networks impractical for many commercial applications. Today, the primary use of fiber optic cable is to extend the distance between stations on a network or to connect two distant networks to one another. The device used to connect a length of fiber optic cable into the LAN or between LANs is a *fiber optic repeater*. The repeater converts the electrical energy of signals flowing on the LAN into light energy for transmission on the fiber optic cable. At the end of the fiber optic cable, a second repeater converts light energy back into electrical energy.

Another common use of fiber optic cable occurs in constructing FDDI networks. Such networks are now primarily used to function as a backbone data highway, connecting two or more local area networks. Although a few organizations have extended fiber to the desktop, its cost as well as the cost of FDDI components currently precludes its widespread adoption as a replacement for other types of local area networks. With the declining cost of the fiber optic cable and fiber optic components, and the continued introduction of improvements that simplify the installation and modification of networks using this type of cable, the next few years may bring a profound movement toward the utilization of fiber optics throughout local area networks.

Ethernet can be categorized as a network for everyone, because of its support of multiple topologies, signaling methods, and transmission media. In addition to twisted-pair and coaxial cable–based Ethernet networks, you can also extend the transmission distance of such networks by the use of fiber optic cable. Thus, the old adage from a presidential campaign, "a choice not an echo," is highly relevant to Ethernet networks.

## Access Method

If the topology of a local area network can be compared to a data highway, then the access method might be viewed as the set of rules that enable data from one workstation to successfully reach its destination via the data highway. Without such rules, it is quite possible for two messages sent by two different workstations to collide, with the result that neither message reaches its destination. The three access methods primarily employed in local area networks are Carrier-Sense Multiple Access/Collision Detection (CSMA/CD), Carrier-Sense Multiple Access/Collision Avoidance (CSMA/CA) and token passing. Each of these access methods is uniquely structured to address the previously mentioned collision and data-destination problems.

Prior to discussing how access methods work, let us first examine the two basic types of devices that can be attached to a local area network to gain an appreciation for the work that the access method must accomplish.

### Listeners and Talkers

We can categorize each device by its operating mode as being a *listener* or a *talker*. Some devices, like printers, only receive data, and thus operate only as listeners. Other devices, such as personal computers, can either transmit or receive data and are capable of operating in both modes. In a baseband signaling environment where only one channel exists, or on an individual channel on a broadband system, if several talkers wish to communicate at the same time, a collision will occur. Therefore, a scheme must be employed to define when each device can talk and, in the event of a collision, what must be done to keep it from happening again.

For data to reach its destination correctly, each listener must have a unique address, and its network equipment must be designed to respond to a message on the net only when it recognizes its address. The primary goals in the design of an access method are to minimize the potential for data collision, to provide a mechanism for corrective action when data does collide, and to ensure that an addressing scheme is employed to enable messages to reach their destinations.

## Carrier-Sense Multiple Access with Collision Detection (CSMA/CD)

*Carrier-Sense Multiple Access with Collision Detection (CSMA/CD)* can be categorized as a *listen then send* access method. CSMA/CD is one of the earliest developed access techniques and is the technique used in Ethernet. Ethernet is a local area network developed by Xerox Corporation; its technology is now licensed to many companies, and was standardized by the Institute of Electrical and Electronic Engineers (IEEE) under its 802.3 standard.

Under the CSMA/CD concept, when a station has data to send, it first listens to determine whether any other station on the network is talking. The fact that the channel is idle is determined in one of two ways, based on whether the network is broadband or baseband.

In a broadband network, the fact that a channel is idle is determined by *carrier-sensing*, or noting the absence of a carrier tone on the cable.

Ethernet, like other baseband systems, uses one channel for data transmission and does not employ a carrier. Instead, Ethernet encodes data using a Manchester code, in which a timing transition always occurs in the middle of each bit, as illustrated in Figure 1.7. Although Ethernet does not transmit data via a carrier, the continuous transitions of the Manchester code can be considered as equivalent to a carrier signal. Carrier-sensing on a baseband network is thus performed by monitoring the line for activity.

In a CSMA/CD network, if the channel is busy, the station will wait until it becomes idle before transmitting data. Since it is possible for two stations to listen at the same time and discover an idle channel, it is also possible that the two stations could then transmit at the same time. When this situation arises, a collision will occur. Upon sensing that a collision has occurred, a delay scheme will be employed to prevent a repetition of the collision. Typically, each station will use either a randomly generated or a predefined time-out period before attempting to retransmit the message that collided. Since this access method requires hardware capable of detecting the occurrence of a collision, additional circuitry required to perform collision detection adds to the cost of such hardware.

Figure 1.9 illustrates a CSMA/CD bus–based local area network. Each workstation is attached to the transmission medium, such as coaxial cable, by a device known as a *bus interface unit (BIU)*. To obtain an overview of the operation of a CSMA/CD network, assume that station A is currently using the channel and stations C and D wish to transmit. The BIUs connecting stations C and D to the network listen to the channel and note that it is busy. Once station A com-

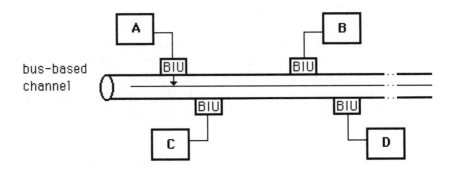

BIU = bus interface unit

**Figure 1.9**  CSMA/CD network operation. In a CSMA/CD network, as the distance between workstations increases, the resulting increase in propagation delay time increases the probability of collisions.

pletes its transmission, stations C and D attempt to gain access to the channel. Since station A's signal takes longer to propagate down the cable to station D than to station C, C's BIU notices that the channel is free slightly before station D's BIU. However, as station C gets ready to transmit, station D now assumes that the channel is free. Within an infinitesimal period of time, C starts transmission, followed by D, resulting in a collision. Here, the collision is a function of the propagation delay of the signal and the distance between two competing stations. CSMA/CD networks therefore work better as the main cable length decreases.

The CSMA/CD access technique is best suited for networks with intermittent transmission, since an increase in traffic volume causes a corresponding increase in the probability of the cable being occupied when a station wishes to talk. In addition, as traffic volume builds under CSMA/CD, throughput may decline, since there will be longer waits to gain access to the network, as well as additional time-outs required to resolve collisions that occur.

## Carrier-Sense Multiple Access with Collision Avoidance (CSMA/CA)

*Carrier-Sense Multiple Access with Collision Avoidance (CSMA/CA)* represents a modified version of the CSMA/CD access technique. Under the CSMA/CA access technique, each of the hardware devices attached to the talkers on the network estimates when a collision is likely to occur and avoids transmission during those times. Since this technique eliminates the requirement for collision-detection hardware, the cost of hardware to implement this access technique is usually less than CSMA/CD hardware. Unfortunately, time delays associated with collision avoidance usually result in a lower level of throughput than that obtainable with CSMA/CD based networks, and this limitation has made CSMA/CA-based networks less popular.

## Token Passing

In a *token-passing* access method, each time the network is turned on, a token is generated. The token, consisting of a unique bit pattern, travels the length of the network, either around a ring or along the length of a bus. When a station on the network has data to transmit, it must first seize a free token. On a Token-Ring network, the token is then transformed to indicate that it is in use. Information is added to produce a frame, which represents data being transmitted from one station to another. During the time the token is in use, other stations on the network remain idle, eliminating the possibility of collisions. Once the transmission is completed, the token is converted back into its original form by the station that transmitted the frame, and becomes available for use by the next station on the network.

Figure 1.10 illustrates the general operation of a token-passing Token-Ring network using a ring topology. Since a station on the network can only transmit when it has a free token, token passing eliminates the requirement for collision detection hardware. Due to the dependence of the network upon the token, the loss of a station can bring the entire network down. To avoid this, the design characteristics of Token-Ring networks include circuitry that automatically removes a failed or failing station from the network, as well as other self-healing features. This additional capability is costly: a Token-Ring adapter card in 1993 was typically priced at two to three times the cost of an Ethernet adapter card.

Due to the variety of transmission media, network structures, and access methods, there is no one best network for all users. Table 1.2 provides a generalized comparison of the advantages and disadvantages of the technical characteristics of local area networks, using the transmission medium as a frame of reference.

workstation with data
to transmit looks for
free token

workstation changes
token into a frame,
adding data to the
frame and its
destination address

destination station
copies data addressed
to it

frame flows back to
originator, which removes
the frame from the
network and generates a
new token

**Figure 1.10**    Token-Ring operation.

**Table 1.2**   Technical characteristics of LANs

| | Transmission medium | | | |
|---|---|---|---|---|
| Characteristic | Twisted-pair wire | Baseband coaxial cable | Baseband coaxial cable | Fiber optic cable |
| Topology | Bus, star, or ring | Bus or ring | Bus or ring | Bus, star, or ring |
| Channels | Single channel | Single channel | Multi-channel | Single, multi-channel |
| Data rate | Normally 2 to 4 Mbps; up to 16 Mbps obtainable | Normally 2 to 10 Mbps; up to 100 Mbps obtainable | Up to 400 Mbps | Up to GMbps |
| Maximum nodes on net | Usually <255 | Usually <1024 | Several thousand | Several thousand |
| Geographical coverage | Thousands of feet | Miles | Tens of miles | Tens of miles |
| Major advantages | Low cost; may be able to use existing wiring | Low cost; simple to install | Supports voice, data, video applications simultaneously | Supports voice, data, video applications simultaneously |
| Major disadvantages | Limited bandwidth; requires conduits; low immunity to noise | Low immunity to noise | High cost; difficult to install; requires RF modems and headend | Cable cost; difficult to splice |

# 1.3 Why Ethernet

After reviewing the basic characteristics of various local area networks, you will note that they present a considerable range of technological characteristics. You can select a network based on its topology, access method, signaling method, and/or support of a particular type of transmission medium. Although there is no one best network for all users, Ethernet represents a diverse mixture of technological characteristics. As such, it provides many more potential networking solutions to user communications requirements than other types of local area networks.

In addition to supporting a broad range of technological characteristics, Ethernet is a declining-cost network. Due to economies of manufacture, as well as the recent support of twisted-pair wiring, Ethernet networks can be established for a fraction of the cost of other types of local area networks. In fact, by early 1994, adapter cards supporting Ethernet that were designed for use in IBM PCs and compatible personal computers could be obtained for under $100. In addition, several notebook and laptop computer vendors were incorporating Ethernet chip sets into their portable computers, enabling computer users who want to transfer files to other computers and printers connected to the network to simply plug their computer into a telephone jack upon returning to the office. Although other types of local area networks, such as FDDI, have recently received more publicity than Ethernet in the trade press, it is worthwhile to note that in terms of adapter board shipments by vendors, Ethernet dominates the market. With over 65 percent of all local area network adapter board shipments and a growth rate exceeding 20 percent per year, we can expect Ethernet networks to continue to be the most viable method of transporting data locally for many years to come.

# CHAPTER **2**

# Networking Standards

Standards can be viewed as the "glue" that binds hardware and software from different vendors so they can operate together. The importance of standards and the work of standards organizations have proved essential for the growth of both local and worldwide communications. In the United States and many other countries, national standards organizations have defined physical and operational characteristics that enable vendors to manufacture equipment compatible with line facilities provided by communications carriers, as well as equipment produced by other vendors. At the international level, standards organizations have promulgated several series of communications-related recommendations. These recommendations, while not mandatory, have become highly influential on a worldwide basis for the development of equipment and facilities, and have been adopted by hundreds of public companies and communications carriers.

In addition to national and international standards, a series of de facto standards has evolved through the licensing of technology among companies. These de facto standards have facilitated, for example, the development of communications software for use on personal computers. Today, communications software can control modems manufactured by hundreds of vendors, since most modems are now constructed to respond to a core set of uniform control codes.

# 2.1 Standards Organizations

In this chapter, we will first focus our attention on two national and two international standards organizations. The national standards organizations we will briefly discuss in this section are the American National Standards Institute (ANSI) and the Institute of Electrical and Electronic Engineers (IEEE). The work of both organizations has been a guiding force in the rapid expansion in the use of local area networks, due to a series of standards they have developed. In the international arena, we will discuss the role of the Consultative Committee for International Telephone and Telegraph (CCITT) and the International Standards Organization (ISO), both of which have developed numerous standards to facilitate the operation of local and wide area networks.

Because of the importance of the ISO's Open Systems Interconnection (OSI) Reference Model and the IEEE's 802 Committee lower layer standards, we will examine each as a separate entity in this chapter. Since we must understand the OSI Reference Model before to examining the effect of the efforts of the IEEE and ANSI upon the lower layers of that model, we will look at the OSI Reference Model before examining the Reference Model layer subdivisions performed by the IEEE and ANSI.

## National Standards Organizations

The two national standards organizations we will briefly discuss are the American National Standards Institute and the Institute of Electrical and Electronic Engineers. In the area of local area networking standards, both ANSI and the IEEE work in conjunction with the ISO to standardize LAN technology.

The ISO delegated the standardization of local area networking technology to ANSI. ANSI, in turn, delegated lower speed LAN standards—defined as operating rates at and below 50 Mbps—to the IEEE. This resulted in ANSI's developing standards for the 100-Mbps Fiber Distributed Data Interface (FDDI), while the IEEE developed standards for Ethernet, Token-Ring, and other local area networks.

Once the IEEE develops and approves a standard, that standard is sent to ANSI for review. If ANSI approves the standard, it is then sent to the ISO. Then, the ISO solicits comments from all member countries to ensure that the standard will work at the international level, resulting in an IEEE- or ANSI-developed standard becoming an ISO standard.

### ANSI

The principal standards forming body in the United States is the American National Standards Institute (ANSI). Located in New York City, this nonprofit, nongovernmental organization was founded in 1918 and functions as the representative of the United States to the ISO.

ANSI standards are developed through the work of its approximately 300 Standards Committees, and from the efforts of associated groups such as the Electronic Industry Association (EIA). Recognizing the importance of the computer industry, ANSI established its X3 Standards Committee in 1960. That committee consists of 25 Technical Committees, each assigned to develop standards for a specific technical area. One of those Technical Committees is the X3S3 committee, more formally known as the Data Communications Technical Committee. This committee was responsible for the ANSI X3T9.5 standard that governs FDDI operations, and that is now recognized as the ISO 9314 standard.

## IEEE

The Institute of Electrical and Electronic Engineers (IEEE) is a US-based engineering society that is very active in the development of data communications standards. In fact, the most prominent developer of local area networking standards is the IEEE, whose subcommittee 802 began its work in 1980 before they had even established a viable market for the technology.

The IEEE Project 802 efforts are concentrated upon the physical interface between network devices and the procedures and functions required to establish, maintain, and release connections among them. These procedures include defining data formats, error control procedures, and other control activities governing the flow of information. This focus of the IEEE actually represents the lowest two layers of the ISO model, physical and link, which are discussed later in this chapter.

## International Standards Organizations

Two important international standards organizations are the Consultative Committee for International Telephone and Telegraph (CCITT) and the International Standards Organization (ISO). The CCITT can be considered a governmental body, because it functions under the auspices of an agency of the United Nations. Although the ISO is a nongovernmental agency, its work in the field of data communications is well recognized.

### CCITT

The Consultative Committee for International Telephone and Telegraph (CCITT) is a group within the International Telecommunications Union (ITU), the latter of which is a specialized agency of the United Nations headquartered in Geneva, Switzerland. The CCITT has direct responsibility for developing data communications standards and consists of 15 Study Groups, each with a specific area of responsibility.

The work of the CCITT is performed on a four-year cycle known as a Study Period. At the conclusion of each Study Period, a Plenary Session occurs. During the Plenary Session, the work of the CCITT during the previous four years is reviewed, proposed recommendations are considered for adoption, and items to be investigated during the next four-year cycle are considered.

The CCITT's Ninth Plenary Session met in 1988 and its tenth session occurred during 1992. Although approval of recommended standards is not intended to be mandatory, CCITT recommendations have the effect of law in some Western European countries, and many of its recommendations have been adopted by communications carriers and vendors in the United States. Perhaps the best-known set of CCITT recommendations is its V-series, which describes the operation of many different modem features—for example, data compression and transmission error detection and correction.

### ISO

The International Standards Organization (ISO) is a nongovernmental entity that has consultative status within the UN Economic and Social Council. The goal of the ISO is to "promote the development of standards in the world with a view to facilitating international exchange of goods and services."

The membership of the ISO consists of the national standards organizations of most countries. There are approximately 100 countries currently participating in its work.

Perhaps the most notable achievement of the ISO in the field of communications is its development of the seven-layer Open Systems Interconnection (OSI) Reference Model.

# 2.2 The ISO Reference Model

The International Standards Organization (ISO) established a framework for standardizing communications systems called the Open Systems Interconnection (OSI) Reference Model. The OSI architecture defines the communications process as a set of seven layers, with specific functions isolated and associated with each layer. Each layer, as illustrated in Figure 2.1, covers lower layer processes, effectively isolating them from higher layer functions. In this way, each layer performs a set of functions necessary to provide a set of services to the layer above it.

| | |
|---|---|
| Application | Layer 7 |
| Presentation | Layer 6 |
| Session | Layer 5 |
| Transport | Layer 4 |
| Network | Layer 3 |
| Data Link | Layer 2 |
| Physical | Layer 1 |

**Figure 2.1**  ISO reference model.

Layer isolation permits the characteristics of a given layer to change without impacting the remainder of the model, provided that the supporting services remain the same. One major advantage of this layered approach is that users can mix and match OSI conforming communications products, and thus tailor their communications systems to satisfy particular networking requirements.

The OSI Reference Model, while not completely viable with many current network architectures, offers the potential to connect networks directly, while using equipment from different vendors. This interconnectivity potential will be of substantial benefit to both users and vendors. For users, interconnectivity will remove the shackles that in many instances tie them to a particular vendor. For vendors, the ability to easily interconnect their products will provide them with access to a larger market. The importance of the OSI model is such that it has been adopted by the CCITT as Recommendation X.200.

## Layered Architecture

As previously discussed, the OSI Reference Model is based on the establishment of a layered, or partitioned, architecture. This partioning effort is derived from the scientific process, in which complex problems are subdivided into several simpler tasks.

As a result of the application of a partitioning approach to communications network architecture, the communications process was subdivided into seven distinct partitions, called *layers*. Each layer consists of a set of functions designed to provide a defined series of services. For example, the functions associated with the physical connection of equipment to a network are referred to as the *physical layer*.

With the exception of layers 1 and 7, each layer is bounded by the layers above and below it. Layer 1, the physical layer, is bound below by the interconnecting medium over which transmission flows, while layer 7 is the upper layer and has no upper boundary. Within each layer is a group of functions that provide a set of defined services to the layer above it, resulting in layer $n$ using the services of layer $n-1$. Thus, the design of a layered architecture enables the characteristics of a particular layer to change without affecting the rest of the system, assuming that the services provided by the layer do not change.

## OSI Layers

The best way to gain an understanding of the OSI layers is to examine a network structure that illustrates the components of a typical wide area network. Figure 2.2 illustrates a network structure that is typical only in the sense that it will be used for a discussion of the components upon which networks are constructed.

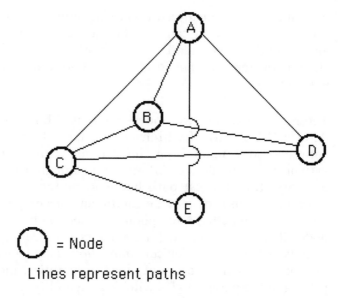

**Figure 2.2**   Generic network structure.

The circles in Figure 2.2 represent nodes, which are points where data enters or exits a network or is switched between two networks connected by one or more paths. Nodes are connected to other nodes via communications cables or circuits, and can be established on any type of communications medium, such as cable, microwave, or radio.

From a physical perspective, a node can be based on any of several types of computers, including a personal computer, minicomputer, mainframe computer, or specialized computer, such as a front-end processor. Connections to network nodes into a wide area network can occur via terminals directly connected to computers, terminals connected to a node via one or more intermediate communications devices, or paths linking one network to another network. In fact, a workstation on an Ethernet local area network that provides access into a wide area network can be considered a network node. In this situation, the workstation can be a bridge, router, or gateway, and provides a connectivity mechanism between other stations on the Ethernet local area network and the wide area network.

The routes between two nodes—such as C-E-A, C-D-A, C-A, and C-B-A, all of which can be used to route data between nodes A and C—are *information paths*. Due to the variability in the flow of information through a wide area network, the shortest path between nodes may not be available for use, or may be inefficient in comparison to other possible paths. A temporary connection between two nodes that is based on such parameters as current network activity is known as a *logical connection*. This logical connection represents the use of physical facilities, including paths and temporary node-switching capability.

The major functions of each of the seven OSI layers are described in the following seven paragraphs.

## Layer 1—The Physical Layer

At the lowest or most basic level, the physical layer (level 1) is a set of rules that specifies the electrical and physical connection between devices. This level specifies the cable connections and the electrical rules necessary to transfer data between devices. Typically, the physical link corresponds to previously established interface standards, such as the RS-232/V.24 interface. This interface governs the attachment of data terminal equipment, such as the serial port of personal computers, to data communications equipment, such as modems, at data rates below 19.2 Kbps.

## Layer 2—The Data Link Layer

The next layer, which is known as the data link layer (level 2), denotes how a device gains access to the medium specified in the physical layer. It also defines data formats, including the framing of data within transmitted messages, error control procedures, and other link control activities. Because it defines data formats, including procedures to correct transmission errors, this layer becomes responsible for the reliable delivery of information. Two examples of data link control protocols that can reside in this layer are IBM's Binary Synchronous Communications (BSC) and the CCITT's High-level Data Link Control (HDLC).

Since the development of OSI layers was originally targeted toward wide area networking, its applicability to local area networks required a degree of modification. Under the IEEE 802 standards, the data link layer was divided into two sublayers: *logical link control (LLC)* and *media access control (MAC)*. The LLC layer is responsible for generating and interpreting commands that control the flow of data and perform recovery operations in the event of errors. In comparison, the MAC layer is responsible for providing access to the local area network, which enables a station on the network to transmit information. Later in this chapter, we will examine the IEEE 802 subdivision of the data link layer into LLC and MAC sublayers, as well as the operation of each layer.

## Layer 3—The Network Layer

The network layer (level 3) is responsible for arranging a logical connection between the source and destination nodes on the network. This responsibility includes the selection and management of a route for the flow of information between source and destination, based on the available data paths in the network. Services provided by this layer are associated with the movement of data packets through a network, including addressing, routing, switching, sequencing, and flow control procedures. In a complex network, the source and destination may not be directly connected by a single path, but instead require a path that consists of many subpaths. Thus, routing data through the network onto the correct paths is an important feature of this layer.

Several protocols have been defined for layer 3, including the CCITT X.25 packet switching protocol and the CCITT X.75 gateway protocol. X.25 governs the flow of information through a packet network, while X.75 governs the flow of information between packet networks.

### Layer 4—The Transport Layer

The transport layer (level 4) is responsible for guaranteeing that the transfer of information occurs correctly after a route has been established through the network by the network level protocol. Thus, the primary function of this layer is to control the communications session between network nodes once a path has been established by the network control layer. Error control, sequence checking, and other end-to-end data reliability factors are the primary concern of this layer, and they enable the transport layer to provide a reliable end-to-end data transfer capability.

### Layer 5—The Session Layer

The session layer (level 5) provides a set of rules for establishing and terminating data streams between nodes in a network. The services that this session layer can provide include establishing and terminating node connections, message flow control, dialogue control, and end-to-end data control.

### Layer 6—The Presentation Layer

The presentation layer (level 6) services are concerned with data transformation, formatting, and syntax. One of the primary functions performed by the presentation layer is the conversion of transmitted data into a display format appropriate for a receiving device. This can include any necessary conversion between ASCII and EBCDIC codes. Data encryption/decryption and data compression/decompression are additional examples of the data transformation that can be handled by this layer.

## Layer 7—The Application Layer

Finally, the application layer (level 7) acts as a window through which the application gains access to all of the services provided by the model. Examples of functions performed at this level include file transfers, resource sharing, and database access. While the first four layers are fairly well defined, the top three layers may vary considerably, depending upon the network used. Figure 2.3 illus-

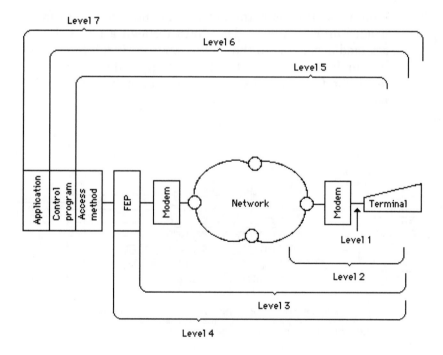

**Figure 2.3** OSI model schematic.

trates the OSI model in schematic format, showing the various levels of the model with respect to a terminal device, such as a personal computer accessing an application on a host computer system.

## Data Flow

As data flows within an ISO network, each layer appends appropriate heading information to frames of information flowing within the network, while removing the heading information added by a lower layer. In this manner, layer *n* interacts with layer *n–1* as data flows through an ISO network.

Figure 2.4 illustrates the appending and removal of frame header information as data flows through a network constructed according to the ISO Reference Model. Since each higher level removes the header appended by a lower level, the frame traversing the network arrives in its original form at its destination.

Legend:
DH, NH, TH, SH, PH and AH are appropriate headers Data Link, Network Header, Transport Header, Session Header, Presentation Header and Application Header added to data as the data flows through an ISO Reference Model network

**Figure 2.4**   Appending and removal of frame header information.

As you will surmise from the previous illustrations, the ISO Reference Model is designed to simplify the construction of data networks. This simplification is due to the eventual standardization of methods and procedures to append appropriate heading information to frames flowing through a network, permitting data to be routed to its appropriate destination following a uniform procedure.

# 2.3 IEEE 802 Standards

The Institute of Electrical and Electronic Engineers (IEEE) Committee 802 was formed at the beginning of the 1980s to develop standards for emerging technologies. The IEEE fostered the development of local area networking equipment from different vendors that can work together. In addition, IEEE LAN standards provided a common design goal for vendors to access a relatively larger market than if proprietary equipment were developed. This, in turn, enabled economies of scale to lower the cost of products developed for larger markets.

## 802 Committees

Table 2.1 lists the organization of IEEE 802 committees involved in local area networks. In examining the lists of committees in Table 2.1, it is apparent that the IEEE early on noted that a number of different systems would be required to satisfy the requirements of a diverse end-user population. Accordingly, the IEEE adopted the CSMA/CD, Token Bus, and Token Ring as standards 802.3, 802.4, and 802.5, respectively.

The IEEE Committee 802 published draft standards for CSMA/CD and Token Bus local area networks in 1982.

**Table 2.1**    IEEE Series 802 committees

| | |
|---|---|
| 802.1 | High Level Interface |
| 802.2 | Logical Link Control |
| 802.3 | CSMA/CD |
| 802.4 | Token-Passing Bus |
| 802.5 | Token-Passing Ring |
| 802.6 | Metropolitan Area Networks |
| 802.7 | Broadband Technical Advisory Group |
| 802.8 | Fiber Optic Technical Advisory Group |
| 802.9 | Integrated Voice and Data Networks |
| 802.10 | Network Security |
| 802.11 | Wireless LANs |

Standard 802.3, which describes a baseband CSMA/CD network similar to Ethernet, was published in 1983. Since then, several addenda to the 802.3 standard have been adopted to govern the operation of CSMA/CD on different types of media. Those addenda include 10BASE-2, which defines a 10-Mbps baseband network operating on thin coaxial cable; 1BASE-5, which defines a 1-Mbps baseband network operating on twisted-pair; 10BASE-T, which defines a 10-Mbps baseband network operating on twisted-pair; and 10BROAD-36, which defines a broadband 10-Mbps network that operates on thick coaxial cable.

The next standard published by the IEEE was 802.4, which describes a token-passing bus–oriented network for both baseband and broadband transmission. This standard is similar to the Manufacturing Automation Protocol (MAP) standard developed by General Motors.

The third LAN standard published by the IEEE was based on IBM's specifications for its Token-Ring network. Known as the 802.5 standard, it defines the operation of token-ring networks on shielded twisted-pair cable at data rates of 1 and 4 Mbps. That standard will more than likely be modified, by the time you read this book, to acknowledge three IBM enhancements to Token-Ring network operations. These enhancements include the 16-Mbps operating rate, the ability to release a token early on a 16-Mbps network, and a bridge routing protocol known as *source routing*.

## Data Link Subdivision

One of the more interesting facets of IEEE 802 standards is the subdivision of the ISO Open System Interconnection Model's data link layer into two sublayers: logical link control and medium access control. Figure 2.5 illustrates the relationship between IEEE 802 local area network standards and the first three layers of the OSI Reference Model.

The separation of the data link layer into two entities provides a mechanism for regulating access to the medium that is independent of the method for establishing, maintaining and terminating the logical link between workstations. The method of regulating access to the medium is defined by the medium access control portion of each local area network standard. This enables the logical link control standard to be applicable to each type of network.

### Medium Access Control

The medium access control sublayer is responsible for controlling access to the network. To accomplish this, it must ensure that two or more stations do not attempt to transmit data onto the network simultaneously. For Ethernet networks, this is accomplished through the use of the CSMA/CD access protocol.

**Figure 2.5**   Relationship between IEEE standards and the OSI Reference Model.

In addition to network access control, the MAC sublayer is responsible for the orderly movement of data onto and off of the network. To accomplish this, the MAC sublayer is responsible for MAC addressing, frame type recognition, frame control, frame copying, and similar frame-related functions.

The MAC address represents the physical address of each station connected to the network. That address can belong to a single station, can represent a predefined group of stations (group address), or can represent all stations on the network (broadcast address). Through MAC addresses, the physical source and destination of frames are identified.

Frame type recognition enables the type and format of a frame to be recognized. To ensure that frames can be processed accurately, frame control prefixes each frame with a preamble, which consists of a predefined sequence of bits. In addition, a frame check sequence (FCS) is computed by applying an algorithm to the contents of the frame; the results of the operation are placed into the frame. This enables a receiving station to perform a similar operation. Then, if the locally computed FCS matches the FCS carried in the frame, the frame is considered to have arrived without error.

Once a frame arrives at a station that has the same address as the destination address in the frame, that station must copy the frame. The copying operation moves the contents of the frame into a buffer area in an Ethernet adapter card. The adapter card removes certain fields from the frame, such as the preamble and start of frame delimiter, and passes the information field into a predefined memory area in the station into which the adapter card is inserted.

Refer to Chapter 4 for detailed information concerning Ethernet frame formats, as well as information concerning how the MAC layer controls the transmission and reception of data on an Ethernet local area network.

## Logical Link Control

Logical link control frames are used to provide a link between network layer protocols and media access control. This linkage is accomplished through the use of Service Access Points (SAPs), which operate in much the same way as a mailbox. That is, both network layer protocols and logical link control have access to SAPs and can leave messages for each other in them.

Like a mailbox in a post office, each SAP has a distinct address. For the logical link control, a SAP represents the location of a network layer process, such as the location of an application within a workstation as viewed from the network. From the network layer perspective, a SAP represents the place to leave messages concerning the network services requested by an application.

LLC frames contain two special address fields, known as the Destination Services Access Point and the Source Services Access Point. The Destination Services Access Point (DSAP) is one byte in length and specifies the receiving network layer process. The Source Service Access Point (SSAP) is also one byte in length. The SSAP specifies the sending network layer process. Both DSAP and SSAP addresses are assigned by the IEEE. Refer to Chapter 4 for detailed information concerning LLC frame formats and data flow.

# CHAPTER 3

# Ethernet Networks

From the title of this chapter, it is apparent that there is more than one type of Ethernet network. From a network access perspective, there is actually only one Ethernet network. However, the CSMA/CD access protocol used by Ethernet, as well as its general frame format and most of its operating characteristics, were used by the Institute of Electrical and Electronic Engineers (IEEE) to develop a series of Ethernet type networks under the IEEE 802.3 umbrella. Thus, this chapter will first focus on the different types of Ethernet networks by closely examining the components and operating characteristics of Ethernet and then comparing its major features to the different networks defined by the IEEE 802.3 standard. Once this is accomplished, we will focus our attention on the wiring, topology, and hardware components associated with each type of IEEE 802.3 Ethernet network. This will enable us to examine the construction of several types of 802.3 networks using a variety of hardware devices and then illustrate how those networks can be connected to one another—a process referred to as *internetworking*.

# 3.1 Ethernet

One of the key concepts behind Ethernet—that of allocating the use of a shared channel—can be traced to the pioneering efforts of Dr. Norman Abramson and his colleagues at the University of Hawaii during the early 1970s. Using a ground-based radio broadcasting system to connect different locations through the use of a shared channel, Abramson and his colleagues developed the concept of listening to the channel prior to transmission, transmitting a frame of information, listening to the channel output to determine whether a collision occurred, and, if it did, waiting a random period of time prior to retransmission. The resulting University of Hawaii ground-based radio broadcasting system, called ALOHA, formed the basis for the development of numerous channel contention systems, including Ethernet. In addition, the subdivision of transmission into frames of data was the pioneering work in the development of packet switching networks. Thus, Norman Abramson and his colleagues can be considered the forefathers of two of the most important communications technologies, contention networks and packet switching networks.

## Evolution

The actual development of Ethernet occurred at the Xerox Palo Alto Research Center (PARC) in Palo Alto, CA. A development team headed by Dr. Robert Metcalfe had to connect over 100 computers on a 1-km cable. The resulting system, which operated at 2.94 Mbps using the CSMA/CD access protocol, was referred to as "Ethernet" in a memorandum authored by Metcalfe. He named it after the luminiferous ether through which electromagnetic radiation was once thought to propagate.

During its progression from a research based network into a manufactured product, Ethernet suffered several identify crises. During the 1970s, it endured such temporary names as the "Alto Aloha Network" and the "Xerox Wire." After reverting to the original name, Xerox decided, quite wisely, that the establishment of Ethernet as an industry standard for local area networks would be expedited by an alliance with other vendors. A resulting alliance with Digital Equipment Corporation and Intel Corporation resulted in the development of a 10-Mbps Ethernet network. It also provided Ethernet with a significant advantage over Datapoint's ARCNet and Wang Laboratories' Wangnet, proprietary local area networks that were the main competitors to Ethernet during the 1970s.

## Network Components

The 10-Mbps Ethernet network standard originally developed by Xerox, Digital Equipment Corporation, and Intel was based on the use of five hardware components. Those components include a coaxial cable, a cable tap, a transceiver, a transceiver cable, and an interface board (also known as an Ethernet controller). Figure 3.1 illustrates the relationships among Ethernet components.

### Coaxial Cable

One of the problems faced by the designers of Ethernet was the selection of an appropriate medium. Although twisted-

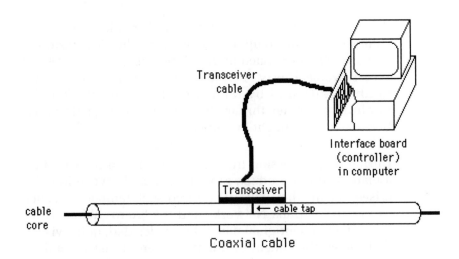

**Figure 3.1** Ethernet hardware components. When thick coaxial cable is used for the bus, an Ethernet cable connection is made with a transceiver cable and a transceiver tapped into the cable.

pair wire is relatively inexpensive and easy to use, the short distances between twists serve as an antenna for receiving electromagnetic and radio frequency interference in the form of noise. Thus, the use of twisted-pair cable restricts the network to relatively short distances. Coaxial cable, however, has a dielectric shielding the conductor. As long as the ends of the cable are terminated, coaxial cable can transmit over greater distances than twisted-pair cable. Thus, the initial selection for Ethernet transmission medium was coaxial cable.

There are two types of coaxial cable that can be used to form the main Ethernet bus. The first type of coaxial cable specified for Ethernet was a relatively thick 50-ohm cable, which is normally colored yellow and is commonly referred to as "thick" Ethernet. This cable has a marking every 2.5 meters to indicate where a tap should occur, if one is required to connect a station to the main cable at a particular location. These markings represent the minimum distance one tap must be separated from another on an Ethernet network.

A second type of coaxial cable used with Ethernet is smaller and more flexible; however, it is capable of providing a transmission distance only one-third of that obtainable on thick cable. This lighter and more flexible cable is referred to as "thin" Ethernet, and also has an impedance of 50 ohms.

Two of the major advantages of thin Ethernet over thick cable are its cost and its use of BNC connectors. Thin Ethernet is significantly less expensive than thick Ethernet. Thick Ethernet requires connections via taps, whereas the use of thin Ethernet permits connections to the bus via industry standard BNC connectors that form T-junctions.

## Transceiver and Transceiver Cable

*Transceiver* is a shortened form of *transmitter-receiver*. This device contains electronics to transmit and receive signals carried by the coaxial cable. The transceiver contains a tap that, when pushed against the coaxial cable, penetrates the cable and makes contact with the core of the cable. In books and technical literature the transceiver, its tap, and its housing are often referred to as the *medium attachment unit (MAU)*.

The transceiver is responsible for carrier detection and collision detection. When a collision is detected during a transmission, the transceiver places a special signal, known as a *jam*, on the cable. This signal, described in Chapter 4, is of sufficient duration to propagate down the network bus and inform all of the other transceivers attached to the bus node that a collision has occurred.

The cable that connects the interface board to the transceiver is known as the *transceiver cable*. This cable can be up to 50 meters (165 feet) in length, and contains five individually shielded twisted pairs. Two pairs are used for data in and data out, and two pairs are used for control signals in and out. The remaining pair, which is not always used, permits the power from the computer in which the interface board is inserted to power the transceiver.

Since collision detection is a critical part of the CSMA/CD access protocol, the original version of Ethernet was modified to inform the interface board that the transceiver collision circuitry is operational. This modification resulted in each transceiver's sending a signal to the attached interface board after every transmission, informing the board that the transceiver's collision circuitry is operational. This signal is sent by the transceiver over the collision pair of the transceiver cable, and must start within 0.6 microseconds after each frame is transmitted. The duration of the signal can vary between 0.5 and 1.5 microseconds. Known as the *Signal Quality Error* and also referred to as the *SQE* or *heartbeat*, this signal is supported by Ethernet Version 2.0, published as a standard in 1982, and by the IEEE 802.3 standard.

### Interface Board

The *interface board*, or *network interface card (NIC)*, is inserted into an expansion slot within a computer, and is responsible for transmitting frames to and receiving frames from the transceiver. This board contains several special chips, including a controller chip that assembles data into an Ethernet frame and computes the cyclic redundancy check used for error detection. Thus, this board is also referred to as an *Ethernet controller*.

Most Ethernet interface boards contain a DB-15 connector for connecting the board to the transceiver. Once thin Ethernet cabling became popular, many manufacturers made their interface boards with both DB-15 and BNC connectors. The latter was used to permit the interface board to be connected to a thin Ethernet cable through the use of a T-connector. Figure 3.2 illustrates the rear panel of a network interface card containing both DB-15 and BNC connectors.

## Cabling Restrictions

Under the Ethernet standard developed by Xerox, Digital Equipment Corporation, and Intel Corporation, a thick coaxial cable is permitted a maximum length of 500 meters

**Figure 3.2**  Ethernet interface board connectors. Many Ethernet interface boards (network interface cards) contain both DB-15 and BNC connectors to support the use of either thick or thin coaxial cable.

(1640 feet). Multiple cable segments can be joined together through the use of repeaters; however, the maximum cable distance between two transceivers is limited to 2.5 km (8200 feet), and no more than four repeaters can be traversed on any path between transceivers.

Each thick trunk cable segment must be terminated with what is known as an *N-series connector* on each end of the cable. The terminator "terminates" the network and blocks electrical interference from flowing onto what would otherwise be exposed cable. One N-series connector also serves as a ground, when used with an attached grounding wire that can be connected to the middle screw of a dual AC electrical power outlet.

Figure 3.3 illustrates a thick Ethernet cable segment after an installer fastened N-series plugs to each cable end. This is normally accomplished after the desired length of coaxial cable is routed to form the required network bus. Next, an N-series terminator connector is fastened onto one N-series plug, while an N-series terminator with ground wire is fastened onto the N-series plug at the opposite end of the cable segment.

In addition, as previously mentioned, attachments to the common bus must be separated by multiples of 2.5 meters. The latter cabling restriction prevents reflections caused by taps in the main cable from adding up in phase and being mistaken by one transceiver for another's transmission. For the total network, up to 1024 attachments are allowed, including all cable sections connected through the use of repeaters; however, no more than 100 transceivers can be on any one cable segment.

## Repeaters

A repeater is a device that receives, amplifies, and retransmits signals. Since a repeater operates at the physical layer,

Thick Ethernet Cable Segment

N-Series
Plugs

N-Series
Jacks

N-Series
Terminator

N-Series
Terminator
With Ground Wire

**Figure 3.3**   Each Ethernet thick coaxial cable segment has N-series plugs on each end. They are terminated through the use of N-series terminators, one of which contains a ground wire or ground wire connection.

it is transparent to data and simply regenerates signals. Figure 3.4 illustrates the use of a repeater to connect two Ethernet cable segments. As indicated, a transceiver is taped to each cable segment to be connected, and the repeater is cabled to the transceiver. When used to connect cable segments, a repeater counts as one station on each connected segment. Thus, a segment capable of supporting up to 100 stations can support only 99 additional stations when a repeater is used to connect cable segments. Although not shown, each cable segment is terminated at each end with an N-series terminator and grounded at one end of one segment.

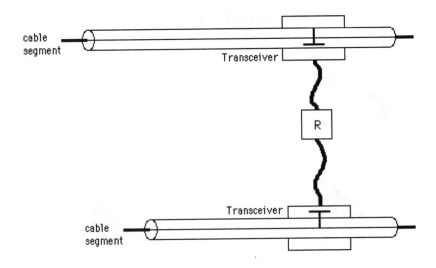

Legend: R = repeater

**Figure 3.4** Using a repeater. Cable segments can be joined together by a repeater to expand the network. The repeater counts as a station on each cable segment.

# 3.2 IEEE 802.3 Networks

The IEEE 802.3 standard is based on Ethernet. However, it has several significant differences, particularly its support of multiple Physical layer options, which include 50- and 75-ohm coaxial cable, unshielded twisted-pair wire, and a proposed implementation of optical fiber that may be a reality by the time you read this book. Other differences between various types of IEEE 802.3 networks and Ethernet include the data rates supported by some 802.3 networks, their methods of signaling, the maximum cable segment lengths permitted prior to the use of repeaters, and their network topologies.

## Network Names

The standards that define IEEE 802.3 networks have been given names that generally follow the form "s type l." Here, *s* refers to the speed of the network in Mbps, *type* is BASE for baseband and BROAD for broadband, and *l* refers to the maximum segment length in 100-meter multiples. Thus, 10BASE-5 refers to an IEEE 802.3 baseband network that operates at 10 Mbps and has a maximum segment length of 500 meters. One exception to this general form is 10BASE-T, which is the name for an IEEE 802.3 network that operates at 10 Mbps using unshielded twisted-pair (UTP) wire.

Table 3.1 compares the operating characteristics of five currently defined IEEE 802.3 networks to Ethernet. Note that the comparisons indicated in Table 3.1 do not consider differences in the composition of Ethernet and IEEE 802.3 frames. Those differences preclude compatibility between Ethernet and IEEE 802.3 networks, and are discussed in detail in Chapter 4.

## 10BASE-5

As indicated in Table 3.1, the IEEE 10BASE-5 standard resembles Ethernet more closely than the other 802.3 standards. In fact, an examination of the operating characteristics of Ethernet and 10BASE-5 indicates that these networks are exactly the same. Similarities between Ethernet and 10BASE-5 include the use of DB-15 connectors on interface boards and transceivers (MAUs) and the

**Table 3.1**    Ethernet and IEEE 802.3 network characteristics

| Operational Characteristics | Ethernet | 10BASE-5 | 10BASE-2 | 1BASE-5 | 10BASE-T | 10BROAD-36 |
|---|---|---|---|---|---|---|
| Operating rate Mbps | 10 | 10 | 10 | 1 | 10 | 10 |
| Access protocol | CSMA/CD | CSMA/CD | CSMA/CD | CSMA/CD | CSMA/CD | CSMA/CD |
| Type of signalling | basebase | baseband | baseband | baseband | baseband | broadband |
| Data encoding | Manchester | Manchester | Manchester | Manchester | Manchester | Manchester |
| Maximum segment length (meters) | 500 | 500 | 185 | 250 | 100 | 1800 |
| Stations/ segment | 100 | 100 | 30 | 12/hub | 12/hub | 100 |
| Medium | 50 ohm coaxial (thick) | 50 ohm coaxial (thick) | 50 ohm coaxial (thin) | unshielded twisted pair | unshielded twisted pair | 75 ohm coaxial |
| Topology | bus | bus | bus | star | star | bus |

termination of 10BASE-5 cable segments with N-series terminators.

However, there are differences in the frame format used by each network, and these differences preclude compatibility between Ethernet and all IEEE 802.3 standards. In addition, under the IEEE 802.3 specification, several network components have different names.

Figure 3.5 illustrates the major terminology changes between Ethernet and the IEEE 802.3 10BASE-5 network. These changes are in the media interface: the transceiver cable is referred to as the *Attachment Unit Interface (AUI)*, and the transceiver, including its tap and housing, is referred to as the *Medium Attachment Unit (MAU)*. The Ethernet controller, also known as an interface board, is now known as the *Network Interface Card (NIC)*. Other similarities between Ethernet and 10BASE-5 include the use of DB-

Legend:
AUI  = Attachment Unit Interface
MAU = Media Attachment Unit
NIC  = Network Interface Card

**Figure 3.5**  Ethernet and 10BASE-5 media interface differences. Terminology changes under the IEEE 10BASE-5 standard resulted in the transceiver being called the *media attachment unit,* while the transceiver cable is known as the *attachment unit interface.*

15 connectors on network interface cards and MAUs and the termination of 10BASE-5 cable segments with the use of N-series terminators at each cable segment end.

Both Ethernet and the IEEE 802.3 10BASE-5 standards support a data rate of 10 Mbps and a maximum cable segment length of 500 meters. 10BASE-5, like Ethernet, requires a minimum spacing of 2.5 meters between MAUs and supports a maximum of five segments in any end-to-end path through the traversal of up to four repeaters in any path. Within any path, no more than three cable segments can be *populated*—have stations attached to the cable—and the maximum number of attachments per segment is limited to 100.

# 10BASE-2

10BASE-2 is a smaller and less expensive version of 10BASE-5. This standard uses a thinner RG-58 coaxial cable, thus earning the names of "cheapnet" and "thinnet," as well as "thin Ethernet." Although 10BASE-2 cable is both less expensive and easier to use than 10BASE-5 cable, it cannot carry signals as far as 10BASE-5 cable.

Under the 10BASE-2 standard, the maximum cable segment length is reduced to 185 meters (607 feet), with a maximum of 30 stations per segment. Another difference between 10BASE-5 and 10BASE-2 concerns the integration of transceiver electronics into the network interface card under the 10BASE-2 standard. This permits the NIC to be directly cabled to the main trunk cable. In fact, under 10BASE-2 the thin Ethernet cable is routed directly to each workstation location and routed through a BNC T-connector, one end of which is pressed into the BNC connector built into the rear of the network interface card. Figure 3.6 illustrates the cabling of a one-segment 10BASE-2 network, which can support a maximum of 30 nodes or stations. BNC barrel connectors can be used to join two lengths of thin 10BASE-2 cable to form a cable segment, as long as the joined cable does not exceed 185 meters in length. A BNC terminator must be attached to each end of each 10BASE-2 cable segment. One of the two terminators on each segment contains a ground wire that should be connected to a ground source, such as the screw on an electrical outlet.

Station 1    Station 2    Station 3                    Station 30

**Figure 3.6**  Cabling a 10BASE-2 network. A 10BASE-2 cable segment cannot exceed 185 meters and is limited to supporting up to 30
nodes or stations.

Because of the similarities between 10BASE-5 and
10BASE-2, several vendors have introduced transceivers
that support both thick and thin coaxial cable. Figure 3.7
illustrates the Universal Ethernet transceiver manufactured
by Transition Engineering of Edina, MN. The transceiver
illustrated in the upper left corner of Figure 3.7 is a
10BASE-2 transceiver. It can be converted into a 10BASE-5
transceiver with an adapter that converts the BNC on the
thin-net transceiver into a "vampire" tap type connector, as
illustrated in the lower right corner of Figure 3.7.

## Expanding a 10BASE-2 Network

You can increase the number of stations that can be
attached to a 10BASE-2 network, the total network distance, or both through the use of repeaters. As with a
10BASE-5 network, between any two nodes there can be
up to five cable segments connected through four
repeaters. Like a 10BASE-5 segment, each end of every
10BASE-2 segment must be terminated with a 50-ohm terminator, with one end of each segment grounded.

Figure 3.8 illustrates an expanded 10BASE-2 network consisting of three populated cable segments; two segments
are used to extend the network span by simply connecting

**Figure 3.7**  Universal Ethernet Transceiver. The Universal Ethernet Transceiver manufactured by Transition Engineering of Edina, MN, supports both 10BASE-2 and 10BASE-5 coaxial cable connections. (Photograph courtesy of Transition Engineering, Inc.)

two repeaters. The latter segments are also commonly referred to as *inter-repeater cable segments (IRCS)*.

**Two-Tier Cabling**  You can further expand a 10BASE-2 network by establishing a two-tier method of cabling. Under this cabling concept, the upper tier can consist of up to 30 repeaters, connected to one another through the use of inter-repeater cable segments. These form a backbone network without direct station attachments, so populated segments on the backbone have to be connected on each segment end to a repeater. The lower tier then consists of repeaters connected to populated cable segments, with the lower tier repeater cabled to the upper tier

**Figure 3.8**  Expanding a 10BASE-2 network. Up to five cable segments connected through the use of four repeaters can be used to expand a 10BASE-2 network.

repeater to obtain a connection to the backbone. Figure 3.9 illustrates the use of a two-tier cabling hierarchy that can be used to extend a 10BASE-2 network. As in Figure 3.8, between any pair of workstations there can be a maximum of five cable segments and four repeaters. Of the five cable segments, up to three can be populated, and each populated segment is limited to a maximum of 30 connections. In addition, the maximum distance between any two stations is limited to 100 meters (328 feet), while the minimum distance between BNC T-connectors is 0.5 meters (1.6 feet).

Legend:
R = Repeater
S = Workstation

**Figure 3.9**  Two-tier thin 10BASE-2 network. A two-tier network permits expansion of a 10BASE-2 network by adding another level of repeaters to the backbone. The segment between repeaters B, C, and D is considered to be populated, since repeater C is counted as one connection on the segment.

## Combining 10BASE-5 and 10BASE-2 Networks

There are many situations in which a combination of thick and thin coaxial cable can better satisfy your cabling requirements than the exclusive use of one type of cable. For example, you may have several clusters of terminals located in different geographically separated areas within a large office complex. Instead of connecting the two clusters through the use of several thin 10BASE-2 cable segments and multiple repeaters, it may be easier to install one or more thick 10BASE-5 cable segments to serve as a backbone network for attachment to two 10BASE-2 cable segments. Thus, the ability of thick coaxial cable to support a longer transmission distance can eliminate or reduce the number of repeaters required in a combined network. In addition, a network built using thin 10BASE-2 cable, which was originally designed for a network span under 925 meters, cannot cover greater distances without mixing network media. Thus, the use of thick coaxial cable may provide the span of coverage not obtainable from the exclusive use of thin coaxial cable.

When thick and thin coaxial cable are combined to form a single cable segment, you must consider the length of each type of cable you anticipate using to develop a combined media cable segment. If the segment is entirely made up of thin cable, its maximum length is 607 feet, while a cable segment made up of thick cable has a maximum length of 1640 feet. Thus, a combined thin and thick cable segment should vary in length between 607 and 1640 feet. If $L$ represents the length of a combined media cable you wish to construct, you can use the following equation to determine the maximum length of thin cable:

$$\text{thin cable} = \frac{1640 - L \text{ feet}}{3.28}$$

For example, suppose you want to construct a cable segment 1400 feet long. Then, the maximum length of thin 10BASE-2 cable you can use becomes:

$$\frac{1640 - 1400}{3.28} = 73 \text{ feet}$$

Thus, you could use 73 feet of 10BASE-2 cable and route that cable through T-connectors, which are fastened to the BNC connectors on the rear of network interface cards. Then, you could use thick cable for the remaining 1327 feet of cable required in the cable segment.

Figure 3.10 shows an example of a combined 10BASE-5 and 10BASE-2 cable segment that connects two groups of stations located at opposite ends of a building without using repeaters. At one end of the building, 10BASE-2

**Figure 3.10**   Combined 10BASE-5 and 10BASE-2 cable segment. A combined thick and thin coaxial segment can be used to economically connect a group of stations clustered in one area of a building to a few stations located a relatively long distance away from the cluster.

cable is used with BNC T-connectors to connect a large number of stations clustered together. At the other end of the building, we will assume there are only a few stations. Thus, we would use 10BASE-5 cable and connect each station to the thick cable through the use of an MAU (transceiver) and an AUI (transceiver cable).

In examining Figure 3.10, note that the end of the thin cable is terminated with a BNC terminator. The connection of thick and thin cable is accomplished through the use of an N-series jack to BNC jack, while the thick cable is terminated with an N-series terminator that has a ground wire.

# 10BROAD-36

10BROAD-36 is the only broadband network based on the CSMA/CD access protocol standardized by the IEEE. Unlike a baseband network, in which Manchester encoded signals are placed directly onto the cable, the 10BROAD-36 standard requires the use of radio frequency (RF) modems. Those modems modulate non-return to zero (NRZ) encoded signals for transmission on one channel at a specified frequency, and demodulate received signals by listening for tones on another channel at a different frequency.

## Cable

A 10BROAD-36 network is constructed with a 75-ohm coaxial cable, similar to the cable used in modern cable television (CATV) systems. Under the IEEE 802.3 broadband standard, either single or dual cables can be used to construct a network. If a single cable is used, the end of the cable (referred to as the *headend*) must be terminated with a frequency translator. That translator converts the signals received on one channel to the frequency assigned to the other channel, retransmitting the signal at the new frequency. Since the frequency band for a transmitted signal is below the frequency band 10BROAD-36 receivers scan, we say the frequency translator *upconverts* a transmitted signal and retransmits it for reception by other stations on the network. If two cables are used, the headend simply functions as a relay point, transferring the signal received on one cable onto the second cable.

## Advantages

A broadband transmission system has several advantages over a baseband system. Two of the primary advantages of broadband are its ability to support multiple transmissions occurring on independent frequency bands simultaneously, and its ability to support a tree structure topology carrying multiple simultaneous transmissions. Using independent frequency bands, you can establish several independent networks. In fact, each network can be used to carry voice, data, and video over a common cable. As for topology, broadband permits the use of a tree structure network, such as the structure shown in Figure 3.11. In this example, the top of the tree would be the headend; it would contain a frequency translator, which would regenerate signals received at one frequency back onto the cable at another predefined frequency.

## Disadvantages

Like the 10BASE-5 network, the 10BROAD-36 system uses an MAU. However, this MAU is more intelligent than a 10BASE-5 MAU, as it is responsible for modifying the 802.3 frame slightly for broadband transmission via a modulator. These frame modifications include the scrambling of the preamble, so that the modulation of the preamble does not result in a loss of clocking, and the addition of a postamble to each frame. The latter assists in the detection of the end-of-frame. Although a 10BASE-5 AUI cable can be connected to a 10BROAD-36 MAU, a 10BROAD-36 MAU obviously cannot be used with a 10BASE-5 network. However, the

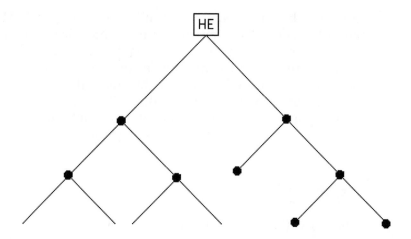

Legend:

HE = Headend

**Figure 3.11** Broadband tree topology support. The headend receives transmissions at one frequency and regenerates the received signals back onto the network at another predefined frequency.

design specifications of the 10BROAD-36 network enable this network to support the connection of CSMA/CD baseband equipment, and also provide a large degree of compatibility and interoperability with baseband systems.

The higher noise immunity of 75-ohm coaxial cable permits a 10BROAD-36 network to span 3600 meters, making this medium ideal for linking buildings on a campus. In addition, the ability of 10BROAD-36 to share channel space on a 75-ohm coaxial cable permits organizations that have an existing CATV system, such as one used for video security, to use that cable for part or all of their broadband CSMA/CD network. Although these advantages can be significant, the cost associated with more intelligent MAUs and RF modems has limited the use of broadband primarily to campus environments that require an expanded network span. In addition, the rapid development and acceptance of 10BASE-T and the decline in the cost of fiber cable to extend the span of 10BASE-T networks have severely limited what many people once anticipated as a promising future for 10BROAD-36 networks.

# 1 BASE-5

The 1BASE-5 standard was based on AT&T's low-cost CSMA/CD network, known as StarLan. Thus, 1BASE-5 is commonly referred to as StarLan, although AT&T uses that term to refer to CSMA/CD networks operating at both 1 and 10 Mbps using unshielded twisted-pair cable. The latter is considered the predecessor to 10BASE-T.

The 1BASE-5 standard differs significantly from Ethernet and 10BASE-5 standards in its use of media and topology, and in its operating rate. The 1BASE-5 standard operates at 1 Mbps and uses unshielded twisted pair (UTP) wiring in a star topology; all stations are wired to a hub, which is known as a *multiple access unit (MAU)*. To avoid confusion with the term "media access unit," we will refer to this wiring concentrator as a *hub*.

## Topology

Each station in a 1BASE-5 network contains a network interface card (NIC), cabled via UTP on a point-to-point basis to a hub port. The hub is responsible for repeating signals and detecting collisions.

The maximum cabling distance from a station to a hub is 250 meters; up to five hubs can be cascaded together to produce a maximum network span of 2500 meters. The highest level hub is known as the *header hub*, and it is responsible for broadcasting news of collisions to all other hubs in the network. These hubs, which are known as *intermediate hubs*, are responsible for reporting all collisions to the header hub.

## Utilization

AT&T's 1-Mbps StarLan network, along with other 1BASE-5 systems, initially received a degree of acceptance for use in small organizations. However, the introduction of 10BASE-T, which provided an operating rate 10 times that obtainable under 1BASE-5, severely limited the further acceptance of 1BASE-5 networks.

The growth in the acceptance of 10BASE-T resulted in economies of scale in the manufacture of 10BASE-T hubs and network interface cards. This, in turn, enabled vendors to match or exceed price cuts of other vendors. One key result of this situation was the ability of end-users to obtain a low-cost, high-performance local area networking capability through the use of 10BASE-T equipment. Needless to say, 10BASE-T has become the preferred network technology of both small and large organizations, and has essentially replaced the use of 1BASE-5.

# 10BASE-T

In the late 1980s, a committee of the IEEE recognized the requirement of organizations for transmitting Ethernet at a 10-Mbps operating rate over low-cost and readily available unshielded twisted-pair cable. Although several vendors had already introduced equipment that permitted Ethernet signaling via UTP cabling, such equipment was based on proprietary designs and was not interoperable. Thus, a new task of the IEEE was to develop a standard for 802.3 networks operating at 10 Mbps using UTP cable. The resulting standard was approved by the IEEE as 802.3i in September, 1990, and is more commonly known as 10BASE-T.

## UTP Use

The 10BASE-T standard supports an operating rate of 10 Mbps at a distance of up to 100 meters (328 feet) over UTP cable without the use of a repeater. The UTP cable requires two pairs of twisted wire. One pair is used for transmitting, while the other pair is used for receiving. Each pair of wires is twisted together, and each twist is 180 degrees. Any electromagnetic interference (EMI) or radio frequency interference (RFI) is therefore received 180 degrees out of phase; this theoretically cancels out EMI and RFI noise while leaving the network signal. In reality, the wire between twists acts as an antenna and receives noise. This noise reception resulted in a 100-meter cable limit, until repeaters were used to regenerate the signal.

Since UTP cable previously installed in commercial buildings contains either three or four wire pairs, the RJ-45 jack used with 10BASE-T has eight-pin connectors. However, only four pins are actually used. Table 3.2 compares the 10BASE-T pin numbers to the RJ-45 jack numbers and indicates the signal names of the pins used with 10BASE-T UTP cable.

## Network Components

A 10BASE-T network can be constructed with network interface cards, UTP cable, and one or more hubs. Each NIC is installed in the expansion slot of a computer and wired on a point-to-point basis to a hub port. When all of the ports on a hub are used, one hub can be connected to another to expand the network, resulting in a physical star, logical bus network structure.

**Table 3.2**   10BASE-T wiring sequence

| 10BASE-T | RJ-45 | 10BASE-T |
|----------|-------|----------|
| *Pin #* | *Pin #* | *Signal Name* |
| 1 | 1 | Transmit Data + |
| 2 | 2 | Transmit Data − |
| 3 | 3 | Receive Data + |
| - | 4 | Not used |
| - | 5 | Not used |
| 6 | 6 | Receive Data − |
| - | 7 | Not used |
| - | 8 | Not used |

**Network Interface Cards**   Most 10BASE-T network interface cards contain multiple connectors, which enable the card to be used with different types of 802.3 networks. For example, the NIC illustrated in Figure 3.12 includes a RJ-45 jack as well as BNC and DB-15 connectors. The RJ-45 jack supports the direct attachment of the NIC to a 10BASE-T network, while the BNC connector permits the NIC to be mated to a 10BASE-2 T-connector. The DB-15 connector enables the NIC to be cabled to a transceiver, and is more commonly referred to as the NIC's *attachment unit interface (AUI)* port.

Depending on the type of connectors built into your NIC, you may have several options to consider for connecting the NIC to a specific type of IEEE 802.3 network. For example, assume that your NIC is limited to supporting a thick or thin coaxial cable connection. In that case, you can still use the NIC to connect to a 10BASE-T network, using a transceiver similar to the one illustrated in Figure 3.13.

**Figure 3.12**   Multiple media network interface card. Some multiple media network interface cards, such as the one illustrated, support the direct attachment to UTP and thin coaxial cable, while the DB-15 connector permits the card to be cabled to an MAU connected to thick coaxial cable.

Figure 3.13 illustrates a 10BASE-T Ethernet transceiver manufactured by Transition Engineering, Inc. This transceiver allows you to connect an existing thick or thin 10BASE-5 or 10BASE-2 NIC's DB-15 AUI port to a 10BASE-T network. To do this, you would cable the NIC's DB-15 AUI port to the DB-15 connector at the left of the

**Figure 3.13** *Transition 10BASE-T transceiver. With a 10BASE-T transceiver, you can connect existing thick or thin 10BASE-5 or 10BASE-2 NICs to a 10BASE-T network. (Photograph courtesy of Transition Engineering, Inc.)*

transceiver. Then, you would cable the transceiver to a hub port using UTP.

**Hub** The wiring hub in a 10BASE-T network functions as a multiport repeater: it receives, retimes, and regenerates signals received from any attached station. The hub also functions as a filter: it discards severely distorted frames.

All hubs that conform to IEEE 10BASE-T specifications perform a core set of tasks in addition to receiving and regenerating signals. 10BASE-T hubs test each port connection, detect and handle excessive collisions, and ignore data that exceeds the maximum 802.3 frame size.

A 10BASE-T hub tests the integrity of the link from each hub port to a connected station by transmitting a special signal to the station. If the device doesn't respond, the hub will automatically shut down the port, and may illuminate a status light-emitting diode (LED) to indicate the status of each port.

Hubs monitor, record, and count consecutive collisions that occur on each individual station link. Since an excessive number of consecutive collisions will prevent data transfer on all of the attached links, hubs are required to cut off or partition any link on which too many collisions have occurred. This partitioning enables the remainder of the network to operate in situations where a faulty NIC transmits continuously. Although the IEEE 802.3 standard does not specify a maximum number of consecutive collisions, the standard does specify that partitioning can be initiated only after 30 or more consecutive collisions occur. Thus, some hub vendors initiate partitioning when 31 consecutive collisions occur, while other manufacturers use a higher value.

Another operating function of 10BASE-T hubs is to ignore continuous data transmissions in which the frame length exceeds the maximum length of 1518 bytes. Such excessive length frames usually result from collisions, and are referred to as *jabbering*. Most hubs also partition a jabbering port, and some hubs include a jabber indicator LED in addition to a partition status LED on each port.

Although a wiring hub is commonly referred to as a *concentrator*, this term is not technically correct. A 10BASE-T wiring hub is a self-contained unit that typically includes 8, 10, or 12 RJ-45 ports for direct connection to stations, and a BNC and/or DB-15 AUI port for expanding the hub to other network equipment. The BNC and AUI ports enable the 10BASE-T hub to be connected to 10BASE-2 and 10BASE-5 networks, respectively. For the latter, the AUI port is cabled to a 10BASE-5 MAU (transceiver), which is tapped into thick 10BASE-5 coaxial cable. One 10BASE-T hub can be connected to another with a UTP link between RJ-45 ports on each hub.

**Figure 3.14** 10BASE-T hub connectors. In addition to 8, 10, or 12 RJ-45 modular jacks for terminal connections, most 10BASE-T hubs contain a BNC and DB-15 port to permit attachment to thin and thick backbone networks.

Figure 3.14 illustrates the connectors on a typical 10BASE-T hub. On some hubs, one RJ-45 jack is labeled uplink/downlink for use in cascading hubs, while other vendors permit any RJ-45 port to be used for connecting hubs.

When one hub is connected to another, a special cable must be used. In that cable, the transmit and receive wire pairs have to be crossed over; that is, the receive pair at one end (pins 1 and 2) must be connected to the transmit pair (pins 3 and 6) at the other end of the cable and vice versa. The only exception to the use of a crossover cable is when a special hub port containing the crossover function is provided. On some hubs this type of port is labeled "crossover," and enables a straight-through cable to be used to cascade one hub to another.

Unlike a hub, a concentrator consists of a main housing into which modular cards are inserted. Although some modular cards may appear to represent hubs, and do indeed function as 10BASE-T hubs, the addition of other modules permits the network to be easily expanded from one location and allows additional features to be supported. For example, the insertion of a fiber optic interrepeater module permits concentrators to be interconnected over relatively long distances of approximately 3 km.

### Expanding a 10BASE-T Network

A 10BASE-T network can be expanded with additional hubs once the number of stations serviced uses up the hub's available terminal ports. In expanding a 10BASE-T network, the wiring that joins each hub together is considered to represent a cable segment, while each hub is considered as a repeater. Thus, under the 802.3 specification, no two stations can be separated by more than four hubs connected together by five cable segments.

Figure 3.15 illustrates the expansion of a 10BASE-T network through the use of five hubs. Note that the connection between station A and station B traverses five segments and four hubs, and so does not violate IEEE 802.3 connection rules.

Since the maximum span of a 10BASE-T network is 100 meters per segment times five segments, or 500 meters, it is quite common for 10BASE-T networks to use a 10BASE-5 or even a 10BASE-2 cable backbone. As in Figure 3.10, in which a 10BASE-5 cable provided a backbone for a 10BASE-2 network, either 10BASE-2 or 10BASE-5 cable can be used to support an extension of a 10BASE-T network. In such situations, the AUI port of a 10BASE-T hub is connected to a MAU (transceiver) connected to the 10BASE-5 (thick coaxial) cable, or the BNC connector is mated to a thin coaxial cable's T-connector. Another reason for using a thin or thick coaxial cable for a backbone is that you can thereby avoid the four-hub cascading limit of 10BASE-T. For example, if you cabled 10 hubs to a 1BASE-5 coaxial cable backbone, each station would traverse at most two hubs, and would

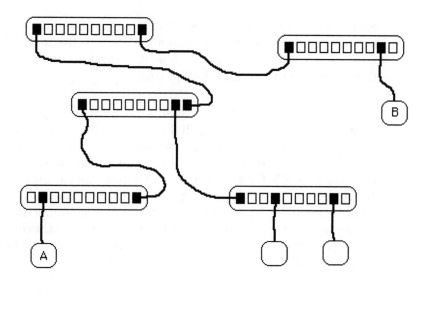

Legend: ◯ = stations

**Figure 3.15** Expanding a 10BASE-T network. No two stations can be separated by more than four hubs in a 10BASE-T network.

thus comply with the IEEE rules. In comparison, you could not connect more than five hubs together in a conventional 10BASE-T network because of IEEE 802.3 rules.

# 3.3 Use of Fiber Optic Technology

A recent addition to Ethernet is known as *FOIRL*, an acronym that stands for *fiber optic repeater link*. Although FOIRL is not an Ethernet network, this specification gov-

erns the transmission of Ethernet across dual fiber cable—
one fiber is used for the transmission of data in the form of
light pulses, while the second fiber is used for the reception of data in the form of light pulses.

The use of fiber permits you to support multiple Ethernet
segments at distances up to 2000 meters (6600 feet) from
one another. At a remote location connected through the
use of FOIRL technology, you can connect a single station
directly using a fiber transceiver, or you can connect a
10BASE-T or fiber hub and support multiple stations. You
would use the AUI port of the hub to provide a connection
via a standard transceiver to different types of Ethernet
networks, while you would use an optical transceiver to
provide a connection to the dual fiber cable.

## Optical Transceiver

An optical transceiver consists of a pulse-generating LED, a
photodetector, and associated transmit and recieve circuitry. Transmit circuitry turns the LED on and off to convert electrical voltages representing data into a series of
light pulses for transmission over the fiber. The photodetector recognizes received light pulses, while the receive
circuitry generates electrical voltages and shapes pulses to
correspond to the received light pulses.

Today, you can purchase a "fiber" network access unit
(NAU), an optical transceiver mounted on an adapter card
for installation in the system unit of a personal computer,
for less than $1000. A second type of optical transceiver
used on Ethernet networks is built into fiber hubs, the use
of which will be covered next in this section. This type of
optical transmitter may be designed to share the use of a
common power source and circuitry, resulting in a per-port
hub cost usually less than the cost of a fiber adapter.

## Fiber Hubs

A fiber hub is a special type of hub that contains a number of FOIRL ports, one AUI port, and usually one or more 10BASE-T ports. For example, AT&T's StarLan fiber hub contains six FOIRL ports, one 10BASE-T port, and one AUI port. In comparison, Transition Engineering's Model 1050 fiber optic hub contains 12 FOIRL ports and one AUI interface port.

In effect, a fiber hub is a grouping of fiber NAUs and one or more 10BASE-T and/or AUI ports. Thus, you can use a fiber hub to support several extended distance Ethernet connections, and then link those connections directly to a 10BASE-T network with a 10BASE-T port built into the fiber hub, or indirectly to any type of Ethernet network with an AUI port built into the fiber hub.

## Fiber Adapter

A third type of hardware product used with FOIRL is a fiber adapter. The fiber adapter is a media conversion device that converts between twisted-pair and fiber optic cable. This device extends the transmission distance between a wire hub and an attached workstation—or another 10BASE-T wire hub—from 100 meters (328 feet) to 2 km. Unless the fiber adapter is connected directly to a fiber hub, an adapter is required at each end of an extended fiber link.

## Wire and Fiber Distance Limits

Figure 3.16 illustrates the transmission distance limits associated with the use of 10BASE-T and fiber hubs and fiber adapters. Note that a fiber network access unit installed in the system unit of a PC can communicate up to 2 km via fiber optic cable, either directly into a fiber hub or to a fiber adapter connected to a wire hub. Also note that in the upper right corner of Figure 3.16, it was assumed that three 10BASE-T wire hubs were installed in a wire closet. If that wire closet is located on a low floor in a building and your organization leases another floor hundreds of feet above the wire closet floor, the use of fiber optic cable provides a mechanism to link two network segments together. Similarly, the wire closet shown in the illustration could be in one building on a university campus, with fiber used to connect that building to another building. This use of fiber optic cable not only extends the transmission distance of the network, but also eliminates the possibility of electromagnetic interference (EMI), since fiber cable is immune to EMI.

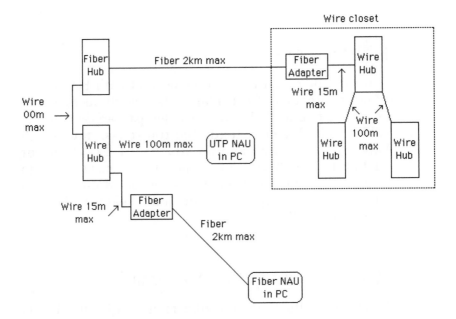

**Figure 3.16**    10BASE-T and FOIRL transmission distance limits.

# CHAPTER **4**

# Frame
# Operations

In this chapter, we will first focus our attention on the
composition of different types of Ethernet frames. In reality, there is only one Ethernet frame, while the CSMA/CD
frame format standardized by the IEEE is technically
referred to as an 802.3 frame. However, as previously
explained in this book, we will refer to CSMA/CD operations collectively as Ethernet, and when appropriate, indicate differences between Ethernet and the IEEE 802.3
Ethernet-based CSMA/CD standard.

One area where Ethernet and the IEEE 802.3 Ethernet-
based CSMA/CD standard differ is their frame formats.
Once we obtain an understanding of the composition of
Ethernet and IEEE 802.3 frames, we will examine the func-

tion of fields within each frame, as well as the manner in which the placement of frames on the media is controlled—a process known as *media access control.*

# 4.1 Frame Composition

Figure 4.1 illustrates the general frame composition of Ethernet and IEEE 802.3 frames. You will note that they differ slightly. An Ethernet frame contains an eight-byte preamble, while the IEEE 802.3 frame contains a seven-byte preamble followed by a one-byte start-of-frame delimiter field. A second difference between the composition of Ethernet and IEEE 802.3 frames concerns the two-byte Ethernet type field. That field is used by Ethernet to specify the protocol carried in the frame, enabling several protocols to be carried independently of one another. Under the IEEE 802.3 frame format, the type field was replaced by a two-byte length field, which specifies the number of bytes that follow that field as data.

Ethernet

| Preamble | Destination Address | Source Address | Type | Data | Frame Check Sequence |
|---|---|---|---|---|---|
| 8 bytes | 6 bytes | 6 bytes | 2 bytes | 46–1500 bytes | 4 bytes |

IEEE 802.3

| Preamble | Start of Frame Delimiter | Destination Address | Source Address | Length | Data | Frame Check Sequence |
|---|---|---|---|---|---|---|
| 7 bytes | 1 byte | 2/6 bytes | 2/6 bytes | 2 bytes | 46–1500 bytes | 4 bytes |

**Figure 4.1** Ethernet and IEEE 802.3 frame formats.

The differences between Ethernet and IEEE 802.3 frames, while minor, make the two incompatible with one another. This means that your network must contain either all Ethernet-compatible network interface cards (NICs) or all IEEE 802.3–compatible NICs. Fortunately, the fact that the IEEE 802.3 frame format represents a standard means that most vendors now market 802.3-compliant hardware and software. Although a few vendors continue to manufacture Ethernet or dual functioning Ethernet/IEEE 802.3 hardware, such products are primarily used to provide organizations with the ability to expand previously developed networks without requiring the wholesale replacement of NICs. Although the IEEE 802.3 standard has essentially replaced Ethernet because of their similarities and the fact that 802.3 was based upon Ethernet, we will consider both to be Ethernet.

Now that we have an overview of the structure of Ethernet and 802.3 frames, let's probe deeper and examine the composition of each frame field. We will take advantage of the similarity between Ethernet and IEEE 802.3 frames to examine the fields of each frame on a composite basis, noting the differences between the two when appropriate.

## Preamble Field

The preamble field consists of eight (Ethernet) or seven (IEEE 802.3) bytes of alternating 1 and 0 bits. The purpose of this field is to announce the frame and to enable all receivers on the network to synchronize themselves to the incoming frame. In addition, this field by itself (under Ethernet) or in conjunction with the start-of-frame delimiter field (under the IEEE 802.3 standard) ensures that there is a minimum spacing period of 9.6 ms between frames for error detection and recovery operations.

## Start-of-Frame Delimiter Field

This field is applicable only to the IEEE 802.3 standard, and can be viewed as a continuation of the preamble. In fact, the composition of this field continues in the same manner as the format of the preamble, with alternating 1 and 0 bits used for the first six bit positions of this one-byte field. The last two bit positions of this field are 11— this breaks the synchronization pattern and alerts the receiver that frame data follows.

Both the preamble field and the start-of-frame delimiter field are removed by the controller when it places a received frame in its buffer. Similarly, when a controller transmits a frame, it prefixes the frame with those two fields (if it is transmitting an IEEE 802.3 frame) or a preamble field (if it is transmitting a true Ethernet frame).

## Destination Address Field

The destination address identifies the recipient of the frame. Although this may appear to be a simple field, in reality its length can vary between IEEE 802.3 and Ethernet frames. In addition, each field can consist of two or more subfields, whose settings govern such network operations as the type of addressing used on the LAN, and whether the frame is addressed to a specific station or more than one station. To obtain an appreciation for the use of this field, let's examine how this field is used under the IEEE 802.3 standard as one of the two field formats applicable to Ethernet.

Figure 4.2 illustrates the composition of the source and destination address fields. As indicated, the two-byte source and destination address fields are applicable only to IEEE 802.3 networks, while the six-byte source and desti-nation address fields are applicable to both Ethernet and

IEEE 802.3 networks. A user can select either a two- or six-byte destination address field; however, with IEEE 802.3 equipment, all stations on the LAN must use the same addressing structure. Today, almost all 802.3 networks use six-byte addressing, since the inclusion of a two-byte field option was designed primarily to accommodate early LANs that use 16-bit address fields.

A. 2 byte field (IEEE 802.3)

B. 6 byte field (Ethernet and IEEE 802.3)

I/G bit subfield   '0' = individual address   '1' = group address
U/L bit subfield   '0' = universally administrated addressing
                   '1' = locally administrated addressing

\* Set to '0' in source address field

**Figure 4.2**   *Source and destination address field formats.*

### I/G Subfield

The one-bit I/G subfield is set to a 0 to indicate that the frame is destined to an individual station, or 1 to indicate that the frame is addressed to more than one station—a *group address*. One special example of a group address is the assignment of all 1s to the address field. Hex "FFFFFFFFFFFF" is recognized as a broadcast address, and each station on the network will receive and accept frames with that destination address.

When a destination address specifies a single station, the address is referred to as a *unicast address*. A group address that defines multiple stations is known as a *multicast address*, while a group address that specifies all stations on the network is, as previously mentioned, referred to as a *broadcast address*.

### U/L Subfield

The U/L subfield is applicable only to the six-byte destination address field. The setting of this field's bit position indicates whether the destination address is an address that was assigned by the IEEE (universally administered) or assigned by the organization via software (locally administered).

### Universal Vs. Locally Administered Addressing

Each Ethernet Network Interface Card (NIC) contains a unique address burned into its read-only memory (ROM) at the time of manufacture. To ensure that this universally administered address is not duplicated, the IEEE assigns blocks of addresses to each manufacturer. These addresses normally include a three-byte prefix, which identifies the manufacturer and is assigned by the IEEE, and a three-byte suffix, which is assigned by the adapter manufacturer to its NIC. For example, the prefix 02608C identifies an NIC manufactured by 3Com, while a prefix of hex 08002 identifies an NIC manufactured by Digital Equipment Company.

Although the use of universally administered addressing eliminates the potential for duplicate network addresses, it does not provide the flexibility obtainable from locally administered addressing. For example, under locally administered addressing, you can configure mainframe software to work with a predefined group of addresses via a gateway PC. Then, as you add new stations to your LAN, you simply use your installation program to assign a locally administered address to the NIC instead of using its universally administered address. As long as your mainframe computer has a pool of locally administered addresses that includes your recent assignment, you do not have to modify your mainframe communications software configuration. Since the modification of mainframe communications software typically requires recompiling and reloading, the attached network must become inoperative for a short period of time. Because a large mainframe may service hundreds to thousands of users, such changes are normally performed late in the evening or on a weekend. Thus, the changes required for locally administered addressing are more responsive to users than those required for universally administered addressing.

## Source Address Field

The source address field identifies the station that transmitted the frame. Like the destination address field, the source address can be either two or six bytes in length.

The two-byte source address is supported only under the IEEE 802.3 standard and requires the use of a two-byte destination address; all stations on the network must use two-byte addressing fields. The six-byte source address field is supported by both Ethernet and the IEEE 802.3 standard. When a six-byte address is used, the first three bytes represent the address assigned by the IEEE to the manufacturer for incorporation into each NIC's ROM. The vendor then normally assigns the last three bytes for each of its NICs.

## Type Field

The two-byte type field is applicable only to the Ethernet frame. This field identifies the higher-level protocol contained in the data field. Thus, this field tells the receiving device how to interpret the data field.

Under Ethernet, multiple protocols can exist on the LAN at the same time. Xerox served as the custodian of Ethernet address ranges licensed to NIC manufacturers and defined the protocols supported by the assignment of type field values. Under the IEEE 802.3 standard, the type field was replaced by a length field, which precludes compatibility between pure Ethernet and 802.3 frames.

## Length Field

The two-byte length field, applicable to the IEEE 802.3 standard, defines the number of bytes contained in the data field. Under both Ethernet and IEEE 802.3 standards, the minimum size frame must be 64 bytes in length from preamble through FCS fields. This minimum size frame ensures that there is sufficient transmission time to enable Ethernet NICs to detect collisions accurately, based on the maximum Ethernet cable length specified for a network and the time required for a frame to propagate the length of the cable. Based on the minimum frame length of 64 bytes and the possibility of using two-byte addressing fields, this means that each data field must be a minimum of 46 bytes in length.

## Data Field

As previously discussed, the data field must be a minimum of 46 bytes in length to ensure that the frame is at least 64 bytes in length. This means that the transmission of 1 byte of information must be carried within a 46-byte data field; if the information to be placed in the field is less than 46 bytes, the remainder of the field must be padded. Although some publications subdivide the data field to include a PAD subfield, the latter actually represents optional fill characters that are added to the information in the data field to ensure a length of 46 bytes. The maximum length of the data field is 1500 bytes.

## Frame Check Sequence Field

The frame check sequence field, applicable to both Ethernet and the IEEE 802.3 standard, provides a mechanism for error detection. Each transmitter computes a cyclic redundancy check (CRC) that covers both address fields, the type/length field, and the data field. The transmitter then places the computed CRC in the four-byte FCS field.

The CRC treats the previously mentioned fields as one long binary number. The $n$ bits to be covered by the CRC are considered to represent the coefficients of a polynomial $M(X)$ of degree $n-1$. Here, the first bit in the destination address field corresponds to the $X^{n-1}$ term, while the last bit in the data field corresponds to the $X^0$ term. Next, $M(X)$ is multiplied by $X^{32}$ and the result of that multiplication process is divided by the following polynomial:

$$G(X)=X^{32}+X^{26}+X^{23}+X^{22}+X^{16}+X^{12}+X^{11}+X^{10}+X^8+X^7+X^5+X^4+X^2+X+1$$

Note that the term $X^n$ represents the setting of a bit to a 1 in position n. Thus, part of the generating polynomial $X^5+X^4+X^2+X^1$ represents the binary value 11011.

This division produces a quotient and remainder. The quotient is discarded, and the remainder becomes the CRC value placed in the four-byte FCS field. This 32-bit CRC reduces the probability of an undetected error to 1 bit in every 4.3 billion, or approximately 1 bit in $2^{32}-1$ bits.

Once a frame reaches its destination, the receiver uses the same polynomial to perform the same operation upon the received data. If the CRC computed by the receiver matches the CRC in the FCS field, the frame is accepted. Otherwise, the receiver discards the received frame, as it is considered to have one or more bits in error. The receiver will also consider a received frame to be invalid and discard it under two additional conditions. Those conditions occur when the frame does not contain an integral number of bytes, or when the length of the data field does not match the value contained in the length field. The latter condition, obviously is only applicable to the 802.3 standard, since an Ethernet frame uses a type field instead of a length field.

# 4.2 Media Access Control

In the first section in this chapter, we examined the frame format by which data is transported on an Ethernet network. Under the IEEE 802 series of standards, the data link layer of the OSI Reference Model is subdivided into two sublayers—logical link control (LLC) and medium access control (MAC). The frame formats examined in Section 4.1 represent the manner in which LLC information is transported. Directly under the LLC sublayer is the MAC sublayer. The MAC sublayer, which is the focus of this section, is responsible for checking the channel and transmitting data if the channel is idle, checking for the occurrence of a collision, and taking a series of predefined steps if a collision is detected. Thus, this layer provides the required logic to control the network.

Figure 4.3 illustrates the relationship between the physical and LLC layers with respect to the MAC layer. The MAC layer is an interface between user data and the physical placement and retrieval of data on the network. To better understand the functions performed by the MAC layer, let

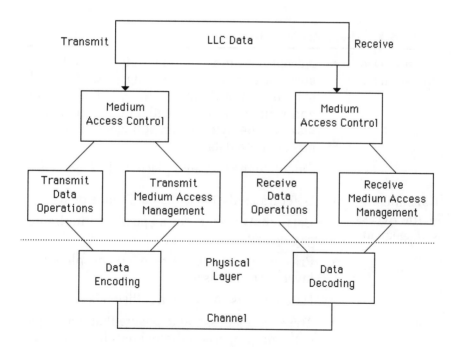

**Figure 4.3** *Medium access control. The medium access control (MAC) layer can be considered an interface between user data and the physical placement and retrieval of data on the network.*

us examine the four major functions performed by that layer—transmitting data operations, transmitting medium access management, receiving data operations, and receiving medium access management. Each of those four functions can be viewed as a functional area, since a group of activities is associated with each area. Table 4.1 lists the four MAC functional areas and the activities associated with each area. Although the transmission and reception of data operations activities are self-explanatory, the transmission and reception of media access management require some elaboration. Therefore, let's focus our attention on the activities associated with each of those functional areas.

**Table 4.1**  MAC functional areas

| | |
|---|---|
| Transmit Data Operations | • Accept data from the LLC sublayer and construct a frame by appending preamble and start-of-frame delimiter; insert destination and source address, length count; if frame is less than 64 bytes, insert sufficient PAD characters in the data field. |
| | • Calculate the CRC and place in the FCS field. |
| Transmit Media Access Management | • Defer transmission if the medium is busy. |
| | • Delay transmission for a specified interframe gap period. |
| | • Present a serial bit stream to the physical layer for transmission. |
| | • Halt transmission when a collision is detected. |
| | • Transmit a jam signal to ensure that news of a collision propagates throughout the network. |
| | • Reschedule retransmissions after a collision until successful, or until a specified retry limit is reached. |

**Table 4.1**  MAC functional areas *(continued)*

| | |
|---|---|
| Receive Data Operations | • Discard all frames not addressed to the receiving station. |
| | • Recognize all broadcast frames and frames specifically addressed to station. |
| | • Perform a CRC check. |
| | • Remove preamble, start-of-frame delimiter, destination and source addresses, length count, and FCS; if necessary, remove PAD fill characters. |
| | • Pass data to LLC sublayer. |
| Receive Media Access Management | • Receive a serial bit stream from the physical layer. |
| | • Verify byte boundary and length of frame. |
| | • Discard frames not an even eight bits in length or less than the minimum frame length. |

## Transmit Media Access Management

CSMA/CD can be described as a *listen-before-acting* access method. Thus, the first function associated with transmit media access management is to find out whether any data is already being transmitted on the network and, if so, to defer transmission. During the listening process, each station attempts to sense the carrier signal of another station, hence the prefix *carrier sense (CS)* for this access method. Although broadband networks use RF modems that generate a carrier signal, a baseband network has no carrier signal in the conventional sense of a carrier as a periodic waveform altered to convey information. Thus, a logical question you may have is how the MAC sublayer on a baseband network can sense a carrier signal if there is no carrier. The answer to this question lies in the use of a digital signaling method, known as

*Manchester encoding*, that a station can monitor to note whether another station is transmitting. Although NRZI encoding is used on broadband networks, the actual data is modulated after it is encoded. Thus, the presence or absence of a carrier is directly indicated by the presence or absence of a carrier signal on a broadband network.

## Collision Detection

As discussed in Chapter 3, under Manchester encoding, a transition occurs at the middle of each bit period. This transition serves as both a clocking mechanism, enabling a receiver to clock itself to incoming data, and as a mechanism to represent data. Under Manchester coding, a binary 1 is represented by a high-to-low transition, while a binary 0 is represented by a low-to-high voltage transition. Thus, an examination of the voltage on the medium of a baseband network enables a station to determine whether a carrier signal is present.

If a carrier signal is found, the station with data to transmit will continue to monitor the channel. When the current transmission ends, the station will then transmit its data, while checking the channel for collisions. Since Ethernet and IEEE 802.3 Manchester encoded signals have a 1-volt average DC voltage level, a collision results at an average DC level of 2 volts. Thus, a transceiver or network interface card can detect collisions by monitoring the voltage level of the Manchester line signal.

## Jam Pattern

If a collision is detected during transmission, the transmitting station will cease transmission of data and initiate transmission of a jam pattern. The jam pattern consists of 32 to 48 bits. These bits can have any value other than the CRC value that corresponds to the partial frame transmitted before the jam. The transmission of the jam pattern ensures that the collision lasts long enough to be detected by all stations on the network.

## Wait Time

Once a collision is detected, the transmitting station waits a random number of slot times before attempting to retransmit. The term *slot* represents 512 bits on a 10-Mbps network, or a minimum frame length of 64 bytes. The actual number of slot times the station waits is selected by a randomization process, formerly known as a *truncated binary exponential backoff*. Under this randomization process, a randomly selected integer $r$ defines the number of slot times the station waits before listening to determine whether the channel is clear. If it is, the station begins to retransmit the frame, while listening for another collision.

If the station transmits the complete frame successfully and has additional data to transmit, it will again listen to the channel as it prepares another frame for transmission. If a collision occurs on a retransmission attempt, a slightly different procedure is followed. After a jam signal is transmitted, the station simply doubles the previously generated random number and then waits the prescribed number of slot intervals prior to attempting a retransmission. Up to 16 retransmission attempts can occur before the station aborts the transmission and declares the occurrence of a multiple collision error condition.

Figure 4.4 illustrates the collision detection process by which a station can determine that a frame was not successfully transmitted. At time $t_0$ both stations A and B are listening and fail to detect the occurrence of a collision, and at time $t_1$ station A commences the transmission of a frame. As station A's frame begins to propagate down the bus in both directions, station B begins the transmission of a frame, since at time $t_2$ it appears to station B that there is no activity on the network.

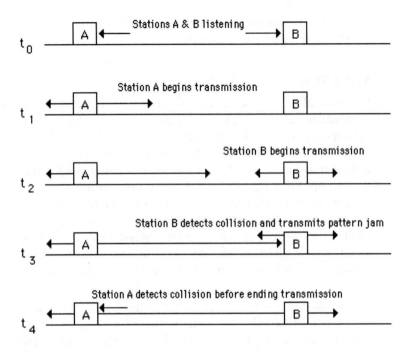

**Figure 4.4**  Collision detection.

Shortly after time $t_2$ the frames transmitted by stations A and B collide, resulting in a doubling of the Manchester encoded signal level for a very short period of time. This doubling of the Manchester encoded signal's voltage level is detected by station B at time $t_3$, since station B is closer to the collision than station A. Station B then generates a jam pattern that is detected by station A.

## Service Primitives

As previously mentioned, the MAC sublayer isolates the physical layer from the LLC sublayer. Thus, one of the functions of the MAC sublayer is to provide services to the LLC. To accomplish this task, a series of service primitives was defined to govern the exchange of LLC data between a local MAC sublayer and its peer LLC sublayer.

The basic MAC service primitives used in all IEEE MAC standards include the medium access data request (MA_DATA.request), medium access data confirm (MA_DATA.confirm), medium access data indicate (MA_DATA.indicate), and medium access data response (MA_DATA.response).

## MA_DATA.request

The medium access data request is generated whenever the LLC sublayer has data to be transmitted. This primitive is passed from layer $n$ to layer $n-1$ to request the initiation of service, and results in the MAC sublayer formatting the request in a MAC frame and passing it to the physical layer for transmission.

## MA_DATA.confirm

The medium access data confirm primitive is generated by the MAC sublayer in response to an MA_DATA.request generated by the local LLC sublayer. The confirm primitive is passed from layer $n-1$ to layer $n$, and includes a status parameter that indicates the outcome of the request primitive.

## MA_DATA.indicate

The medium access data indicate primitive is passed from layer $n-1$ to layer $n$ to indicate that a valid frame has arrived at the local MAC sublayer. Thus, this service primitive denotes that the frame was received without CRC, length, or frame-alignment error.

### MA_DATA.response

The medium access data response primitive is passed from layer *n* to layer *n–1*. This primitive acknowledges the MA_DATA.indicate service primitive.

## Primitive Operations

To illustrate the use of MAC service primitives, let us assume that station A on a network wants to communicate with station B. As illustrated in Figure 4.5, the LLC sublayer of station A requests transmission of a frame to the MAC sublayer service interface via the issuance of an MA_DATA.request service primitive. In response to the MA_DATA.request, a frame is transmitted to station B. Upon receipt of that frame, the MAC sublayer at that sta-

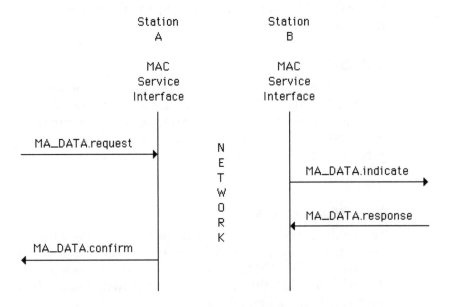

**Figure 4.5**  Relationship of medium access control service primitives.

tion generates an MA_DATA.indicate to inform the LLC sublayer of the arrival of the frame. The LLC sublayer accepts the frame and generates an MA_DATA.response to inform the MAC sublayer that it has the frame. That response flows across the network to station A, where the MAC sublayer generates an MA_DATA.confirm to inform the LLC sublayer that the frame was received without error.

# 4.3 Logical Link Control

As discussed in Chapter 2, the logical link control (LLC) sublayer was defined under the IEEE 802.2 standard to make the method of link control independent of a specific access method. Thus, the 802.2 method of link control spans Ethernet (IEEE 802.3), Token Bus (IEEE 802.4), and Token-Ring (IEEE 802.5) local area networks. Functions performed by the LLC include generating and interpreting commands to control the flow of data, including recovery operations for when a transmission error is detected.

Link control information is carried within the data field of an IEEE 802.3 frame as an LLC Protocol Data Unit. Figure 4.6 illustrates the relationship between the IEEE 802.3 frame and the LLC Protocol Data Unit.

As discussed in Chapter 2, Service Access Points (SAPs) function much like a mailbox. Since the LLC layer is bounded below the MAC sublayer and bounded above by the network layer, SAPs provide a mechanism for exchanging information between the LLC layer and the MAC and network layers. For example, from the network layer perspective, a SAP represents the place to leave messages about the services requested by an application. The Destination Services Access Point (DSAP) is one byte in

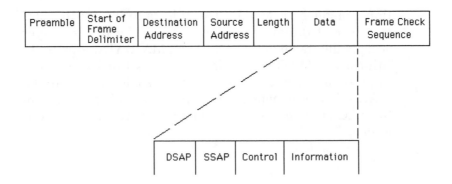

**Figure 4.6**    Formation of LLC protocol data unit. Control information is carried within a MAC frame.

length, and is used to specify the receiving network layer process. The Source Service Access Point (SSAP) is also one byte in length. The SSAP specifies the sending network layer process. Both DSAP and SSAP addresses are assigned by the IEEE. For example, hex address "FF" represents a DSAP broadcast address.

## Types and Classes of Service

Under the 802.2 standard, there are three types of service available for sending and receiving LLC data. These types are discussed in the next three paragraphs. Figure 4.7 provides a visual summary of the operation of each LLC service type.

### Type 1

Type 1 is an unacknowledged connectionless service. The term *connectionless* refers to the fact that transmission does not occur between two devices as if a logical connection were established. Instead, transmission flows on the

Type 1  Unacknowledged connectionless service

Type 2  Connection-oriented service

Type 3  Acknowledged connectionless source

Legend:
PDU = protocol data unit
ACK = acknowledgement
A,B  = stations on the network

**Figure 4.7**  Local link control service types.

channel to all stations; however, only the destination address acts upon the data. As the name of this service implies, there is no provision for the acknowledgement of frames. Neither are there provisions for flow control or for error recovery. Therefore, this is an unreliable service.

Despite those shortcomings, Type 1 is the most commonly used service, since most protocol suites use a reliable transport mechanism at the transport layer, thus eliminating the need for reliability at the link layer. In addition, by eliminating the time needed to establish a virtual link and the overhead of acknowledgements, a Type 1 service can provide a greater throughput than other LLC types of services.

## Type 2

The Type 2 connection-oriented service requires that a logical link be established between the sender and the receiver prior to information transfer. Once the logical connection is established, data will flow between the sender and receiver until either party terminates the connection. During data transfer, a Type 2 LLC service provides all of the functions lacking in a Type 1 service, using a sliding window for flow control.

## Type 3

The Type 3 acknowledged connectionless service contains provision for the setup and disconnection of transmission; it acknowledges individual frames using the stop-and-wait flow control method. Type 3 service is primarily used in an automated factory process-control environment, where one central computer communicates with many remote devices that typically have a limited storage capacity.

### Classes of Service

All logical link control stations support Type 1 operations. This level of support is known as Class I service. The classes of service supported by LLC indicate the combinations of the three LLC service types supported by a station. Class I supports Type 1 service, Class II supports both Type 1 and Type 2, Class III supports Type 1 and Type 3 service, and Class IV supports all three service types. Since service Type 1 is supported by all classes, it can be considered a least common denominator, enabling all stations to communicate using a common form of service.

## Service Primitives

The LLC sublayer uses service primitives similar to those that govern the exchange of data between the MAC sublayer and its peer LLC sublayer. In doing so, the LLC sublayer supports the Request, Confirm, Indicate, and Response primitives described in Section 4.2 of this chapter. The major difference between the LLC and MAC service primitives is that the LLC sublayer supports three types of services. As previously discussed, the available LLC services are unacknowledged connectionless, connection-oriented, and acknowledged connectionless. Thus, the use of LLC service primitives varies in conjunction with the type of LLC service initiated. For example, a connection-oriented service uses service primitives in the same manner as that illustrated in Figure 4.5. If the service is unacknowledged connectionless, the only service primitives used are the Request and Indicate, since there is no Response nor Confirmation.

# CHAPTER **5**

# Internet Hardware and Networking Software

Until this chapter, our primary hardware focus was on generic products designed to construct Ethernet type networks at a single location. Although we discussed the use of electrical fiber optic repeaters, that discussion was limited to a few network expansion examples. In addition, until now we have essentially avoided discussing the use of bridges, routers, and gateways to extend Ethernet connectivity beyond a single network, and the role of network software and how it relates to your personal computer's operating system. In this chapter, we will focus our attention on those two areas.

First, we will focus our attention on the basic operation of several hardware components that are the building blocks essential to extending the connectivity capability of an Ethernet local area network: repeaters, bridges, routers, brouters, gateways, servers, and wiring hubs. Next, we will discuss the role and operation of three major types of software required for local area network operations: computer operating systems, LAN operating systems, and application programs. This will be followed by a discussion of the software used to route data from one LAN to another using different internet hardware products. By examining hardware and software, we will obtain an appreciation for the methods used to link LANs both directly and through wide area networks.

In this chapter and throughout this book, we will use the terms *local area network* and *network* synonymously. We will use the term *internetwork* or just *internet* to refer to the joining of two or more local area networks. Note that we will use the latter term to refer to the combining of networks and not to the specific network called the Internet, whose first letter is capitalized.

# 5.1 Hardware Components

In this section we will examine hardware products essential to the construction and interconnection of local area networks. These products provide us with the ability to extend the distance of local area network coverage, connect local networks to distant ones, and obtain access to centralized computational facilities.

## Repeaters

A repeater is the simplest type of hardware component in terms of design, operation, and functionality. This device operates at the physical layer of the ISO Open Systems

a. OSI operation

b. Signal regeneration process

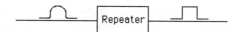

**Figure 5.1**    Repeater operation. A repeater connects two local area networks or network segments at the OSI physical layer (cable) by regenerating the signal received on one LAN or LAN segment onto the other network or network segment.

Interconnection Reference Model, regenerating a signal received on one cable segment and then retransmitting the signal onto another cable segment. Figure 5.1 illustrates the operation of a repeater with respect to the ISO OSI Reference Model.

## Types

There are two basic types of repeaters. An *electrical repeater* simply receives an electrical signal and then regenerates the signal. During the signal regeneration process, a new signal is formed which matches the original characteristics of the received signal. This process is illustrated in the lower portion of Figure 5.1. By transmitting a new signal, the repeater removes any previous distortion and attenuation, enabling an extension in the permissible transmission distance. Although several network segments can be connected by the use of repeaters to extend the coverage of a network, there are constraints that govern the maximum permissible length of a LAN. For example, a 50-ohm coaxial bus-based Ethernet supports a maximum cabling distance of 2.3 km, and that distance cannot be extended through the use of repeaters.

The second type of repeater commonly used is an *electrical-optical device*, such as the FOIRL repeater, the use and general operation of which were discussed in Chapter 3. This type of repeater converts an electrical signal into an optical signal for transmission and performs a reverse function when receiving a light signal. Similar to an electrical repeater, the electrical-optical repeater extends the distance that a signal can be carried on a local area network.

Since a repeater is restricted to operating at the OSI physical layer, it is transparent to data flow. This restricts the use of a repeater to linking identical networks or network segments. For example, you could use repeaters to connect two Ethernet or two Token-Ring network segments, but not to connect an Ethernet network to a Token-Ring network.

## Utilization

Figure 5.2 illustrates the use of a repeater to connect two Ethernet bus-based LANs, one serving the accounting department, and the other network serving the data processing department. In this situation, all messages on one

Connecting Ethernet bus-based local area networks

Legend:

□  workstations
MSAU  multistation access unit
R  repeaters

**Figure 5.2**  Using a repeater to link separate network segments. When a repeater is used to connect separate network segments, traffic on each segment is regenerated onto the other segment.

local area network are passed to the other, regardless of their intended recipient. The use of repeaters in this manner increases the sum of the traffic on each LAN. If this system is implemented without knowledge of the traffic flow and utilization levels on each network, performance problems may result when separate networks are interconnected through the use of repeaters.

## Bridges

Unlike repeaters, which lack intelligence and are restricted to linking similar LANs and LAN segments, bridges are intelligent devices that can connect similar and dissimilar local area networks. To obtain an appreciation for the functions performed by bridges, let us examine the use of this type of networking product.

## Operation

Figure 5.3 illustrates the operation of a bridge with respect to the OSI Reference Model, as well as its use to connect two separate Ethernet local area networks. Although the use of the bridge in the lower portion of Figure 5.3 looks similar to the use of a repeater previously shown in Figure 5.2, the operation of each device includes a number of key differences.

When a bridge begins to operate, it examines each frame transmitted on connected local area networks at the data link layer—a process beyond the capability of a repeater, which operates transparent to data. By reading the source address included in each frame, the bridge assembles a table of local addresses for each network. In addition to reading each source address, the bridge also reads the destination address contained in the frame. If the destination address is not contained in the local address table that the bridge constructs, this fact indicates that the frame's destination is not on the current network or network segment. In this situation, the bridge transmits the frame onto the other network or network segment. If the destination address is contained in the local address table, this indicates that the frame should remain on the local network. In this situation, the bridge simply repeats the frame without altering its routing.

The previously described method of bridging operation is referred to as *transparent bridging*. Refer to Chapter 6 for detailed information concerning different methods of bridge operations.

We can summarize the operation of the bridge illustrated in the lower portion of Figure 5.3 as follows:

**OSI operation**

**Application Example**

Legend:  ☐ = workstations

**Figure 5.3**   Bridge operation. A bridge connects two local area networks or network segments at the data link layer.

- Bridge reads all frames transmitted on network A.
- Frames with destination address on network A are repeated back onto that network.

- Frames with destination address on network B are removed from network A and retransmitted onto network B.

- The above process is reversed for traffic on network B.

**Filtering and Forwarding** The process of examining each frame is known as *filtering*. The *filtering rate* of a bridge is directly related to its level of performance. That is, the higher the filtering rate of a bridge, the lower the probability it will become a bottleneck to network performance. A second performance measurement associated with bridges is their *forwarding rate*. The forwarding rate is expressed in frames per second and denotes the maximum capability of a bridge to transmit traffic from one network to another. In Chapter 6, we will expand our examination of bridges to determine their maximum filtering and forwarding rates when used on Ethernet networks.

## Types

There are two general types of bridges: transparent and translating. Each type of bridge can be obtained as a local or remote device; a remote device includes a wide area network interface and the ability to convert frames into a WAN transmission protocol. Refer to Chapter 5 for information concerning wide area network transmission facilities, services, and protocols.

**Transparent Bridge** A transparent bridge provides a connection between two local area networks that employ the same data link protocol. Thus, the bridge shown in the lower portion of Figure 5.3 is a transparent bridge. At the physical layer, some transparent bridges have multiple ports that support different media. Thus, a transparent bridge does not have to be transparent at the physical level, although the majority of such bridges are.

Although a transparent bridge provides a high level of performance for a small number of network interconnections, its level of performance decreases as the number of interconnected networks increases. The rationale for this loss in performance is based on the method used by transparent bridges to develop a route between LANs. Refer to Chapter 6 for specific information concerning bridge routing and performance issues.

**Translating Bridge** A translating bridge provides a connection capability between two local area networks that employ different protocols at the data link layer. Since networks using different data link layer protocols normally use different media, a translating bridge also provides support for different physical layer connections.

Figure 5.4 illustrates the use of a translating bridge to interconnect a Token-Ring and an Ethernet local area network. In this example, the bridge functions as an Ethernet node on the Ethernet, and as a Token-Ring node on the Token-Ring. When a frame from one network has a destination on the other network, the bridge will perform a series of operations, including frame and transmission rate conversion. For example, consider an Ethernet frame destined to the Token-Ring network. The bridge will strip the frame's preamble and FCS, then it will convert the frame into a Token-Ring frame format. Once the bridge receives a free token, the new frame will be transmitted onto the Token-Ring; however, the transmission rate will be at the Token-Ring network rate and not at the Ethernet rate. For frames going from the Token-Ring to the Ethernet, the process is reversed.

One of the problems associated with the use of a translating bridge is the conversion of frames from their format on one network to the format required for use on another network. As indicated in Chapter 2, the information field of an

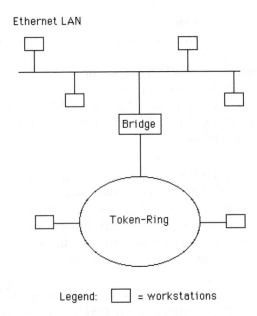

Ethernet LAN

Bridge

Token-Ring

Legend: ☐ = workstations

**Figure 5.4** Translating bridge operation. A translating bridge connects local area networks that employ different protocols at the data link layer. In this example, the translating bridge is used to connect an Ethernet local area network to a Token-Ring network.

Ethernet frame can vary from 64 to 1500 bytes. In comparison, a Token-Ring can have a maximum information field size of 4500 bytes when the ring operates at 4 Mbps, or 18000 bytes when the ring operates at 16 Mbps. If a station on a Token-Ring network has a frame with an information field that exceeds 1500 bytes in length, the bridging of that frame onto an Ethernet network cannot occur. This is because there is no provision within either protocol to inform a station that a frame flowing from one network to another was fragmented and requires reassembly. Using a bridge effectively in this situation requires that software on each workstation on each network be configured to use the smallest maximum frame size of any interconnected network. In this example, Token-

Ring workstations would not be allowed to transmit information fields greater than 1500 bytes.

## Features

The functionality of a bridge is based on the features incorporated into this device. Below is a list of the 11 major bridge features that define both the functionality and the performance level of a bridge.

- Filtering and forwarding rate
- Selective forwarding capability
- Multiple port support
- Wide area network interface support
- Local area network interface support
- Transparent operation at the data link layer
- Translating operation to link dissimilar networks
- Encapsulation operation to support wide area network use
- Standalone and adapter-based fabrication
- Self-learning (transparent) routing
- Source routing

**Filtering and Forwarding**   The filtering and forwarding rates indicate the ability of the bridge to accept, examine, and regenerate frames on the same network (filtering) and transfer frames onto a different network (forwarding). Higher filtering and forwarding rates indicate better bridge performance.

**Selective Forwarding**   Some bridges have a selective forwarding capability. Bridges with this feature can be configured to forward frames selectively, based on predefined source and destination addresses. With a selective forwarding capability, you can develop predefined routes for frames to take when flowing between networks, and enable or inhibit the transfer of information between predefined workstations.

Figure 5.5 illustrates the use of the selective forwarding capability of two bridges to provide two independent routes for data transfer between an Ethernet and a Token-Ring network. In this example, you might enable all workstations with source address 1 or 2 to have data destined to

Legend:   ☐ = workstations

**Figure 5.5**   Using bridge selective forwarding capability. Using the selective forwarding capability of bridges enables the data flow between networks to be distributed based upon source or destination addresses.

the Token-Ring flow over bridge 1, while workstations with a source address of 3 or 4 are configured to use bridge 2. Although the bridges illustrated in Figure 5.5 appear to form a closed loop, in effect the previously described method of selective forwarding results in a single logical path for each station on the Ethernet. This ensures there are no closed loops—a condition that would violate the spanning tree bridging algorithm supported by Ethernet bridges. The operation of that algorithm is described in Chapter 6.

**Multiple Port Support**    The multiple port support capability of a bridge is related to its local and wide area network media interface support. Some bridges support additional ports beyond the two that make up a basic bridge. Doing so enables a bridge to provide connectivity between three or more local area networks.

Figure 5.6 illustrates one potential use of a multiple port bridge to link an Ethernet network to two Token-Ring networks.

**Local and Wide Area Interface Support**    Local area media interfaces supported by bridges can include thin and thick Ethernet coaxial cable, IEEE 10BASE-T, and other types of twisted-pair cable. Wide area network interfaces are incorporated into remote bridges that are designed to provide an internetworking capability between two or more geographically dispersed LANs linked by a WAN. Common WAN media interfaces can include RS-232 for data rates at or below 19.2 Kbps, CCITT X.21 for packet network access at data rates up to 128 Kbps, CCITT V.35 for data rates between 48 Kbps and 128 Kbps, and a T1/E1 interface for operations at 1.544 Mbps and 2.048 Mbps, respectively.

**Transparent Operation**    Although bridges are thought of as transparent to data, this is not always true. For intercon-

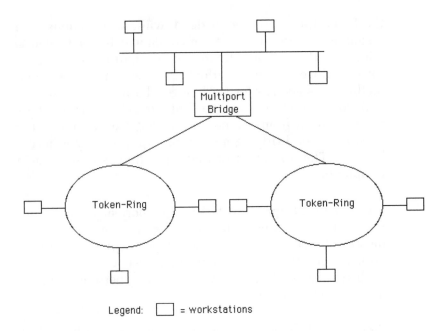

**Figure 5.6**  Using a multiport bridge. With a multiport bridge, you can interconnect three or more local area networks.

necting different networks located in the same geographical area, bridges are normally transparent to data. However, some remote bridges use data compression algorithms to reduce the quantity of data transmitted between bridges connected via a wide area network. Such compression performing bridges are not transparent to data, although they restore data to its original form.

**Frame Translation**   For interconnecting different types of local area networks, bridges must perform a translation of frames. For example, an Ethernet frame must be changed into a Token-Ring frame when the frame is routed from an Ethernet to a Token-Ring network. As previously mentioned, since frames cannot be fragmented at the data link layer, you must set the workstations on the Token-Ring network to the smallest maximum information field of an Ethernet frame, 1500 bytes.

When data is transferred between co-located local area networks, the frame format on one network is suitable for transfer onto the other network; it is modified for transfer when the media access control layers differ. When a bridge is used to connect two local area networks via a wide area network facility, a WAN protocol is employed to control data transfer. The wide area network protocol is better suited for transmission over the WAN, as it is standardized to incorporate error detection and correction, enable a large number of unacknowledged WAN frames to exist to speed information transfer, and support full-duplex data transfers. Examples of such wide area network protocols include IBM's SDLC, Digital Equipment Corporation's DDCMP, and the CCITT's HDLC and X.25.

**Frame Encapsulation**   Figure 5.7 illustrates the operation of a pair of remote bridges connecting two local area networks via a wide area network. For transmission from network A to network B, user data from a network A station is first converted into logical link control and media access control frames. The bridge then encapsulates one or more LAN frames into the bridging protocol frame used for communications over the wide area network. Since the local area network frame is wrapped in another protocol, we say the LAN frame is *tunneled* within the WAN protocol. At the opposite end of the wide area network, the distant remote bridge performs a reverse operation, removing the WAN protocol header and trailer from each frame.

**Fabrication**   Some bridges are manufactured as stand-alone products. Such devices are called *plug and play*, because you simply connect the bridge to the media and turn it on. Other bridges are manufactured as adapter cards

| Location | Frame Composition |
|---|---|
| 1, 9 | User data |
| 2, 8 | LLC-H \| User data |
| 3, 4, 6, 7 | MAC-H \| LLC-H \| User data \| LLC-T |
| 5 | Link-H \| MAC-H \| LLC-H \| User data \| LLC-T \| Link-T |

**Figure 5.7** Remote bridge operation. A remote bridge wraps the logical link control (LLC) and media access control (MAC) frames in another protocol for transmission over a wide area network.

for insertion into the system unit of a personal computer, workstation, or reduced instruction set computer (RISC). Through the use of software developed in conjunction with hardware, you may obtain more flexibility with this type of bridge than with a standalone device whose software is fixed in ROM.

**Routing Method** The routing capability of a bridge governs its capability to interconnect local area networks and its level of performance. A transparent bridge automatically develops routing tables. Thus, this device is known as a *self-learning bridge*, and represents the most elementary type of bridge routing. In the IBM Token-Ring frame, there is an optional routing field that can be used to develop routing information for frames routed through a series of bridges—a technique referred to as *source routing*.

Refer to Chapter 6 for an in-depth discussion of bridge routing methods.

## Routers

A router is a device that operates at the network layer of the ISO OSI Reference Model, as illustrated in Figure 5.8. Although this level of operation may appear to be insignificant compared to that of a bridge operating at the data link layer, there is actually a considerable difference in the routing capability of bridges and routers.

### Operation

The ability to operate at the network layer enables a router to extend networking across multiple data links in an

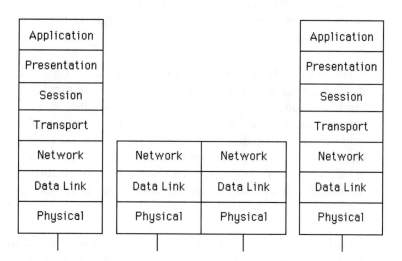

**Figure 5.8**   Router operation. A router operates at the network layer of the ISO OSI Reference Model. This enables a router to provide network layer services, such as flow control and frame fragmentation.

orderly and predefined manner. This means that a router can determine the best path through a series of data links from a source network to a destination network. To accomplish this, the router operates under a network protocol, such as the Internet Protocol (IP), Digital Equipment Corporation's DECnet Phase V, or Novell's IPX. This networking protocol must operate on both the source and destination network when protocol-dependent routers are used. If you use protocol-independent routers, you can interconnect networks using different protocols. The protocol independent router can be considered a sophisticated transparent bridge. Its operation and utilization are described in detail in Chapter 7.

In comparison, since a bridge operates at the data link layer, it can always be used to transfer information between networks operating under different network protocols. This makes a bridge more efficient for linking networks that only have one or a few paths, while a router is more efficient for interconnecting multiple network links via multiple paths.

**Network Address Utilization**   Unlike a bridge, which must monitor all frames at the media access control layer, a router is specifically addressed at the network layer. This means that a router has to examine only frames explicitly addressed to that device. In communications terminology, the monitoring of all frames is referred to as a *promiscuous* mode of operation, while the selective examination of frames is referred to as a *nonpromiscuous* mode of operation.

Another difference between the operation of bridges and routers is the structure of the addresses on which they operate. Bridges operate at the data link layer, which means that they typically examine physical addresses that are contained in ROM on adapter cards and used in the generation of frames. In comparison, routers operate at the network layer, where addresses are normally assigned by a network administrator to a group of stations having a common characteristic, such as being connected on an Ethernet in one area of a building. This type of address is known as a *logical address*, and can be assigned and modified by the network administrator.

**Table Operation** Like bridges, routers make forwarding decisions using tables. However, unlike a bridge, which may employ a simple table look-up procedure to determine if a destination address is on a particular network, a router may employ much more sophisticated forwarding decision criteria. For example, a router may be configured to analyze several paths using an algorithm and dynamically select a path based upon the results of the algorithm. Routing algorithms and protocols are discussed in Chapter 7.

**Advantages of Use** The use of routers provides a number of significant advantages over the use of bridges. To illustrate these advantages, we will examine the use of routers in Figure 5.9, in which four corporate offices containing seven local area networks are interconnected through the use of four routers. In this example, networks A and B are located in a building in Los Angeles, networks C and D are located in New York, network E is located in Washington, DC, and networks F and G are located in Miami.

**Multiple Path Transmission and Routing Control** Suppose a station on network A in Los Angeles requires transmission to a station on network G in Miami. Initially, router R1 might use the path R1-R4 to transmit data between networks. If the path should fail, or if an excessive amount of traffic flows between Los Angeles and Miami using that path, router R1 can seek to establish other paths, such as R1-R3-R4 or even R1-R2-R3-R4. In fact, many routers will con-

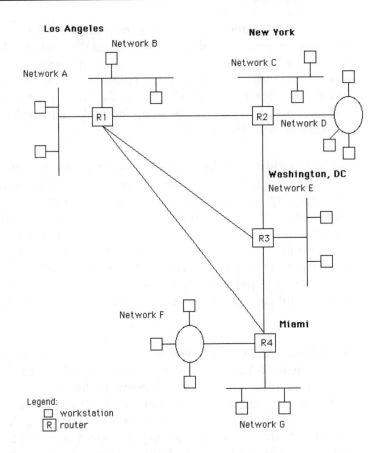

**Figure 5.9**  Building an internet using routers. Routers can be used to establish complex networks in which traffic is varied over network facilities. This variation is based on the operational status and utilization of different network paths.

sider each packet as a separate entity, routing the packet to its destination over the best available path at the time of transmission. Although this could conceivably result in packets arriving at R4 out of sequence, routers have the capability to resequence packets into their original order before passing data onto the destination network.

**Flow Control**   As data flows through multiple paths toward its destination, a link can become congested. For example, data from stations on network C and network E routed to network G might build up to the point where the path R3-R4 becomes congested. To eliminate the possibility of packet loss, routers will use flow control. That is, they will inhibit transmission onto a link and notify other routers to inhibit data flow until there is an available level of bandwidth for traffic.

**Frame Fragmentation**   As previously mentioned, bridges cannot break a frame into a series of frames when transmission occurs between networks with different frame sizes. This situation requires workstations to be configured to use the smallest maximum frame size of any of the networks to be connected together. In comparison, most network protocols supported by routers include a provision for fragmentation and reassembly of packets.

The higher level of functionality of routers over bridges is not without a price. That price is in terms of packet processing, software complexity, and cost. Since routers provide a more complex series of functions than bridges, their ability to process packets is typically one-half to two-thirds of the processing capability of bridges. In addition, the development time required to program a more complex series of functions adds to the cost of routers. Thus, routers are generally more expensive than bridges. Table 5.1 summarizes the major differences between bridges and routers in terms of their operation, functionality, complexity, and cost.

## Brouters

A brouter is a hybrid device, representing a combination of bridging and routing capabilities.

**Table 5.1** Bridge/router comparison

| Characteristic | Bridge | Router |
|---|---|---|
| Routing based upon an algorithm or protocol | Normally no | yes |
| Protocol transparency | yes | only protocol-independent router |
| Uses network addresses | no | yes |
| Promiscuous mode of operation | yes | no |
| Forwarding decision | elementary | can be complex |
| Multiple path transmission | limited | high |
| Routing control | limited | high |
| Flow control | no | yes |
| Frame fragmentation | no | yes |
| Packet processing rate | high | moderate |
| Cost | less expensive | more expensive |

## Operation

When a brouter receives a frame, it examines that frame to determine whether it is destined for another local area network. If it is, the brouter then checks the protocol of the frame to determine whether it is supported at the network layer supported by the router function. If the frame's protocol is supported, the brouter will route the frame as if it were a router. However, if the brouter does not support the protocol, it will instead bridge the frame using layer 2 information.

In comparison to routers, brouters provide an additional level of connectivity between networks, although that connectivity takes place at a lower level in the OSI Reference Model hierarchy. This is because a router would simply ignore a frame for which it does not support the network protocol, while a brouter would bridge the frame.

### Utilization

The key advantage of using a brouter is the ability of this device to both bridge and route data. Its ability to perform this dual function enables a brouter to replace the use of separate bridges and routers in some networking applications. For example, consider the use of a separate bridge and router in the top portion of Figure 5.10. In this example, the bridge provides an interconnection capability between two neighboring networks, while the router provides an interconnection capability to distant networks. By replacing the separate bridge and router with a brouter, you can obtain the same level of functionality, as illustrated in the lower portion of Figure 5.10. Of course, you want to ensure that the filtering and forwarding rates of the brouter are sufficient to be used in the manner illustrated. Otherwise, the replacement of separate bridges and routers by brouters may introduce delays that affect network performance. Refer to Chapters 6 and 7 for information concerning the processing requirements of bridges and routers.

## Gateway

The well-known phrase "one person's passion is another's poison" can, in many ways, apply to gateways. The term *gateway* was originally coined to refer to a device providing a communications path between two local area networks, or between a LAN and a mainframe computer, from the physical layer through the application layer. Figure

Using a separate bridge and router

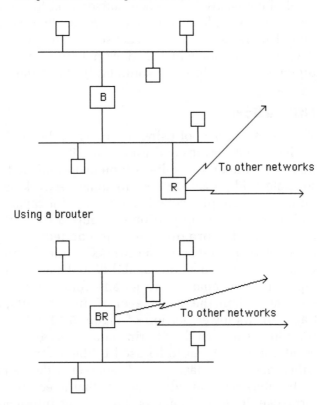

Using a brouter

**Figure 5.10**    Replacing a separate bridge and router with a brouter.

5.11 illustrates the operation of a gateway with respect to the ISO OSI Reference Model.

Since its original operational description, the term *gateway* has been used more loosely to describe a range of products, ranging from bridges that simply interconnect two local area networks to protocol converters that provide asynchronous dial-up access into an IBM SNA network.

| Application | Application | Application | Application |
| Presentation | Presentation | Presentation | Presentation |
| Session | Session | Session | Session |
| Transport | Transport | Transport | Transport |
| Network | Network | Network | Network |
| Data Link | Data Link | Data Link | Data Link |
| Physical | Physical | Physical | Physical |

**Figure 5.11**   Gateway operation. A gateway operates at all seven layers of the ISO OSI Reference Model.

## Definition

In this book, we will use the term *gateway* as it was originally intended, to describe a product that performs protocol conversion through all seven layers of the ISO OSI Reference Model. As such, a gateway performs all of the functions of a router, as well as protocol conversion.

## Operation

Gateways are protocol-specific in function, typically used to provide access to a mainframe computer. Some vendors manufacture multi-protocol gateways. Such products are normally manufactured as adapter cards, containing separate processors that are installed in the system unit of a personal computer or in a specially designed vendor hardware platform. When used in conjunction with appropriate vendor software, this type of gateway is actually an N-in-1 gateway, where N is the number of protocol conversions and separate connections the gateway can perform.

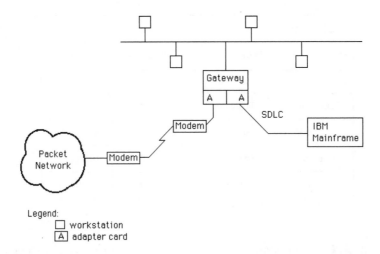

Legend:
□ workstation
Ⓐ adapter card

**Figure 5.12** Multi-protocol gateway operation. A multi-protocol gateway can be used to provide local area network stations access to different computational facilities, either directly or through the use of a packet network.

Figure 5.12 shows a multi-protocol gateway used to link LAN stations to an IBM mainframe via an SDLC link and an X.25 connection to a packet switching network. Once connected to the packet switching network, LAN traffic may be further converted by gateway facilities built into that network, or traffic may be routed to a packet network node and transmitted from that node to its final destination in its X.25 packet format.

Gateways are primarily designed and used for LAN-WAN connections and not for inter-LAN communications. Because they perform more sophisticated functions than routers, they are slower in providing network throughput. In addition, because the configuration of a gateway requires the consideration of a large number of protocol options, a gateway installation is considerably more difficult than the setup of a router. Refer to Chapter 8 for specific information concerning the operation and utilization of gateways.

## File Server

The file server is the central repository of information upon which a local area network is normally constructed. The file server is normally a personal computer or workstation that has a very powerful microprocessor, such as an Intel 80486 or a RISC chip, and a large amount of fast access on-line storage. The on-line storage is used to hold the local area network operating system and the application programs that other stations on the network may use. Several software vendors have split application programs, enabling portions of a program to be run on a network station, while other portions, such as the updating of a database, occur on the server. This technique is known as *client–server processing*.

### Connectivity Functions

As the heart of a local area network, the server supports every network application. It is therefore in an ideal position to perform connectivity functions. Some servers are designed to function as asynchronous gateways, providing access to one or more modems that individual network stations can access for communications via the switched telephone network. Here, software on the server considers the group of modems as a pool for access purposes. Hence, the term *modem pooling* is used to refer to a server used to provide this service.

Other servers contain software and hardware to provide access to mainframe computers via a specific protocol, such as SDLC, X.25, or TCP/IP. Depending on the capabilities of the network operating system used on the server, the server may support server-to-server communications on an intra- and inter-LAN basis. When supporting intra-LAN server-to-server communications, you can assign network users to a specific default server for an initial network logon, distributing the use of servers so that no one server becomes overused. Then, the network operating system would support the transfer of information between servers, such as an electronic mail message created by a network user assigned to one server, who addresses the message to another employee assigned to a different server. If your network operating system supports inter-LAN server-to-server communications, the server in effect functions as a remote bridge.

## Location Considerations

Figure 5.13 illustrates a file server used both in its traditional role as a repository for application programs and for modem pooling and gateway operations. The transmission of information between workstations and servers far exceeds transmission between workstations. The location

**Figure 5.13**   Server placement. The location of a server on a network is critical for ensuring network performance. In this example, since each workstation requires access to the server, its location requires the greatest transmission distance between individual workstations and the server. This, therefore, is probably a poor server location.

of file servers on an Ethernet local area network is there-fore critical for ensuring that network performance remains at an acceptable level. In the example shown in Figure 5.13, the server is located at a point on an Ethernet bus-based local area network in which the transmission dis-tance between each workstation and the server is maximized. This location results in the greatest propaga-tion delay for the transmission of data between each work-station and the server. This is probably a poor location with respect to network performance if each workstation requires a similar level of access to the server.

## Wire Hubs

As mentioned in Chapter 3, 10BASE-T Ethernet networks use wiring concentrators, or *hubs*. Hubs are typically located in telephone wiring closets, with stations cabled to the hub in the form of a star. Hubs are then connected to one another to form a bus. Only if the closest workstations to the server require a disproportionate level of server access, in comparison to other workstations, is the server location shown in Figure 5.13 correct. If each workstation has an equal level of server access, the server should be relocated to the middle of the network. This move would minimize propagation delays between the workstations and the server—which, in turn, would minimize the proba-bility of collisions. Since collisions result in the occur-rence of a random backoff time interval during which no data can be transferred on the network, the proper location of a server can increase network transmission efficiency.

### Advantages

Ethernet 10BASE-T hubs employ standard wiring between stations and the hub in the form of twisted-pair cable. Since workstations are connected to a single point, administration of a hub-based network is normally simple and economical, since a central point allows network configuration and reconfiguration, monitoring, and management. Due to the value of hubs in local area networking, several vendors have introduced products commonly referred to as *intelligent hubs.* This product provides users with the ability to build local area networks, ranging in scope from a single LAN with a small number of nodes to mixed protocol LANs with several thousand nodes that can be monitored, modified, and analyzed from a single point.

## Intelligent Hubs

An intelligent hub represents a tremendous advance in functionality and capability over conventional wire hubs. The intelligent hub includes its own microprocessor and memory, which not only provide a network management capability, but, in addition, may provide the ability to interconnect separate networks through integrated bridges and routers.

Most intelligent hubs include a multibus backplane, which enables bridges and routers to access and route data originating over multiple types of media. When operating in this manner, the intelligent hub can be viewed as a PBX, providing connectivity between any station on any network connected through the hub, while providing a centralized management and control capability.

Through the use of an intelligent hub, the administrator can enable or disable network ports from a network management workstation, segment a network to balance traffic better and improve performance, and facilitate troubleshooting and maintenance operations. As networks have become more sophisticated, intelligent hubs have evolved to facilitate their operation and management. With the ability of some intelligent hubs to bring together various media flavors of different local area networks, this device also provides a mechanism for the integration of prior piece-by-piece planning, or for the correction of a plan gone astray. Thus, the use of an intelligent hub may provide you with an umbrella mechanism to bring together separate networks and media previously installed in a building.

# 5.2 Networking Software

The installation of a local area network requires a variety of hardware and software products. At minimum, each workstation on the network normally requires the installation of an interface card into its system unit. This interface card contains a number of ROM modules and specialized circuitry, as well as a microprocessor that implements the access method used to communicate on the common cable.

In some local area networks, one personal computer must be reserved to process the network commands and functions. Since it services these commands and functions, it is normally called the *network server.* A combination of specialized software that overlays the operating system on each workstation and software placed on the server governs the operation of the network; this relationship provides a *client–server processing* capability. In comparison, the flow of data from one workstation to another without the use of a server is known as *peer-to-peer processing.* Since the vast majority of Ethernet LANs use servers, we will focus our attention in this section on the software required to support client–server operations. To understand the role of the network server and the functions of LAN software, let us first review how a personal computer operates under a conventional version of the disk operating system (DOS) used in the IBM PC personal computer environment.

## DOS

DOS is a single-user operating system designed to provide access to peripherals attached to the system and control of those peripherals, interpretation of commands to perform various functions on the system, and management of disk storage and memory. Under DOS, your keyboard is the standard input device and your display is the standard output device, and control of the personal computer is limited to one user. When you turn on your PC, one of the functions performed by DOS is to load a command processor into a predefined area of your computer's memory. The command processor contains coding that examines your keyboard entries, and coding that performs predefined functions when certain commands are recognized from your keyboard entries. The commands for which the command processor immediately executes code are known as *internal commands*. When other commands are recognized, the command processor loads a predefined file into memory and then executes its contents. These commands are known as *external commands*, since the code used to perform the functions associated with these commands reside on a file external to the command processor's code in memory.

## Network Software Components

As soon as a networked personal computer is initialized, its network software routines are added to DOS, permitting the computer to interact with the rest of the network. Prior to the introduction of DOS Version 3.1, this software was normally an overlay to DOS that served to filter commands, and that translated those commands requiring network access into code to transmit data via the LAN adapter card. Unfortunately, each network operating system vendor developed code to interface the adapter card in a proprietary manner, and software developed to work with one manufacturer's adapter card may not necessarily work with another manufacturer's adapter card.

When a command is issued on the PC, the software overlay permits the command to pass directly to DOS for execution. If a command is issued that refers to the network, the software overlay intercepts or filters the command from reaching DOS and, in conjunction with the adapter board, transmits the command onto the network. If the network is server-based, the non-local commands must be sent to a server for additional processing. The left-hand portion of Figure 5.14 illustrates the hardware and software components required when LAN software is designed as an overlay to DOS.

**Figure 5.14**  Potential PC LAN hardware and software relationships in an IBM PC environment.

Prior to the introduction of DOS 3.1, most LAN operating system vendors developed proprietary methods to access the LAN adapter card, and either developed proprietary methods to lock files and records or ignored incorporating such features. In effect, this limited their networks to simple file-swapping and printer-sharing applications. Since there was no Network Basic Input/Output System (NETBIOS), a proprietary network BIOS was developed and accessed via the vendor's LAN overlay software to send and receive data from the LAN adapter card. Here, NETBIOS is the lowest level of software on a local area network, translating commands to send and receive data via the adapter card into the instructions that actually perform the requested functions.

With the introduction of IBM's first local area network, referred to as the PC Network, in August 1984, IBM released all three components required to implement an IBM local area network using IBM equipment: the IBM PC Network Program, PC DOS 3.1, and the IBM PC Network Adapter. The IBM PC Network Program was actually a tailored version of Microsoft Corporation's Microsoft Networks (MS-NET) software, which is essentially a program that overlays DOS and permits workstations on a network to share their disks and peripheral devices. DOS 3.1, also developed by Microsoft, added file- and record-locking capabilities to DOS, permitting multiple users to access and modify data. Without file- and record-locking capabilities in DOS, custom software was required to obtain these functions—without them, the last person saving data onto a file would overwrite changes made to the file by other persons. Thus, DOS 3.1 provided networking and application programmers with a set of standards they could use in developing network software.

Included on the IBM PC Network Adapter card in ROM is an extensive number of programming instructions, known as NETBIOS. The middle portion of Figure 5.14 illustrates the hardware and software components of an IBM PC LAN network.

When the IBM Token-Ring Network was introduced, NET-BIOS was removed from the adapter card and incorporated as a separate software program, activated from DOS. The right-hand column of Figure 5.14 illustrates this new relationship between hardware and software. At first, NET-BIOS was designed to operate with Token-Ring adapter cards. Later, IBM extended NETBIOS to work with CSMA/CD Ethernet adapter cards.

Due to the standardization of file-and-record locking under DOS 3.1, any multi-user software program written for DOS Version 3.1 or later will run on any LAN that supports this version of DOS. Although DOS 3.1 supports many networking functions, it is not a networking operating system. In fact, a variety of networking operating systems support DOS 3.1 and later versions of DOS, including MS-NET, IBM's PC Network Program, IBM's Token-Ring Program, and Novell's NetWare. You can therefore select a third-party network operating system to use with IBM or non-IBM network hardware, or you can consider obtaining both third-party hardware and software to construct your local area network.

## Network Operating System

A modern network operating system operates as an overlay to the personal computer's operating system, providing the connectivity that enables personal computers to communicate with one another and share such network resources as hard disks, CD-ROM drives, and printers, and even obtain access to mainframes and minicomputers. Three of the more popular LAN operating systems are Microsoft Corporation's LAN Manager, a later version of that vendor's MS-NET, and Novell Corporation's NetWare.

Both LAN Manager and NetWare are file server–based network operating systems. This means that most network modules reside on the file server. A shell program loaded into each workstation works in conjunction with the server modules. The shell program workstation filters commands, directing user-entered commands to DOS or to the network modules residing on the server. Communications between the shell and the server modules occur at the OSI Reference Model's Network Layer. Microsoft's LAN Manager uses the IP protocol, while Novell's NetWare uses its Internetwork Packet Exchange (IPX) protocol as the language in which the workstation communicates with the file server. In fact, both IP and IPX are sophisticated network protocols that enable multiple servers to be located on a network and route information to their appropriate destination on a network, or between servers located on different networks.

## Services

The process by which the shell enables a workstation to communicate with a set of services residing on a server is known as a *client–server relationship*. Services provided by network modules on the server can range in scope from file access and transfer, shared printer utilization, and printer queuing to electronic mail. Other features available in most network operating systems include the ability to partition disk storage and allocate such storage to different network users, and the assignment of various types of security levels to individual network users, groups of users, directories, files, and printers. Some network operating systems include a disk mirroring feature and a remote console dial-in capability.

Since file information in the form of updated accounting, payroll, and engineering data can be critical to the health of a company, it is often very important to have duplicate copies of information in case a hard disk should fail. Disk mirroring is a feature that duplicates network information on two or more disks simultaneously. Thus, if one disk fails, network operations can continue.

A remote console dial-in capability enables a network user to gain access to the network from a remote location. This feature can be particularly advantageous for people who travel and wish to transmit and receive messages with people back at the office or obtain access to information residing on the network. Since the administration of a network can be a complex process, a remote dial-in feature may also make life less taxing for a network administrator. Working at home or at another location, the administrator can reassign privileges and perform other network functions that may not be possible in an eight-hour day.

## Looking at NetWare

Since the best way to obtain information concerning the relationship of a network operating system to network hardware is to examine the software, we will do so. We will discuss Novell Corporation's NetWare, as that network operating system (NOS) is by far the most popular of all network operating systems used.

## Architecture

The architecture or structure of NetWare can be mapped to the OSI Reference Model. It provides an indication of the method by which this network operating system provides support for different types of hardware, and includes the capability for the routing of packets between networks. Figure 5.15 illustrates the general relationship between NetWare and the OSI Reference Model.

In examining Figure 5.15, note that NetWare supports numerous types of local area networks. This means that you can use NetWare as the network operating system on Ethernet, Token-Ring, ARCnet, and other types of net-

**Figure 5.15**    NetWare and the OSI Reference Model.

works. In fact, NetWare also supports different types of personal computer operating systems, such as DOS, OS/2, UNIX, and Macintosh's Finder. This means that NetWare is capable of supporting different types of local area networks as well as workstations that use different operating systems.

Using NetWare on a PC requires the loading of two Novell files whenever you turn on your computer or perform a system reset. Those files are IPX and NETx, where x indicates a specific version of the NET file used with a specific version of DOS, such as NET3 used with DOS 3.

Both IPX and NET are workstation shell programs that interpret and filter commands entered from the keyboard and provide a mechanism for communications between the workstation and the server. Prior to NetWare Version 2.1, the shell was known as ANET3.COM, and was combined with IPX and NETx into one file. Later versions of NetWare separated IPX from NETx.

To automate the loading of NetWare on your workstation to establish a network connection, you would normally insert appropriate commands into your computer's AUTO-EXEC.BAT file. Those commands would include:

```
IPX
NETx
F:
LOGIN <servername/username>
```

**IPX**    The command IPX would cause Novell's IPX.COM file to be loaded and executed. This file is a driver that establishes communications with the network interface board, and it is responsible for providing communications with servers and other stations on the network using a network protocol known as IPX. At the network layer, Novell's IPX protocol performs addressing and internet routing functions. To accomplish this, an IPX packet contains both the source and destination network addresses. Those addresses are assigned by a network administrator, and they provide the mechanism for the routing of data between networks by routers which examine the network layer.

IPX is a connectionless network layer protocol that does not guarantee the delivery of data. To provide a reliable delivery mechanism, Novell developed its Sequenced Packet eXchange (SPX)—a transport level interface that provides a connection-oriented packet delivery service.

**NCP**    At the session and presentation layers, NetWare uses a NetBIOS emulator, which provides an interface between application programs written in compliance with NetBIOS and NetWare. As previously mentioned, the NetWare shell operates on each workstation and communicates with a core set of modules that reside on servers. That core set of modules is known as the NetWare Core Protocol (NCP). NCP provides such functions as workstation and network naming management, file partitioning, access and locking capabilities, accounting, and security.

**NET**   The command NETx loads NETx.COM, which is the true workstation shell, since it interprets and filters commands entered from the keyboard. In addition, NETx supports a large number of NetWare commands, which, when entered, are converted into IPX packets and transmitted to the server for processing. The NetWare Core Protocol decodes the command request, processes the request, and then transmits a response to the workstation using one or more IPX packets. The workstation's NET module then processes and displays the response. For example, typing the NetWare command CHKVOL at the workstation transmits a request to the server to obtain statistics concerning the logical driver (volume) assigned to the workstation user. The results of that request are transmitted back to the workstation and displayed on its screen the same way a DOS CHKDSK command is displayed.

When the shell (NETx) is loaded, it normally establishes a connection to a network server by sending a request to IPX to broadcast a Get Nearest Server command. The first server that responds to the request then establishes a connection to the workstation and displays the message "Attached to server <servername>" on your computer's console. You can also specify a preferred server by adding the PS= parameter to the NETx command; this provides you with the ability to distribute workstation server usage over a number of servers.

Once a connection to a NetWare server occurs, the command F: in the AUTOEXEC.BAT file moves the workstation user to the server's SYS:LOGIN directory. That directory is designated or mapped to drive F: on your DOS operated workstation. Once this is accomplished, the command LOGIN initiates the LOGIN module on the server. If you include the servername and username, LOGIN will then request only your password to obtain access to the server.

**Versions**   Several versions of NetWare have been marketed during the past few years. NetWare 286, which was renamed NetWare 2.2, is designed to operate on Intel 286-based servers. This operating system supports up to 100 users. A more modern version of NetWare, NetWare 386 (renamed NetWare 3.1), operates on Intel 386-based servers. This network operating system supports up to 250 users.

## Application Software

The third major component of software required for productive work to occur on a local area network is application software. These application programs support electronic mail, multiple access to database records, or the use of spreadsheet programs; they operate at the top layer of the OSI Reference Model.

Until the mid-1980s, most application programs used on LANs were not tailored to operate correctly in a multi-user environment. A large part of their inability to work correctly was due to the absence of file- and record-locking capabilities on PC operating systems—a situation that was corrected with the introduction of DOS 3.1. A second problem associated with application programs occurred when the program was written to bypass the personal computer's BIOS. Although this action in many instances would speed up screen displays, disk access, and other operations, in this case it resulted in nonstandardized program actions.

This made it difficult, if not impossible, for some network operating systems to support ill-defined programs, because an interrupt clash could bring the entire network to a rapid halt.

Today, most application programs use BIOS calls and are well defined. Such programs are easily supported by network operating systems. A few programs that bypass BIOS may also be supported, since the application program that caused operating system vendors to tailor their software to support such applications was so popular.

# CHAPTER **6**

# Bridge Routing Methods and Network Performance Issues

In Chapter 5, an overview of bridge operations was presented, along with information concerning the functionality of other local area network hardware and software components. That chapter deferred until now a detailed examination of bridge routing methods, their network utilization, and performance issues. In this chapter, we will focus our attention on those issues, examining different methods that bridges use for routing frames, performance issues that govern their ability to examine and forward frames without introducing network bottlenecks, and their typical employment for the construction of networks.

# 6.1 Routing Methods

Bridges operate by examining MAC layer addresses, using the destination and source addresses within a frame as a decision criterion to make their forwarding decisions. Operating at the MAC layer, bridges are not addressed, and must therefore examine all frames that flow on a network.

## Address Issues

Since bridges connect networks, it is important to ensure that duplicate MAC addresses do not occur on joined networks—a topology we will refer to as an *internet.* While duplicate addresses will not occur when universally administered addressing is used, when locally administered addressing is used duplicate addresses become possible. Thus, the addresses assigned to stations on separate networks joined to form an internet should be reviewed prior to using bridges to connect two or more separate networks.

Two primary routing methods are used by bridges for connecting local area networks: transparent or self-learning and source routing. Transparent bridges were originally developed to support the connection of Ethernet networks, as briefly described in Chapter 5.

## Transparent Bridging

A transparent bridge examines media access control frames to learn the addresses of stations on the network, storing information in internal memory in the form of an address table. Thus, this type of bridge is also known as a *self-learning bridge.* To understand the operation of a transparent bridge in more detail and realize some of the limitations associated with the use of this device, consider the simple internet illustrated in Figure 6.1. This internet consists of one Ethernet and two Token-Ring local area networks connected through the use of two self-learning bridges. For simplicity of illustration, only two workstations are shown and labeled on each local area network.

As previously mentioned, transparent bridges were originally developed to interconnect Ethernet local area networks. This type of bridge can also be used to connect Ethernet and Token-Ring networks; however, for this purpose, the bridge must at least be capable of performing frame conversion.

## Frame Conversion

The frame formats used by Ethernet and Token-Ring networks, while similar, are not equal to one another. For

| Bridge 1 Address/Routing Table | |
|---|---|
| Port 1 | Port 2 |
| A | C |
| B | D |
|  | E |
|  | F |

| Bridge 2 Address/Routing Table | |
|---|---|
| Port 1 | Port 2 |
| A | E |
| B | F |
| C |  |
| D |  |

**Figure 6.1** *Transparent bridge operation. A transparent or self-learning bridge examines the source and destination addresses to form address or routing tables in memory.*

example, Ethernet frames are prefixed with a preamble field, which is followed by a Starting Delimiter field. The Ethernet preamble field is not used in a Token-Ring frame, and the Ethernet starting delimiter field differs in composition from its Token-Ring equivalent field. Similarly, each Token-Ring frame is prefixed with a starting delimiter field, which is quite different from the field with that name used on an Ethernet frame. Another significant difference between Ethernet and Token-Ring networks concerns the methods used for bridging. Ethernet networks use transparent bridging, employing a spanning tree algorithm. IBM Token-Ring networks support an optional routing method known as *source routing*. If that routing method is not used, an IBM bridge can support transparent bridging. In addition, a recently adopted standard known as *Source Routing Transparent (SRT)* bridging provides the ability for bridges to support both methods in constructing Ethernet and IBM Token-Ring networks. The spanning tree algorithm used by transparent bridges, the source routing algorithm used by source routing bridges, and the operation of SRT bridges are discussed in detail later in this chapter.

### Address/Routing Table Construction

In examining the construction of bridge address/routing tables for the network shown in Figure 6.1, we will assume that each bridge operates as a transparent bridge. As frames flow on the Ethernet, bridge 1 examines the source address of each frame. Eventually, after both stations A and B have become active, the bridge associates their address as being on port 1 of that device. Any frames with a destination address other than stations A or B are considered to be on another network. Thus, bridge 1 would eventually associate addresses C, D, E, and F with port 2, once it receives frames with those addresses in their destination address fields. Similarly, bridge 2 constructs its own address/routing table. Since frames from Ethernet 1 and Token-Ring 1 can have source addresses of A, B, C, or D, eventually the address/routing table of bridge 2 associates those addresses with port 1 of that device. Since frames from Ethernet 1 or Token-Ring 1 with a destination address of E or F are not on those local area networks, bridge 2 then associates those addresses with port 2 of that device.

## Advantages

One of the key advantages of a transparent bridge is that it operates independently of the contents of the information field and is protocol-independent. Since this type of bridge is self-learning, it requires no manual configuration and is essentially a "plug and play" device. Thus, this type of bridge is attractive for connecting a few local area networks together, and is usually sufficient for most small and medium-sized businesses. Unfortunately, its use limits the development of certain interconnection topologies, as we will soon see.

## Disadvantages

To see the disadvantages associated with transparent bridges, consider Figure 6.2, in which the three Ethernet local area networks are interconnected through the use of three bridges. In this example, the internet forms a *circular* or *loop topology*. Since a transparent bridge views stations as being connected to either port 1 or port 2, a circular or loop topology will create problems. Those problems can result in an unnecessary duplication of frames, which not only degrades the overall level of performance of the internet, but will quite possibly confuse the end stations. For example, consider a frame whose source address is A and whose destination address is F. Both bridge 1 and bridge 2 will forward the frame. Although bridge 1 will forward the frame to its appropriate network using the most direct route, the frame will also be forwarded by bridge 3 to Ethernet 2, resulting in a duplicate frame arriving at workstation F. At station F, a mechanism would be required to

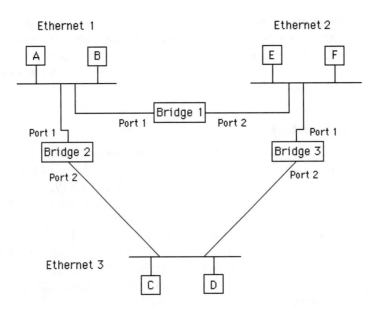

**Figure 6.2** Transparent bridges do not support network loops. The construction of a circular or loop topology with transparent bridges can result in an unnecessary duplication of frames, and may confuse end stations. To avoid these problems, the Spanning Tree Protocol (STP) opens a loop by placing one bridge in a standby mode of operation.

reject duplicate frames. Even if such a mechanism is available, the additional traffic flowing across multiple internet paths would result in an increase in network utilization approaching 100 percent. This, in turn, would saturate some networks, while significantly reducing the level of performance of other networks. For these reasons, transparent bridging is prohibited from creating a loop or circular topology. However, transparent bridging supports concurrently active multiple bridges, using an algorithm known as the *spanning tree* to determine which bridges should forward and which bridges should only filter frames.

# Spanning Tree Protocol

The problem of active loops was addressed by the IEEE Committee 802 in the 802.1D standard with an intelligent algorithm known as the Spanning Tree Protocol (STP). The STP, based on graph theory, converts a loop into a tree topology by disabling a link. This action ensures there is a unique path from any node in an internet to every other node. Disabled nodes are then kept in a standby mode of operation until a network failure occurs. At that time, the spanning tree protocol will attempt to construct a new tree using any of the previously disabled links.

## Operation

To illustrate the operation of the spanning tree protocol, we must first become familiar with the difference between the physical and active topology of bridged networks. In addition, there are a number of terms associated with the spanning tree algorithm, as defined by the protocol, that we should become familiar with. Thus, we will also review those terms before discussing the operation of the algorithm.

**Physical Versus Active Topology**    In transparent bridging, a distinction is made between the physical and active topology resulting from bridged local area networks. This distinction enables the construction of a network topology in which inactive but physically constructed routes can be placed into operation if a primary route should fail, and in which the inactive and active routes would form an illegal circular path violating the spanning tree algorithm if both routes were active at the same time.

The top of Figure 6.3 illustrates one possible physical topology of bridged networks. The cost (C) assigned to each bridge will be discussed later in this chapter. The lower portion of Figure 6.3 illustrates a possible active

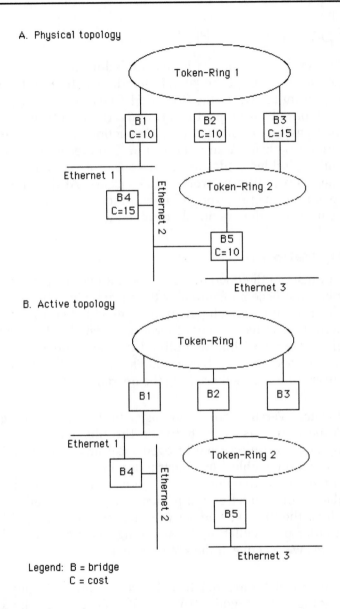

A. Physical topology

B. Active topology

Legend: B = bridge
C = cost

**Figure 6.3** Physical versus active topology. When transparent bridges are used, the active topology cannot form a closed loop in the internet.

topology for the physical configuration shown at the top of that illustration.

When a bridge is used to construct an active path, it will forward frames through those ports used to form active paths. The ports through which frames are forwarded are said to be in a *forwarding state of operation*. Ports that cannot forward frames because their operation forms a loop are said to be in a *blocking state of operation*.

Under the spanning tree algorithm, a port in a blocking state can be placed into a forwarding state to provide a path that becomes part of the active network topology. This new path usually occurs because of the failure of another path, bridge component, or the reconfiguration of interconnected networks, and must not form a closed loop.

**Spanning Tree Algorithm**  The basis for the spanning tree algorithm is a tree structure, since a tree forms a pattern of connections that has no loops. The term *spanning* is used because the branches of a tree structure span or connect subnetworks.

Similar to the root of a tree, one bridge in a spanning tree network will be assigned to a unique position in the network. Known as the *root bridge*, this bridge is assigned as the top of the spanning tree, and because of this position, it has the potential to carry the largest amount of internet traffic.

Since bridges and bridge ports can be active or inactive, a mechanism is required to identify bridges and bridge ports. Each bridge in a spanning tree network is assigned a unique bridge identifier. This identifier is the MAC address on the bridge's lowest port number and a two-byte bridge priority level. The priority level is defined when a bridge is installed and functions as a bridge number. Similar to the bridge priority level, each adapter on a bridge that functions as a port has a two-byte port identifier. Thus, the unique bridge identifier and port identifier enable each port on a bridge to be uniquely identified.

Under the spanning tree algorithm, the difference in physical routes between bridges is recognized, and a mechanism is provided to indicate the preference for one route over another. That mechanism is accomplished by the ability to assign a path cost to each path. Thus, you could assign a low cost to a preferred route and a high cost to a route you only want to be used in a backup situation.

Once path costs are assigned to each path in an internet, each bridge will have one or more costs associated with different paths to the root bridge. One of those costs is lower than all other path costs. That cost is known as the bridge's *root path cost*, and the port used to provide the least path cost toward the root bridge is known as the *root port*.

As previously discussed, the spanning tree algorithm does not permit active loops in an interconnected network. To prevent this situation from occurring, only one bridge linking two networks can be in a forwarding state at any particular time. That bridge is known as the designated bridge, while all other bridges linking two networks will not forward frames and will be in a blocking state of operation.

**Constructing the Spanning Tree**   The spanning tree algorithm employs a three-step process to develop an active topology. First, the root bridge is identified. In Figure 6.3B we will assume bridge 1 was selected as the root bridge. Next, the path cost from each bridge to the root bridge is determined, and the minimum cost from each bridge becomes the root path cost. The port in the direction of the least path cost to the root bridge, known as the root port, is then determined for each bridge. If the root path cost is the same for two or more bridges linking LANs, then the bridge with the highest priority will be selected to furnish the minimum path cost. Once the paths are selected, the designated ports are activated.

In examining Figure 6.3A, let us now use the cost entries assigned to each bridge. Let us assume that bridge 1 was selected as the root bridge, since we expect a large amount of traffic to flow between Token-Ring 1 and Ethernet 1 networks. Therefore, bridge 1 will become the designated bridge between Token-Ring 1 and Ethernet 1 networks.

In examining the path costs to the root bridge, note that the path through bridge 2 was assigned a cost of 10, while the path through bridge 3 was assigned a cost of 15. Thus, the path from Token-Ring 2 via bridge 2 to Token-Ring 1 becomes the designated bridge between those two networks. Hence, Figure 6.3B shows bridge 3 inactive by the omission of a connection to the Token-Ring 2 network. Similarly, the path cost for connecting the Ethernet 3 network to the root bridge is lower by routing through the Token-Ring 2 and Token-Ring 1 networks. Thus, bridge 5 becomes the designated bridge for the Ethernet 3 and Token-Ring 2 networks.

**Bridge Protocol Data Unit**   One question that is probably in your mind by now is how each bridge knows whether to participate in a spanned tree topology. Bridges obtain topology information by the use of Bridge Protocol Data Unit (BPDU) frames.

The root bridge is responsible for periodically transmitting a "HELLO" BPDU frame to all networks to which it is connected. According to the spanning tree protocol, HELLO frames must be transmitted every 1 to 10 seconds. The

BPDU has the group MAC address 800143000000, which is recognized by each bridge. A designated bridge will then update the path cost and timing information and forward the frame. A standby bridge will monitor the BPDUs, but will not update nor forward them.

When a standby bridge is required to assume the role of the root or designated bridge, the HELLO BPDU will indicate that a standby bridge should become a designated bridge. The process by which bridges determine their role in a spanning tree network is iterative. As new bridges enter a network, they assume a listening state to determine their role in the network. Similarly, when a bridge is removed, another iterative process occurs to reconfigure the remaining bridges.

Although the STP algorithm procedure eliminates duplicate frame and degraded internet performance, it can be a hindrance for situations where multiple active paths between networks are desired. Another disadvantage of the spanning tree protocol occurs when it is used in remote bridges connecting geographically dispersed networks. For example, returning to Figure 6.2, suppose Ethernet 1 were located in Los Angeles, Ethernet 2 in New York, and Ethernet 3 in Atlanta. If the link between Los Angeles and New York were placed in a standby mode of operation, all frames from Ethernet 2 routed to Ethernet 1 would be routed through Atlanta. Depending on the traffic between networks, this situation might require an upgrade in the bandwidth of the links connecting each network to accommodate the extra traffic flowing through Atlanta. Since the yearly cost of upgrading a 56- or 64-Kbps circuit to a 128-Kbps fractional T1 link can easily exceed the cost of a bridge or router, you might wish to consider the use of routers to accommodate this networking situation. In comparison, when using local bridges, the higher operating rate of local bridges in interconnecting local area networks normally allows an acceptable level of performance when LAN traffic is routed through an intermediate bridge.

## Protocol Dependency

Another problem associated with the use of transparent bridges concerns the differences between Ethernet and IEEE 802.3 frame field compositions. As noted in Chapter 4, the Ethernet frame contains a type field that indicates the higher layer protocol in use. Under the IEEE 802.3 frame format, the type field is replaced by a length field, and the data field is subdivided to include logical link control (LLC) information in the form of destination (DSAP) and source (SSAP) service access points. Here, the DSAP and SSAP are similar to the type field in an Ethernet frame: they also point to a higher level process. Unfortunately, this small difference can create problems when you are using a transparent bridge to interconnect Ethernet and IEEE 802.3 networks.

The top portion of Figure 6.4 shows the use of a bridge to connect an AppleTalk network supporting several Macintosh computers to an Ethernet network on which a Digital Equipment Corporation VAX computer is located. Although the VAX may be capable of supporting DecNet Phase IV, which is true Ethernet, and AppleTalk if both modules are resident, a pointer is required to direct the IEEE 802.3 frames generated by the Macintosh to the right protocol on the VAX. Unfortunately, the Ethernet connection used by the VAX will not provide the required pointer. This explains why you should avoid connecting Ethernet and IEEE 802.3 networks via transparent bridges. Fortunately, almost all Ethernet network interface cards (NICs) manufactured today are IEEE 802.3–compatible to alleviate this problem; however, older NICs may operate as true Ethernets and result in the previously mentioned problem.

## Source Routing

Source routing is a bridging technique developed by IBM for connecting Token-Ring networks. The key to the implementation of source routing is the use of a portion of the information field in the Token-Ring frame to carry routing information and the transmission of "discovery" packets to determine the best route between two networks.

**Figure 6.4**  Protocol differences preclude linking IEEE 802.3 and Ethernet networks using transparent bridges. A Macintosh computer connected on an IEEE 802.3 network using AppleTalk will not have its frame pointed to the right process on a VAX on an Ethernet. Thus, the differences between Ethernet and IEEE 802.3 networks require transparent bridges for interconnecting similar networks.

The presence of source routing is indicated by the setting of the first bit position in the source address field of a Token-Ring frame to a binary 1. When set, this indicates that the information field is preceded by a route information field (RIF), which contains both control and routing information.

## The RIF Field

Figure 6.5 illustrates the composition of a Token-Ring (RIF). This field is variable in length and is developed during a discovery process, described later in this section.

The control field contains information that defines how information will be transferred and interpreted and what size the remainder of the RIF will be. The three broadcast bit positions indicate a non-broadcast, all-routes broadcast, or single-route broadcast situation. A non-broadcast designator indicates a local or specific route frame. An all-routes broadcast designator indicates that a frame will be transmitted along every route to the destination station. A single-route broadcast designator is used only by designated bridges to relay a frame from one network to another. In examining the broadcast bit settings shown in Figure 6.5, note that the letter $X$ indicates an unspecified bit setting that can be either a 1 or 0.

The length bits identify the length of the RIF in bytes, while the D bit indicates how the field is scanned, left to right or right to left. Since vendors have incorporated different memory in bridges which may limit frame sizes, the LF bits enable different devices to negotiate the size of the frame. Normally, a default setting indicates a frame size of 512 bytes. Each bridge can select a number, and if it is supported by other bridges, that number is then used to represent the negotiated frame size. Otherwise, a smaller number used to represent a smaller frame size is selected

Field Format

B are broadcast bits

| bit settings | designator |
|---|---|
| 0XX | non-broadcast |
| 10X | all-routes broadcast |
| 11X | single route broadcast |

L are length bits which denote length of the RIF in bytes
D is direction bit
LF identifies largest frame

| bit settings | size in bytes |
|---|---|
| 000 | 516 |
| 001 | 1500 |
| 010 | 2052 |
| 011 | 4472 |
| 100 | 8191 |
| 101 | reserved |
| 110 | reserved |
| 111 | used in all-routes broadcast frame |

R are reserved bits

**Figure 6.5** Token-Ring route information field. The Token-Ring route information field is variable in length.

and the negotiation process is repeated. Note that a 1500-byte frame is the largest frame size supported by Ethernet IEEE 802.3 networks. Thus, a bridge used to connect Ethernet and Token-Ring networks cannot support the use of Token-Ring frames exceeding 1500 bytes.

Up to eight route number subfields, each consisting of a 12-bit ring number and a 4-bit bridge number, can be contained in the routing information field. This permits two to eight route designators, enabling frames to traverse up to eight rings across seven bridges in a given direction. Both ring numbers and bridge numbers are expressed as hexadecimal characters, with three hex characters used to denote the ring number and one hex character used to identify the bridge number.

## Operation Example

To illustrate the concept behind source routing, consider the internet illustrated in Figure 6.6. In this example, let us assume that two Token-Ring networks are located in Atlanta and one network is located in New York.

Each Token-Ring and bridge is assigned a ring or bridge number. For simplicity, ring numbers R1, R2, and R3 are

**Figure 6.6** Source routing discovery operation. The route discovery process results in each bridge entering the originating ring number and its bridge number into the route information field.

used here, although as previously explained, those numbers are actually represented in hexadecimal. Similarly, bridge numbers are shown here as B1, B2, B3, B4, and B5 instead of hexadecimal characters.

When a station wants to originate communications, it is responsible for finding the destination by transmitting a discovery packet to network bridges and other network stations whenever it has a message to transmit to a new destination address. If station A wishes to transmit to station C, it sends a route discovery packet containing an empty route information field and its source address, as indicated in the upper left portion of Figure 6.6. This packet is recognized by each source routing bridge in the network. When a source routing bridge receives the packet, it enters the packet's ring number and its own bridge identifier in the packet's routing information field. The bridge then transmits the packet to all of its connections except the connection on which the packet was received, a process known as *flooding*. Depending on the topology of the interconnected networks, it is more than likely that multiple copies of the discovery packet will reach the recipient. This is illustrated in the upper right corner of Figure 6.6, in which two discovery packets reach station C. Here, one packet contains the sequence R1B1R1B2R30—the zero indicates that there is no bridging in the last ring. The second packet contains the route sequence R1B3R2B4R2B5R30. Station C then picks the best route, based on either the most direct path or the earliest arriving packet, and transmits a response to the discover packet originator. The response indicates the specific route to use, and station A then enters that route into memory for the duration of the transmission session.

Under source routing, bridges do not keep routing tables like transparent bridges. Instead, tables are maintained at each station throughout the network. Thus, each station must check its routing table to determine what route frames must traverse to reach their destination station. This routing method results in source routing using distributed routing tables instead of the centralized routing tables used by transparent bridges.

## Advantages

There are several advantages associated with source routing. One advantage is the ability to construct mesh networks with loops for a fault-tolerant design; this cannot be accomplished with the use of transparent bridges. Another advantage is the inclusion of routing information in the information frames. Several vendors have developed network management software products which use that information to provide statistical information concerning internet activity. Those products may assist you in determining how heavily your wide area network links are being used, and whether you need to modify the capacity of those links; they may also inform you if one or more workstations are hogging communications between networks.

## Disadvantages

Although the preceding advantages are considerable, they are not without a price. That price includes a requirement to identify bridges and links specifically, higher bursts of network activity, and an incompatibility between Token-Ring and Ethernet networks. In addition, because the structure of the Token-Ring route information field supports a maximum of seven entries, routing of frames is restricted to crossing a maximum of seven bridges.

When using source routing bridges to connect Token-Ring networks, you must configure each bridge with a unique bridge/ring number. In addition, unless you wish to accept the default method by which stations select a frame during the route discovery process, you will have to reconfigure your LAN software. Thus, source routing creates an administrative burden not incurred by transparent bridges.

Due to the route discovery process, the flooding of discovery frames occurs in bursts when stations are turned on or after a power outage. Depending upon the complexity of an internet, the discovery process can degrade network performance. This is perhaps the most problematic for organizations that require the interconnection of Ethernet and Token-Ring networks.

A source routing bridge can be used only to interconnect Token-Ring networks, since it operates on route information field data that is not included in an Ethernet frame. Although transparent bridges can operate in Ethernet, Token-Ring, and mixed environments, their use precludes the ability to construct loop or mesh topologies, and inhibits the ability to establish operational redundant paths for load sharing. Another problem associated with bridging Ethernet and Token-Ring networks also involves the route information field in a Token-Ring frame. Unfortunately, different LAN operating systems use the RIF data in different ways. Thus, the use of a transparent bridge to interconnect Ethernet and Token-Ring networks may require the same local area network operating system on each network. To alleviate these problems, several vendors introduced source routing transparent (SRT) bridges, which function in accordance with the IEEE 802.1D standard that was approved during 1992.

## Source Routing Transparent Bridges

A source routing transparent bridge supports both IBM's source routing and the IEEE transparent spanning tree protocol operations. This type of bridge can be considered two bridges in one; it has been standardized by the IEEE 802.1 committee as the IEEE 802.1D standard.

## Operation

Under source routing, the media access control packets contain a status bit in the source field that identifies whether source routing is to be used for a message. If source routing is indicated, the bridge forwards the frame as a source routing frame. If source routing is not indicated, the bridge determines the destination address and processes the packet using a transparent mode of operation, using routing tables generated by a spanning tree algorithm.

## Advantages

There are several advantages associated with source routing transparent bridges. First and perhaps foremost, they enable different networks to use different local area network operating systems and protocols. This capability enables you to interconnect networks developed independently of one another, and allows organization departments and branches to use LAN operating systems without restriction. Secondly, also a very important consideration, source routing transparent bridges can connect Ethernet and Token-Ring networks while preserving the ability to mesh or loop Token-Ring networks. Thus, their use provides an additional level of flexibility for network construction.

# 6.2 Network Utilization

In this section, we will examine the use of bridges to interconnect separate local area networks and to subdivide networks to improve performance. In addition, we will focus our attention on how we can increase network availability by employing bridges to provide alternate communications paths between networks.

## Serial and Sequential Bridging

The top of Figure 6.7 illustrates the basic use of a bridge to interconnect two networks serially. Suppose that monitoring of each network indicates a high level of intra-network utilization. One possible configuration to reduce intra-LAN traffic on each network can be obtained by moving some stations off each of the two existing networks to form a third network. The three networks would then be interconnected through the use of an additional bridge, as illustrated in the middle portion of Figure 6.7. This extension results in *sequential* or *cascaded bridging*, and is appropriate when intra-LAN traffic is necessary but minimal. This internet topology is also extremely useful when the length of an Ethernet must be extended beyond the physical cabling of a single network. By locating servers appropriately within each network segment, you may be able to minimize inter-LAN transmission. For example, the first network segment could be used to connect marketing personnel, while the second and third segments could be used to connect engineering and personnel departments. This might minimize the use of a server on one network by persons connected to another network segment. Both serial and sequential bridging are applicable to transparent, source routing, and source routing transparent bridges that do not provide redundancy nor the ability to balance traffic flowing between networks. Each of these deficiencies can be alleviated through the use of parallel bridging. However, this bridging technique creates a loop and is only applicable to source routing and source routing transparent bridges.

## Parallel Bridging

The lower portion of Figure 6.7 illustrates the use of parallel bridges to interconnect two Token-Ring networks. This bridging configuration permits one bridge to back up the other, providing a level of redundancy for linking the two networks as well as a significant increase in the availability

**Figure 6.7**    *Serial, sequential, and parallel bridging.*

of one network to communicate with another. For example, assume the availability of each bridge used at the top of Figure 6.7 (serial bridging) and bottom of Figure 6.7 (parallel bridging) is 90 percent. The availability through two serially connected bridges would be $0.9 \times 0.9$ (unavailability of bridge 1 × unavailability of bridge 2), or 81 percent. In comparison, the availability through parallel bridges would be $1-(0.1 \times 0.1)$, which is 99 percent.

The dual paths between networks also improve inter-LAN communications performance, because communications between stations on each network can be load balanced. The use of parallel bridges can thus be expected to provide a higher level of inter-LAN communications than the use of serial or sequential bridges. However, as previously noted, this topology is not supported by transparent bridging.

## Star Bridging

With a multiport bridge, you can connect three or more networks to form a star internet topology. The top portion of Figure 6.8 shows the use of one bridge to form a star topology by interconnecting four separate networks. This topology, or a variation on this topology, could be used to interconnect networks on separate floors within a building. For example, the top network could be on floor N+1, while the bottom network could be on floor N–1 in a building. The bridge and the two networks to the left and right of the bridge might then be located on floor N.

Although star bridging permits several networks located on separate floors within a building to be interconnected, all internet data must flow through one bridge. This can result in both performance and reliability constraints to traffic flow. Thus, to internet separate networks on more than a

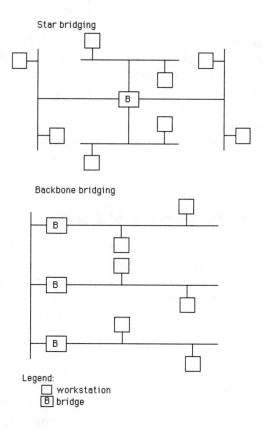

**Figure 6.8** *Star and backbone bridging.*

few floors in a building, you should consider using of backbone bridging.

## Backbone Bridging

The lower portion of Figure 6.8 illustrates the use of back-bone bridging. In this example, one network runs vertically through a building with Ethernet "ribs" extending from the backbone onto each floor. Depending upon the amount of internet traffic and the vertical length required for the backbone network, the backbone can be either a conventional Ethernet bus-based network or a fiber optic backbone. For the latter, you might consider using a 100-Mbps FDDI network that could serve as a "super highway" to transport data among many individual Ethernet networks installed on separate floors within a building.

# 6.3 Performance Issues

The key to obtaining an appropriate level of performance when interconnecting networks is planning. The actual planning process will depend upon several factors, such as whether separate networks are in operation, the type of networks to be connected, and the type of bridges to be used—local or remote.

## Traffic Flow

If separate networks are in operation and you have appropriate monitoring equipment, you can determine the traffic flow on each of the networks to be interconnected. Once this is accomplished, you can expect an approximate 10 to 20 percent increase in network traffic. This additional traffic represents the flow of information between networks after an interconnection links previously separated local area networks. Although this traffic increase represents an average encountered by the author, your network traffic may not represent the typical average. To explore further, you can examine the potential for internet communications in the form of electronic messages that may be transmitted to users on other networks, potential file transfers of word processing files, and other types of data that would flow between networks.

## Network Types

The types of networks to be connected will govern the rate at which frames are presented to bridges. This rate, in turn, will govern the filtering rate at which bridges should operate so that they do not become bottlenecks on a network. For example, the maximum number of frames per second will vary between different types of Ethernet and Token-Ring networks, as well as between different types of the same network. The operating rate of a bridge may thus be appropriate for connecting some networks while inappropriate for connecting other types of networks.

## Type of Bridge

Last but not least, the type of bridge—local or remote—will have a considerable bearing upon performance issues. Local bridges pass data between networks at their operating rates. In comparison, remote bridges pass data between networks using wide area network transmission facilities, which typically provide a transmission rate that is only a fraction of a local area network operating rate. Now that we have discussed some of the aspects governing bridge and internet performance using bridges, let's probe deeper by estimating network traffic.

## Estimating Network Traffic

If we do not have access to monitoring equipment to analyze an existing network, or if we are planning to install a new network, we can spend some time to develop a reasonable estimate of network traffic. To do so, we should attempt to classify stations into groups based on the type of general activity performed, and then estimate the network activity for one station per group. This will enable us to multiply the number of stations in the group by the station activity to determine the group network traffic. Adding up the activity of all groups will then provide us with an estimate of the traffic activity for the network.

As an example of local area network traffic estimation, let us assume that our network will support 20 engineers, 5 managers, and 3 secretaries. Table 6.1 shows how we would estimate the network traffic in terms of the bit rate for each station group and the total activity per group, and then sum up the network traffic for the three groups that will use the network. In this example, which for the sake of simplicity does not include the transmission of data to a workstation printer, the total network traffic was estimated to be slightly below 50,000 bps.

**Table 6.1**  Estimating network traffic

**Engineering Workstations**

| Activity | Message Size (Bytes) | Frequency | Bit Rate* |
|---|---|---|---|
| Request Program | 1,500 | 1/hour | 4 |
| Load program | 480,000 | 1/hour | 1,067 |
| Save files | 120,000 | 2/hour | 533 |
| Send/receive E-mail | 2,000 | 2/hour | 9 |
| | | | 1,613 |

Total Engineering Activity = 1,613 × 20 = 32,260 bps

**Table 6.1**   Estimating network traffic *(continued)*

**Managerial Workstations**

| Activity | Message Size (Bytes) | Frequency | Bit Rate* |
|---|---|---|---|
| Request Program | 1,500 | 2/hour | 7 |
| Load program | 320,000 | 2/hour | 1,422 |
| Save files | 30,000 | 2/hour | 134 |
| Send/receive E-mail | 3,000 | 4/hour | 27 |
| | | | 1,590 |

Total Managerial Activity = 1,590 × 5 = 7,950 bps

**Secretarial Workstations**

| Activity | Message Size (Bytes) | Frequency | Bit Rate* |
|---|---|---|---|
| Request Program | 1,500 | 4/hour | 14 |
| Load program | 640,000 | 2/hour | 2,844 |
| Save files | 12,000 | 8/hour | 214 |
| Send/receive E-mail | 3,000 | 6/hour | 40 |
| | | | 3,112 |

Total Secretarial Activity = 3,112 × 3 = 9,336 bps

Total Estimated Network Activity = 45,546 bps

*Note: Bit rate is computed by multiplying message rate by frequency by 8 bits/byte and dividing by 3,600 seconds/hour.

To plan for the interconnection of two or more networks through the use of bridges, our next step should be to perform a similar traffic analysis for each of the remaining networks. After this is accomplished, we can use the network traffic to estimate inter-LAN traffic, using 10 to 20 percent of total intra-network traffic as an estimate of the internet traffic that will result from the connection of separate networks.

## Internet Traffic

To illustrate the traffic estimation process for the interconnection of separate LANs, let us assume that network A's traffic was determined to be 50,000 bps, while network B's traffic was estimated to be approximately 100,000 bps. Figure 6.9 illustrates the flow of data between networks connected by a local bridge. Note that the data flow in each direction is expressed as a range, based on the use of an industry average of 10 to 20 percent of network traffic routed between interconnected networks.

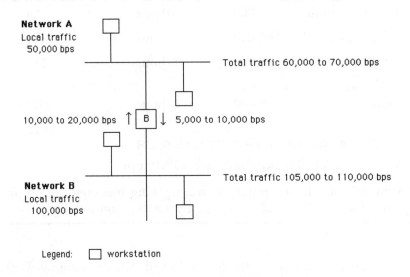

**Figure 6.9** *Considering internet data flow. To determine the traffic flow on separate networks after they are interconnected, you must consider the flow of data onto each network from the other network.*

## Network Types

Our next area of concern is to examine the types of networks to be interconnected. In doing so, we should focus our attention on the operating rate of each LAN. If network A's traffic was estimated to be approximately 50,000 bps, then the addition of 10,000 to 20,000 bps from network B onto network A will raise network A's traffic level to between 60,000 and 70,000 bps. Similarly, the addition of traffic from network A onto network B will raise network B's traffic level to between 105,000 and 110,000 bps. In this example, the resulting traffic on each network is well below the operating rate of all types of local area networks, and will not present a capacity problem for either network.

## Bridge Type

As previously mentioned, local bridges transmit data between networks at the data rate of the destination network. This means that a local bridge will have a lower probability of being an internet bottleneck than a remote bridge, since the latter provides a connection between networks using a wide area transmission facility, which typically operates at a fraction of the operating rate of a LAN.

In examining the bridge operating rate required to connect networks, we will use a bottom-up and a top-down approach. That is, we will first determine the operating rate in frames per second for the specific example previously discussed. This will be followed by computing the maximum frame rate supported by an Ethernet network.

For the bridge illustrated in Figure 6.9, we previously computed that its maximum transfer rate would be 20,000 bps from network B onto network A. This is equivalent to 2,500 bytes per second. If we assume that data is transported in 512-byte frames, this would be equivalent to 6 frames per second—a minimal transfer rate supported by every bridge manufacturer. However, when remote bridges are used, the frame forwarding rate of the bridge will more than likely be constrained by the operating rate of the wide area network transmission facility.

## Bridge Operational Considerations

A remote bridge wraps a LAN frame into a higher level protocol packet for transmission over a wide area network communications facility. This operation requires the addition of a header, protocol control, error detection, and trailer fields and results in a degree of overhead. A 20000-bps data flow from network B to network A therefore could not be accommodated by a transmission facility operating at that data rate.

In converting LAN traffic onto a wide area network transmission facility, you can expect a protocol overhead of approximately 20 percent. Thus, your actual operating rate must be at least 24000 bps before the wide area network communications link becomes a bottleneck and degrades internet communication. Now that we have examined the bridging performance requirements for two relatively small networks, let us focus our attention on determining the maximum frame rates of an Ethernet network. This will provide us with the ability to determine the rate at which the frame processing rate of a bridge becomes irrelevant, since any processing rate above the maximum network rate will not be useful. In addition, we can use the maximum network frame rate when estimating traffic, because if we approach that rate, network performance will begin to degrade significantly when utilization exceeds between 60 to 70 percent of that rate.

## Ethernet Traffic Estimation

An Ethernet frame can vary between a minimum of 72 bytes and a maximum of 1,526 bytes. Thus, the maximum frame rate on an Ethernet will vary with the frame size.

Ethernet operations require a dead time between frames of 9.6 usec. The bit time for a 10-Mbps Ethernet is $1/10^7$ or 100 nsec. Based upon the preceding, we can compute the maximum number of frames/second for 1526 byte frames. Here, the time per frame becomes:

9.6 usec + 1,526 bytes × 8 bits/byte

or      9.6 usec + 12,208 bits × 100 nsec/bit

or      1.23 msec

Thus, in one second there can be a maximum of 1/1.23 msec or 812 maximum size frames. For a minimum frame size of 72 bytes, the time per frame is:

9.6 usec + 72 bytes × 8 bits/byte × 100 nsec/bit

or      $67.2 × 10^{-6}$ second.

Thus, in one second there can be a maximum of $1/67.2 × 10^{-6}$ or 14,880 minimum-size 72-byte frames. Table 6.2 summarizes the frame processing requirements for a 10-Mbps Ethernet under 50 percent and 100 percent load conditions, based on minimum and maximum frame sizes. Note that those frame processing requirements define the frame examination (filtering) operating rate of a bridge connected to an Ethernet. That rate indicates the number of frames per second a bridge connected to a 10-Mbps Ethernet local area network must be capable of examining under heavy (50 percent load) and full (100 percent load) traffic conditions.

**Table 6.2**  Ethernet frame processing requirements (frames per second)

| Average Frame Size (bytes) | Frame Processing Requirements | |
| --- | --- | --- |
| | 50% Load | 100% Load |
| 1526 | 405 | 812 |
| 72 | 7,440 | 14,880 |

We can extend our analysis of Ethernet frames by considering the frame rate supported by different link speeds. For example, let us consider a pair of remote bridges connected by a 9.6-kbps line. The time per frame for a 72-byte frame at 9.6 kbps is:

$$9.6 \times 10^{-6} + 72 \times 8 \times 0.0001041 \text{s/bit or } 0.0599712$$

seconds per frame. Thus, in one second the number of frames is 1/.0599712, or 16.67 frames per second. Table 6.3 compares the frame-per-second rate supported by different link speeds for minimum and maximum size Ethernet frames. As expected, the frame transmission rate supported by a 10-Mbps link for minimum and maximum size frames is exactly the same as the frame processing requirements under 100 percent loading, as indicated in Table 6.2.

In examining Table 6.3, note that the entries in this table do not consider the effect of the overhead of a protocol used to transport frames between two networks. You should therefore decrease the frame-per-second rate by approximately 20 percent for all link speeds through 1.536 Mbps. The reason the 10-Mbps rate should not be adjusted is that it represents a local bridge connection that does not

**Table 6.3**   Link speed versus frame rate

| Link Speed | Frames Per Second Minimum | Maximum |
|---|---|---|
| 9.6 Kbps | 16.67 | 0.79 |
| 19.2 Kbps | 33.38 | 1.58 |
| 56.0 Kbps | 97.44 | 4.60 |
| 64.0 Kbps | 111.17 | 5.25 |
| 1.536 Mbps | 2,815.31 | 136.34 |
| 10.0 Mbps | 14,880.00 | 812.00 |

require the use of a wide area network protocol to transport frames. Also note that the link speed of 1.536 Mbps represents a T1 transmission facility that operates at 1.544 Mbps. However, since the framing bits on a T1 circuit use 8 Kbps, the effective line speed available for the transmission of data is 1.536 Mbps.

## Predicting Throughput

Until now, we have assumed that the operating rate of each LAN linked by a bridge is the same. However, in many organizations this may not be true, because LANs are implemented at different times using different technologies. Thus, accounting may be using a 10-Mbps LAN, while the personnel department might be using a 1-Mbps LAN.

Suppose we wanted to interconnect the two LANs via the use of a multimedia bridge. To predict throughput between LANs, let us use the network configuration illustrated in Figure 6.10. Here, the operating rate of LAN A is assumed to be $R_1$ bps, while the operating rate of LAN B is assumed to be $R_2$ bps.

In one second, $R_1$ bits can be transferred on LAN A and $R_2$ bits can be transferred on LAN B. Similarly, it takes $1/R_1$

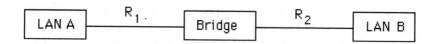

**Figure 6.10** Linking LANs with different operating rates. When LANs with different operating rates ($R_1$ and $R_2$) are connected via a bridge, access of files across the bridge may result in an unacceptable level of performance.

seconds to transfer one bit on LAN A and $1/R_2$ seconds to transfer one bit on LAN B. So, to transfer one bit across the bridge from LAN A to LAN B, ignoring the transfer time at the bridge:

$$\frac{1}{R_T} = \frac{1}{R_1} + \frac{1}{R_2}$$

or

$$R_T = \frac{1}{\dfrac{1}{R_1} + \dfrac{1}{R_2}}$$

We computed that a 10-Mbps Ethernet would support a maximum transfer of 812 maximum-sized frames per second. If we assume that the second LAN operating at 1 Mbps is also an Ethernet, we would compute its transfer rate to be approximately 81 maximum-sized frames per second. The throughput in frames per second would then become:

$$R_T = \frac{1}{\dfrac{1}{812} + \dfrac{1}{81}} = 73 \text{ frames per second}$$

Knowing the transfer rate between LANs can help us answer many common questions. It can also provide us with a mechanism for determining whether we should alter the location of application programs on different servers. For example, suppose that a program located on a server on LAN B suddenly became popular for use by workstations on LAN A. If the program required 320 K of storage, we could estimate the minimum transfer time required to load that program and, depending on the results of our calculation, we might want to move the program onto a server on LAN A. For this example, the data transfer rate would be 73 frames/second × 1,500 bytes/frame or 109,500 bytes per second. Dividing the data to be transferred by the data transfer rate, we obtain:

$$\frac{320 \text{ K bytes} \times 1024 \text{ bytes/K}}{109500 \text{ bytes/seconds}} = 2.99 \text{ seconds}$$

The preceding computation represents a best-case scenario, in which the use of each network is limited to the user on LAN A loading a program from a server on LAN B. In reality, the average number of users using the resources of each network must be used to adjust the values of $R_1$ and $R_2$. For example, suppose that through monitoring you determined that the average number of active users on LAN A was 3 and on LAN B was 2. In that case, you would adjust the value of $R_1$ by dividing 812 by 3 to obtain 270.6, and adjust the value of $R_2$ by dividing 81 by 2 to obtain 40.5. You would then use the new values of $R_1$ and $R_2$ to obtain the average value of $R_T$, based on the fact that the program loading operation would be performed concurrently with other operations on each network. Once you computed the average frame transfer rate, you would divide that value into the quantity of data to be transferred to obtain the average expected transfer time.

# CHAPTER 7

# Routers

In Chapter 5, we examined the basic operation and utilization of a variety of local area networking components, including routers. Information presented in that chapter will serve as a foundation for the more detailed discussion of the operation and utilization of routers presented in this chapter.

## 7.1 Router Operation

By operating at the ISO Reference Model Network Layer, a router becomes capable of making intelligent decisions concerning the flow of information in a network. To accomplish this, routers perform a variety of functions that are significantly different from those performed by bridges. Unlike bridges, routers are addressable. Routers examine frames that are directly addressed to them by looking at the network address within each frame to make their forwarding decisions.

## Basic Operation and Use of Routing Tables

To see the basic operation of routers, consider the simple mesh structure formed by the use of three routers labeled R1, R2, and R3 in Figure 7.1A. In this illustration, three Ethernet networks are interconnected through the use of three routers.

The initial construction of three routing tables is shown in Figure 7.1B. Unlike bridges, which learn MAC addresses, most routers are initially configured, and routing tables are established at the time of equipment installation. Thereafter, periodic communication between routers updates routing tables to take into consideration any changes in internet topology and traffic.

In examining Figure 7.1B, note that the routing table for router R1 indicates which routers it must communicate with to access each interconnected Ethernet network. Router R1 would communicate with router R2 to reach Token-Ring network 2, and with router R3 to reach Token-Ring network 3.

Figure 7.1C illustrates the composition of a packet originated by station S2 on Ethernet 1 that is to be transmitted to station S12 on Ethernet 2. Router R1 first examines the destination network address and notes that it is on another network. The router searches its routing table and finds that the frame should be transmitted to router R2 to reach Ethernet network 2. Router R1 forwards the frame to router R2. Router R2 then places the frame onto Ethernet network 2 for delivery to station S12 on that network.

Since routers use the network addresses instead of MAC addresses for making their forwarding decisions, it is possible to have duplicate locally administered MAC

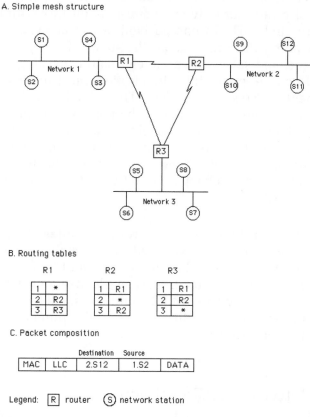

**Figure 7.1** Basic router operation.

addresses on each network interconnected by a router. The use of bridges, on the other hand, requires you to review and then eliminate any duplicate locally administered addresses. This process can be time-consuming when large networks are connected.

Another difference between bridges and routers is that a router can support the transmission of data on multiple paths between local area networks. Although a multiport bridge with a filtering capability can perform intelligent routing decisions, the result of a bridge operation is normally valid for only one point-to-point link within a wide area network. In comparison, a router may be able to acquire information about the status of a large number of paths and select an end-to-end path consisting of a series of point-to-point links. In addition, most routers can fragment and reassemble data. This permits packets to flow over different paths and to be reassembled at their final destination. With this capability, a router can route each packet to its destination over the best possible path at a particular instant in time, and change paths dynamically to correspond to changes in network link status on traffic activity.

For example, each of the routing tables illustrated in Figure 7.1B can be expanded to indicate a secondary path to each network. While router R1 would continue to use the entry of R2 as its primary mechanism to reach network 2, a secondary entry of R3 could be established to provide an alternative path to network 2 via routers R3 and R2, rather than directly via router R2.

## Networking Capability

For an illustration of the networking capability of routers, see Figure 7.2. It shows three geographically dispersed locations that have a total of four Ethernet and three Token-Ring networks, interconnected through the use of four routers and four wide area network transmission circuits or links. For simplicity, modems and DSUs on the wide area network are not shown. This figure will be referred to several times in this chapter to illustrate different types of router operations.

In addition to supporting a mesh structure that is not obtainable from the use of transparent bridges, routers offer other advantages in the form of addressing, message processing, link utilization, and priority of service. A router is known to stations that use its service. Packets can thus be addressed directly to a router. This eliminates the necessity for the device to examine in detail every packet flowing on a network, and results in the router having to process only messages that are addressed to it by other devices.

**Figure 7.2**   Router operation. Routers enable the transmission of data over multiple paths, alternate path routing, and the use of a mesh topology that transparent bridges cannot support.

Assume that a station on E1 transmits to a station on TR3. Depending on the status and traffic on network links, packets could be routed via L1 and use TR2 to provide a transport mechanism to R4, from which the packets are delivered to TR3. Alternatively, links L2 and L4 could be used to provide a path from R1 to R4. Although link availability and link traffic usually determine routing, routers can support prioritized traffic, and may store low priority traffic for a small period of time to allow higher priority traffic to gain access to the wide area transmission facility. Because of these features, which are essentially unavailable with bridges, the router is a more complex and more expensive device.

# 7.2 Communication, Transport, and Routing Protocols

For routers to be able to operate in a network, they must normally be able to speak the same language at both the data link and network layers. The key to accomplishing this is the ability to support common communication, transport, and routing protocols.

## Communication Protocol

Communication protocols support the transfer of data from a station on one network to a station on another network; they occur at the OSI network layer. In examining Figure 7.3, which illustrates several common protocol implementations with respect to the OSI Reference Model, you will note that Novell's NetWare uses IPX as its network communications protocol, while IBM LANs use the PC LAN Support Program, and Microsoft's LAN Manager uses the Internet Protocol (IP). This means that a router linking networks

| OSI Layer | Common Protocol Implementation | | | |
|---|---|---|---|---|
| Application | Application Programs | | | |
| | Application Protocols | | | |
| Presentation | Novell Network File Server Protocol (NFSP) | | IBM Server Message Block (SMB) | Microsoft LAN Manager |
| Session | Xerox Networking System (XNS) | N e t B I O S | NetBIOS | NetBIOS Advanced Peer-to-Peer Communications |
| Transport | Sequenced Packet Exchange (SPX) | | PC LAN Support Program | Transmission Control Protocol (TCP) Transport Protocol Class 4 (TCP4) |
| Network | Internetwork Packet Exchange (IPX) | | | Internet Protocol (IP) |
| Data Link | Logical Link Control 802.2 | | | |
| | Media Access Control | | | |
| Physical | Transmission Media: Twisted pair, coax, fiber optic | | | |

**Figure 7.3**  *Common protocol implementations. Although Novell, IBM, and Microsoft LAN operating system software support standardized physical and data link operations, they differ considerably in their use of communication and routing protocols.*

based on Novell, IBM, and Microsoft LAN operating systems must support those three communication protocols. Router communication protocol support is a very important criterion in determining whether a particular product is capable of supporting your networking requirements.

## Routing Protocol

The routing protocol is the method used by routers to exchange routing information; it forms the basis for providing a connection across an internet. In evaluating routers, it is important to determine the efficiency of the routing protocol, its effect upon the transmission of information, the method used and memory required to construct routing tables, and the time required to adjust those tables. Examples of router-to-router protocols include Xerox Network Systems' (XNS) Routing Information Protocol (RIP), the Transmission Control Protocol/Internet Protocol's (ICP/IP) RIP, Open Shortest Path First (OSPF), and Hello routing protocols.

## Transport Protocol

The transport protocol represents the format by which information is physically transported between two points. Here, the transport protocol represents the data link layer illustrated in Figure 7.3. Examples of transport protocols include Token-Ring and Ethernet MAC for LANs and X.25 and Frame Relay for WANs.

There are a wide variety of communication and transport protocols in use today. Some of these protocols, such as Apple Computer's AppleTalk, were designed specifically to operate on local area networks. Other protocols, such as X.25 and Frame Relay, were developed as wide area network protocols.

16 popular communication and transport protocols are listed below. Many routers support only a subset of these protocols.

- AppleTalk
- Applo Domain VINES
- Banyan

- CHAOSnet
- DECnet Phase IV
- DECnet Phase V
- DDN X.25
- Frame Relay
- ISO CLNS
- HDLC
- NOVELL IPX
- SDLC
- TCP/IP
- Xerox XNS
- X.25
- Ungermann-Bass Net/One

# 7.3 Router Classifications

Depending upon their support of communication and transport protocols, routers can be classified into two groups: protocol-dependent and protocol-independent.

## Protocol-Dependent Routers

To understand the characteristics of a protocol-dependent router, consider the internet illustrated in Figure 7.2. If a station on network E1 wishes to transmit data to a second station on network E3, router R1 must know that the second station resides on network E3, and it must know the best path to use to reach that network. The method used to determine the destination station's network also determines the protocol dependency of the router.

If the station on network E1 tells router R1 the destination location, it must supply a network address in every LAN packet it transmits. This means that all routers in the internet must support the protocol used on network E1. Otherwise, stations on network E1 could not communicate with stations residing on other networks, and vice versa.

### NetWare IPX Example

To illustrate the operation of a protocol-dependent router, let us assume that networks E1 and E3 use Novell's NetWare as their LAN operating system. The routing protocol used at the network layer between a station and server on a Novell network is known as IPX. This protocol can also be used between servers.

Under NetWare's IPX, a packet addressed to a router will contain the destination address in the form of network and host addresses, and the origination address in the form of the source network and source host addresses. Here, the IPX term *host* is actually the physical address of a network adapter card.

Figure 7.4A illustrates in simplified format the IPX packet composition for workstation A on network E1, transmitting data to workstation B on network E3, under Novell's NetWare IPX protocol.

After router R1 receives and examines the packet, it notes that the destination address E3 requires the routing of the packet to router R2. It converts the first packet into a router (R1) to router (R2) packet, as illustrated in Figure 7.4B. At router R2, the packet is again examined. Router R2 notes that the destination network address (E3) is con-

A. Packet from workstation A, network E1 to router R1

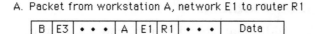

B. Router (R1) to router (R2) packet

C. Router R2 converts packet for placement on network E3

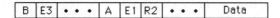

**Figure 7.4**   NetWare IPX routing.

nected to that router, so it reconverts the packet for delivery onto network E3. It does this by converting the destination router address to a source router address and transmitting the packet onto network E3. This is illustrated in Figure 7.4C.

## Addressing Differences

In the preceding example, note that each router uses the destination workstation and network addresses to transfer packets. If all protocols used the same format and addressing structure, routers would be protocol-insensitive at the network layer. Unfortunately, this is not true. For example, TCP/IP addressing conventions are very different from those used by NetWare. This means that networks using different operating systems require the use of multiprotocol routers configured to perform address translation. Each multiprotocol router must maintain separate routing tables for each supported protocol, requiring additional memory and time.

## Other Problems

Two additional problems associated with protocol-dependent routers are the time required for packet examination and the fact that not all LAN protocols are routable. If a packet must traverse a large network, the time required by a series of routers to modify the packet and assure its delivery to the next router can significantly degrade router performance. To overcome this problem, organizations should consider the use of a Frame Relay service.

In addition to providing an enhanced data delivery service by eliminating error detection and correction within the network, the use of a Frame Relay service can significantly reduce the cost of routers. Consider, for example, the network in Figure 7.2, in which four routers are interconnected through the use of five links. To support transmission on five links, the routers require ten ports. Normally, each router port is obtained as an adapter card installed in a high performance computer. If a Frame Relay service is used, the packet network providing that service also provides the routing paths to interconnect routers, as illustrated in Figure 7.5. This reduces the number of required router ports to four. This reduction can result in a considerable hardware savings.

A second problem associated with protocol-dependent routers is the fact that some LAN protocols cannot be routed using that type of device. This is because some LAN protocols, such as NetBIOS and IBM's LAN Server—and unlike NetWare, DECnet and TCP/IP—do not include routing information within a packet. Instead, those protocols employ a user-friendly device-naming convention instead of using network and device addresses. This convention permits such names as "Gil's PC" and "Accounting Printer" to be used. For example, IBM's Network Basic Input/Output System (NetBIOS) was designed to facilitate program-to-program communication by hiding the complexities of network addressing from the user. Thus, NetBIOS uses names up to 16

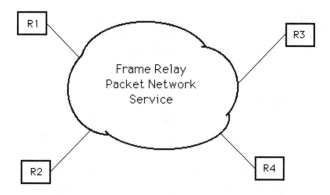

**Figure 7.5** Using a frame relay service. If a frame relay service is used, the packet network provides the capability for interconnecting each network access port to other network access ports. Thus, only one router port is required to obtain an interconnection capability to numerous routers connected to the network.

alphanumeric characters long to define clients and servers on a network. Unfortunately, NetBIOS does not include a facility to distinguish one network from another, since it lacks a network addressing capability. Such protocols are restricted to using the physical addresses of adapter cards, such as Token-Ring source and destination addresses. Since a protocol-dependent router must know the network on which a destination address is located, it cannot route such protocols. A logical question, then, is how a router interconnects networks using an IBM LAN protocol. The answer to this question is bridging. That is, a protocol-dependent router must operate as a bridge in the previously described situation.

## Protocol-Independent Routers

A protocol-independent router functions as a sophisticated transparent bridge. That is, it addresses the problem of network protocols that do not have network addresses. It does this by examining the source addresses on connected networks to learn automatically what devices are on each network. The protocol-independent router assigns network identifiers to each network whose operating system does not include network addresses in its network protocol. This activity enables both routable and nonroutable protocols to be serviced by a protocol-dependent router.

In addition to building address tables automatically like a transparent bridge, a protocol-independent router exchanges information concerning its routing directions with other internet routers. This enables each router to build a map of the internet. The method used to build the network map falls under the category of a link state routing protocol, which is described later in this chapter.

## Advantages

There are two key advantages to using protocol-independent routers. Those advantages are the abilities of routers to learn network topology automatically and to service nonroutable protocols. The ability to learn network topology automatically can considerably simplify the administration of an internet. For example, in a TCP/IP network, each workstation has an IP address and must know the IP addresses of other LAN devices it wants to communicate with.

IP addresses are assigned by a network administrator, and they must be changed if a station is moved to a different network, or if a network is segmented because of a high level of traffic or other reason. In such situations, all LAN users must be notified about the new IP address, or they will not be able to locate the moved station. Obviously, the movement of stations within a building between different LANs could become a considerable administrative burden. The ability of a protocol-independent router to learn addresses automatically removes the administrative burden of notifying users of changes in network addresses.

The ability to route nonroutable protocols can be of considerable assistance in integrating IBM System Architecture (SNA) networks into an enterprise network. Otherwise, without the use of protocol-independent routers, organizations may have to maintain separate transmission facilities for SNA and LAN traffic.

## Supporting SNA Traffic

Figure 7.6 illustrates the use of protocol-independent routers to support both interLAN and SNA traffic. In this example, an IBM SNA network, a 3174 control unit with a Token-Ring adapter (TRA) at a remote site provides communications connectivity to an IBM 3745 communications controller at a central site. Routers must be capable of routing both SNA and LAN traffic to enable the use of a common transmission facility between the central and remote site.

**Figure 7.6** Supporting SNA traffic. A protocol-independent router can support SNA traffic and other LAN traffic over a common transmission facility.

**Methods to Consider**    There are essentially two methods by which SNA and LAN traffic can be combined for routing over a common network: encapsulation and protocol-independent routing. Under the encapsulation method, SNA packets are modified so that another protocol's header, addressing, and trailer fields surround each SNA packet. For example, a TCP/IP protocol–dependent router would encapsulate SNA into TCP/IP packets for routing through a TCP/IP network. Since a TCP/IP packet has over 60 bytes of overhead, and the average SNA packet is 30 bytes in length, encapsulation can reduce performance considerably when transmission occurs over low-speed links. A second disadvantage of encapsulation is that it requires the existence of a corporate network using the encapsulation protocol. Otherwise, you would have to build this network to obtain an encapsulation capability.

The second method by which an SNA network can be integrated with LAN traffic is through protocol-independent routing. Protocol-independent routers assign a LAN device address to each SNA control unit and communications controller. Then, SNA packets are prefixed with source and destination addresses to permit their routing through the internet. At the destination router, the addressing information is removed, and the SNA packets are delivered to their destination in their original form. Since the addition of source and destination addresses adds a significantly lower number of bytes than an encapsulation process, overhead is reduced. This, in turn, enables you to consider using lower-speed circuits to interconnect locations.

Another advantage of protocol-independent routing over encapsulation relates directly to the operation of SNA networks. Although such networks are discussed in detail in Chapter 8, several SNA operational characteristics now warrant attention. They will help us appreciate the advantages of protocol-independent routing, and they will explain the rationale for such routers' requiring a traffic priority mechanism to support SNA traffic efficiently.

**Need For Priority Mechanism**  In its current incarnation, SNA is a hierarchically structured network, as shown in Figure 7.7. Here, the communications controller communicates with control units, which in turn communicate with attached terminal devices. The communications controller periodically polls each control unit, and the control unit periodically polls each terminal device. If there is no data to transmit in response to a poll, each polled device indicates this fact to the higher level device by responding negatively to the poll. Thus, the communications controller expects to receive a response to each poll it generates. In fact, if it does not receive a response within a predefined period of time (typically less than five seconds), the com-

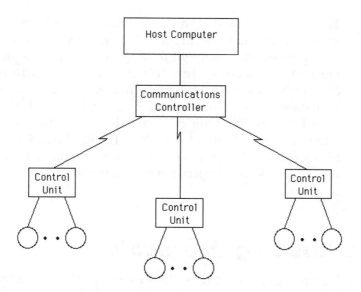

**Figure 7.7**  SNA network hierarchy. In an SNA network, communications controllers poll control units, which in turn poll attached devices.

munications controller will assume that the control unit has malfunctioned, terminate any active sessions to devices attached to the control unit, and then attempt to re-establish communications by sending an initialization message to the control unit.

When SNA and LAN traffic is integrated into a common router-based network, the operation of routers can adversely affect SNA traffic because of the time delays associated with routing and encapsulation. For example, routers may alter the path used to transmit data, depending on internet traffic and circuit availability. If path switching makes the SNA traffic exceed its timeout threshold, the communications controller will terminate sessions and reinitialize control units that fail to respond to its poll within the predefined time period. Similarly, delays caused by encapsulation can also result in unintended timeouts.

To prevent unintended timeouts caused by path switching, some vendors have added a traffic priority mechanism to their protocol-independent routing capability. This priority mechanism enables users to assign a higher priority to SNA traffic than to LAN traffic, thus enabling SNA data to be forwarded across wide area networks ahead of other inter-LAN traffic. This can considerably reduce or even eliminate the potential for LAN traffic to obstruct the flow of SNA data; it may also result in unintended timeouts, inadvertently causing session terminations.

# 7.4 Routing Protocols

The routing protocol is the key element to transferring information across an internet in an orderly manner. The protocol is responsible for developing paths between routers, using a predefined mechanism.

# Types of Routing Protocols

There are two types of routing protocols: interior and exterior domain. Here, we use the term *domain* to refer to the connection of a group of networks to form a common entity, such as a corporate or university enterprise network.

## Interior Domain Routing Protocols

An *interior domain routing protocol* is used to control the flow of information within a series of separate networks that are interconnected to form an internet. Thus, interior domain routing protocols provide a mechanism for the flow of information within a domain and are also known as *intra-domain* routing protocols. Such protocols create routing tables for each autonomous system within the domain, using such metrics as the hop count or time delay to develop routes from one network to another within the domain. Examples of interior domain routing protocols include RIP, OSPF, and Hello.

## Exterior Domain Routing Protocols

*Exterior domain routing protocols* are used to connect separate domains together. Thus, they are also referred to as *inter-domain* routing protocols. Currently, inter-domain routing protocols are defined only for OSI and TCP/IP. Example of inter-domain routing protocols include the Exterior Gateway Protocol (EGP), the Border Gateway Protocol (BGP), and the Inter-Domain Routing Protocol (IDRP). Unlike interior domain routing protocols, which are focused on the construction of routing tables for data flow within a domain, inter-domain routing protocols specify the method by which routers exchange information concerning what networks they can reach on each domain.

Figure 7.8 illustrates the use of interior and exterior domain routing protocols. In this example, OSPF is the intra-domain protocol used in Domain A, while RIF is the intra-domain

**Figure 7.8** Interior and exterior routing protocols. An interior routing protocol controls the flow of information within a collection of interconnected networks known as a *domain*. An exterior routing protocol provides routers with the ability to determine what networks on other domains they can reach.

protocol used in Domain B. Routers in Domains A and B use the inter-domain routing protocols EGP and/or BGP to determine what networks on other domains they can reach.

**Exterior Gateway Protocol**   There are four basic functions performed by the Exterior Gateway Protocol. First, the EGP performs an acquisition function, which enables a router in one domain to request information exchange with a router on another domain. Since routers also serve as a gateways to the domain, they are sometimes referred to as *gateways*. A second function performed by the router gateway is to test periodically whether its EGP neighbors are responding. The third and most important function performed by the EGP is to enable router gateways to exchange information concerning the networks in each domain by transmitting routing update messages. The fourth function involves terminating an established neighbor relationship between gateways on two domains.

To accomplish its basic functions, EGP defines nine message types. Figure 7.9 illustrates EGP message types associated with each of the three basic features performed by the protocol.

Under the EGP, once a neighbor is acquired, Hello messages must be transmitted at a minimum of 30-second intervals. In addition, routing updates must be exchanged at a minimum of two-minute intervals. This exchange of information at two-minute intervals can result in the use of a considerable amount of the bandwidth linking domains when the number of networks on each domain is large, or when the circuits linking domains consist of low-speed lines. The Border Gateway Protocol was developed to alleviate those potential problems.

**Border Gateway Protocol**   The Border Gateway Protocol represents a follow-on to the EGP. Unlike the EGP, in which all network information is exchanged at two-minute or shorter intervals, the BGP transmits incremental updates as changes occur. This can significantly reduce the quantity of data exchanged between router gateways, thus freeing up a considerable amount of circuit bandwidth for the transmission of data. Both the EGP and the BGP run over TCP/IP and are standardized by Internet documents RFC904 and RFC1105, respectively.

| Function | Message Type |
| --- | --- |
| Acquiring Neighbors | Acquisition Request → |
| | ← Acquisition Confirm |
| | or |
| | ← Acquisition Refuse |
| Neighbor Reachability | Hello → |
| | ← I Heard You |
| Routing Update | Poll Request → |
| | ← Routing Update |
| De-acquiring Neighbors | Cease Request → |
| | ← Cease Confirm |

Domain A

Domain B

**Figure 7.9**  Exterior gateway protocol message types.

## Interior Domain Routing Protocols

As previously discussed, interior domain routing protocols govern the flow of information between networks. This is the type of routing protocol that is of primary interest to most organizations. Interior domain routing protocols can be further subdivided into two broad categories, based on the method they use for building and updating the contents of their routing tables: vector distance and link state.

**Vector Distance Protocol**  A vector distance protocol constructs a routing table in each router, and periodically broadcasts the contents of the routing table across the internet. When the routing table is received at another router, that device examines the set of reported network destinations and the distance to each destination. The receiving router then determines whether it knows a shorter route to a network destination, finds a destination it does not have in its routing table, or finds a route to a destination through the sending router where the distance to the destination changed. If any one of these situations occurs, the receiving router will change its routing tables.

The term *vector distance* relates to the information transmitted by routers. Each router message contains a list of pairs, known as vector and distance. The *vector* identifies a network destination, while the *distance* is the distance in hops from the router to that destination.

Figure 7.10 illustrates the initial distance vector routing table for the routers R1 and R2 shown in Figure 7.2. Each table contains an entry for each directly connected network and is broadcast periodically throughout the internet. The distance column indicates the distance in hops to each network from the router.

At the same time router R1 is constructing its initial distance vector table, other routers are performing a similar operation. The lower portion of Figure 7.10 illustrates the composition of the initial distance vector table for router R2.

**a. Router R1**

| Destination | Distance |
|---|---|
| E1 | 0 |
| E2 | 0 |

**b. Router R2**

| Destination | Distance |
|---|---|
| E3 | 0 |
| TR1 | 0 |

**Figure 7.10** Initial distance vector routing tables.

As previously mentioned, under a distance vector protocol, the contents of each router's routing table are periodically broadcast. When routers R1 and R2 broadcast their initial distance vector routing tables, each router uses the received routing table to update its initial routing table. Figure 7.11 illustrates the result of this initial routing table update process for routers R1 and R2.

**a. Router R1**

| Destination | Distance | Route |
|---|---|---|
| E1 | 0 | direct |
| E2 | 0 | direct |
| E3 | 1 | R2 |
| TR1 | 1 | R2 |

**b. Router R2**

| Destination | Distance | Route |
|---|---|---|
| E1 | 1 | R1 |
| E2 | 1 | R1 |
| E3 | 0 | direct |
| TR1 | 0 | direct |

**Figure 7.11** Initial routing table update.

As additional routing tables are exchanged, the routing table in each router will converge with respect to the internet topology. However, to ensure that each router knows the state of all links, routing tables are periodically broadcast by each router. Although this process has a minimal effect upon small networks, its use with large networks can significantly reduce available bandwidth for actual data transfer. This is because the transmission of lengthy router tables will require additional transmission time in which data cannot flow between routers.

Popular vector distance routing protocols include the TCP/IP Routing Information Protocol (RIP), the AppleTalk Routing Table Management Protocol (RTMP), and Cisco's Interior Gateway Routing Protocol (IGRP).

**Routing Information Protocol**　　Under RIP, participants are either active or passive. *Active* participants are normally routers that transmit their routing tables, while *passive* machines listen and update their routing tables based upon information supplied by other devices. Normally, host computers are passive participants, while routers are active participants.

Under RIP, an active router broadcasts its routing table every 30 seconds. Each routing table entry contains a network address and the hop count to the network. However, unlike the previous vector distance example, in which a directly connected network has a hop count distance of 0, RIP uses a hop count of 1. Similarly, RIP uses a hop count of 2 for networks that are reachable through one router.

One key limitation of RIP is the maximum hop distance it supports. This distance is 16 hops, which means that an alternative protocol must be used for large networks.

**Routing Table Maintenance Protocol** The Routing Table Maintenance Protocol (RTMP) was developed by Apple Computer for use with that vendor's AppleTalk network. Under RTMP, each router transmits messages to establish routing tables and update them periodically. The update process, during which information on an internet is exchanged between routers, also serves as a mechanism for implementing alternate routing. This is because the absence of update information for a greater than expected period of time converts the status of an entry in other router routing tables from "good" to "suspect" and then to "bad."

RTMP is delivered by AppleTalk's Data Delivery Protocol (DDP), which is a network layer connectionless service operating between two upper layer processes referred to as *sockets*. Four types of packets are specified by RTMP: data, request, route data request, and response. Routing updates are transmitted as data packets. End nodes transmit request packets to acquire information about the identity of the internet routers (IRs) to which they can transmit non-local packets. IRs respond to route request packets with response packets, while end nodes that want to receive an RTMP data packet indicate this by sending a route data request packet. The latter packet type is also used by nodes that require routing information from IRs not directly connected to their network.

In the AppleTalk routing process, the source node first examines the destination network number. If the packet has a local network address, it is passed to the data link layer for delivery. Otherwise, the packet is passed to any of the IRs that reside on a network segment. The IR will examine the destination address of the packet and then check its routing tables to determine the next hop, routing the packet on a specific port that enables it to flow toward the next hop. Thus, a packet will travel through the internet on a hop by hop basis. When the packet reaches an IR connected to the destination network, the data link layer is used to deliver the packet to its local destination.

Figure 7.12 illustrates a sample AppleTalk network and the routing table for one router. Each AppleTalk routing table has five entries, as indicated. The *network range* defines the range of network numbers assigned to a particular network segment. The *distance* entry specifies the number of routers that must be traversed prior to the destination being reached, and *port* defines the router port used to provide access to a destination location. The *next IR* entry indicates the identifier of the next IR on the internet, and

**Routing table for router R1**

| Network Range | Distance | Port | Next IR | Entry State |
|---|---|---|---|---|
| 1-3 | 0 | 2 | 0 | Good |
| 7-7 | 0 | 1 | 0 | Good |
| 4-6 | 1 | 1 | R2 | Good |
| 8-10 | 1 | 1 | R3 | Good |
| 11-11 | 1 | 1 | R3 | Good |
| 12-12 | 2 | 1 | R3 | Good |

**Figure 7.12**   AppleTalk routing table example.

*entry state* defines the status of receiving routing updates. An entry state can go from "good" to "suspect" to "bad" if routing updates are not received within predefined time intervals.

**Interior Gateway Routing Protocol**   Cisco's proprietary Interior Gateway Routing Protocol is a distance vector protocol in which updates are transmitted at 90-second intervals. Each IGRP gateway operates on a local basis to determine the best route for forwarding data packets. Unlike protocols that require each router to have a complete routing table, each IGRP router computes only a portion of the routing table, based on its perspective of the internet. This enables the IGRP to support distributed routing without requiring each router to have a complete view of the internet.

Other features of the IGRP include the ability to establish routes automatically, perform load balancing dynamically over redundant links, and detect and remove bad circuits from the internet routing tables it develops. Routes are declared inaccessible if an update is not received within three update periods (270 seconds). After five update periods (450 seconds), the route is removed from the routing table.

**Link State Protocols**   A link state routing protocol addresses the traffic problem associated with any large networks that use a vector distance routing protocol. It does this by transmitting routing information only when there is a change in one of its links. A second difference between vector difference and link state protocols concerns the manner in which a route is selected when multiple routes are available between destinations. For a vector distance protocol, the best path is the one that has the fewest intermediate routers on hops between destinations. A link state protocol, however, can use multiple paths to provide traffic balancing between locations. In addition, a link state protocol permits routing to occur based on link delay, capacity and reliability. This provides the network manager with the ability to specify a variety of route development situations.

**SPF Algorithms**    Link state routing protocols are implemented by a class of algorithms known as Shortest Path First (SPF). Unfortunately, this is a misnomer, since routing is not based on the shortest path.

The use of SPF algorithms requires each participating router to have complete knowledge of the internet topology. Each router participating in an SPF algorithm then performs two tasks: status testing of neighboring routers and periodic transmission of link status information to other routers.

To test neighboring routers, a short message is periodically transmitted. If the neighbor replies, the link is considered to be up. Otherwise, the absence of a reply after a predefined period of time indicates that the link is down.

To provide link status information, each router will periodically broadcast a message indicating the status of each of its links. Unlike the vector distance protocol, in which routes are specified, an SPF link status message simply indicates whether communications are possible between pairs of routers. Using information in the link status message, routers are able to update their network maps.

Unlike vector distance protocols, in which tables are required to be exchanged, link state protocols such as SPF algorithms exchange a much lower volume of information in the form of link status queries and replies. Then, SPF participating routers simply broadcast the status of each of their links, and other routers use this information to update their internet maps. This routing technique permits each router to compute routes independently of other routers, and eliminates the potential for the table flooding that can occur when a vector state protocol is used to interconnect a large number of networks.

To illustrate the operation of a link state routing protocol, let us return to the internet configuration previously illustrated in Figure 7.2. Figure 7.13 indicates the initial network map for router R1. This map lists the destination of all networks on the internet from router R1, with their distances and routes. Note that if multiple routes exist to a destination, each route is listed. This defines a complete network topology, and allows alternate routes to be selected if link status information indicates that one or more routes cannot be used.

| Destination | Distance | Route | Status |
| --- | --- | --- | --- |
| E1 | 0 | direct | up |
| E2 | 0 | direct | up |
| E3 | 1 | R2 | up |
| E3 | 2 | R3,R2 | up |
| E3 | 3 | R3,R4,R2 | up |
| E4 | 2 | R2,R4 | up |
| E4 | 2 | R3,R4 | up |
| E4 | 3 | R3,R2,R4 | up |
| TR1 | 1 | R2 | up |
| TR1 | 2 | R3,R2 | up |
| TR1 | 3 | R3,R4,R2 | up |
| TR2 | 1 | R3 | up |
| TR2 | 2 | R2,R3 | up |
| TR2 | 2 | R2,R4 | up |
| TR3 | 2 | R3,R4 | up |
| TR3 | 2 | R2,R4 | up |
| TR3 | 3 | R3,R2,R4 | up |

**Figure 7.13**    Router R1 initial network map.

Let us suppose that at a particular point in time, the link status messages generated by the routers in the internet are as indicated in Figure 7.14. Note that both routers R2 and R3 have determined that link L3 is down. Using this information, router R1 would then update the status column for its network map. Since link L3 is down, all routes that require a data flow between R2 and R3 would have their status changed to "down." For example, for destination E3 via route R3, R2 would have its status changed to "down." Since the minimum distance to E3 is 1 hop via router R2, the failure of link L3 would not affect data flow from router R1 to network E3. Now consider the effect of link L2 becoming inoperative. This would affect route R2, which

**R1 link status**

| Link | Status |
|------|--------|
| L1   | Up     |
| L2   | Up     |

**R2 link status**

| Link | Status |
|------|--------|
| L2   | Up     |
| L3   | Down   |
| L4   | Up     |

**R3 link status**

| Link | Status |
|------|--------|
| L1   | Up     |
| L3   | Down   |

**R4 link status**

| Link | Status |
|------|--------|
| L4   | Up     |
| L5   | Up     |

**Figure 7.14**  Link status messages.

has the minimum distance to network E3. It would still leave route R3 = R4 = R2, although this route would have a distance of three hops. Of course, when a new link status message indicates that a previously declared down link is up, each router's network map is updated accordingly.

Examples of link state protocols include Open Shortest Path First (OSPF), OSI Intermediate System to Intermediate System (IS-IS), DecNet Phase V, and IBM's Advanced Peer-to-Peer Networking (APPN). Due to space limitations, we will review briefly the operational features of only the first of these link state protocols.

**Open Shortest Path First Protocol**   The OSPF protocol is an interior domain routing protocol that uses the SPF algorithm. Like the EGP, the OSPF protocol consists of a small core of different types of messages. Under the OSPF protocol, five message types are defined.

A Hello message is used to test the reachability of other devices. A database description message passes the topology. The remaining message types include a link status request, a link status update, and a link status acknowledgement message.

Initially, OSPF generates database description messages to initialize its network topology database. These messages are flooded through the domain. However, once a topological database is formed, routing table updates are transmitted at 30-minute intervals unless there is a change in the network, in which case there is an immediate update.

Like the EGP, OSPF routers use a Hello message to discover their neighbors. One of the key features of the OSPF protocol is its ability to authenticate messages. This means that you can't entice routers to transmit packets to a specific computer for examination or interception by generating low-cost routes. Another key feature of the OSPF protocol is its ability to support multiple active paths of equal weight: it selects each path in a round robin manner. Table 7.1 provides a summary of 16 common routing protocol abbreviations, their meanings, and a short description of each protocol.

**Table 7.1**  Common routing protocols

| | |
|---|---|
| AURP | AppleTalk Update Routing Protocol. This routing protocol is implemented in Apple networks and sends changes to routing tables via updates. |
| BGP | Border Gateway Protocol. This is a TCP/IP interdomain routing protocol. |
| CLNP | Connectionless Network Protocol. This is the OSI version of the IP routing protocol. |
| DDP | Datagram Delivery Protocol. This routing protocol is used in Apple's AppleTalk network. |
| EGP | Exterior Gateway Protocol. This TCP/IP protocol is used to locate networks on another domain. |
| IDRP | Inter-Domain Routing Protocol. This is the OSI interdomain routing protocol. |
| IGP | Interior Gateway Protocol. This TCP/IP protocol is used by routers to move information within a domain. |
| IGRP | Interior Gateway Routing Protocol. This is a proprietary routing protocol developed by Cisco Systems. |
| IP | Internet Protocol. This is the network layer protocol of the TCP/IP (Transmission Control Protocol/Internet Protocol) suite of protocols. |
| IPX | Internet Packet Exchange. This routing protocol is based on Xerox's XNS, was developed by Novell, and is implemented in Novell's NetWare. |
| IS-IS | Intermediate-Station-to-Intermediate-Station. This is an OSI link-state routing protocol that routes both OSI and RIP traffic. |

*(continued)*

**Table 7.1**  Common routing protocols *(continued)*

| | |
|---|---|
| NCP | NetWare Core Protocol. This is Novell's NetWare specific routing protocol. |
| OSPF | Open Shortest Path First. This is a TCP/IP link-state routing protocol that provides an alternative to RIP. |
| RIP | Routing Information Protocol. This routing protocol is used in TCP/IP, XNS, and IPX. Under RIP, a message is broadcast to find the shortest route to a destination based on a hop count. |
| RTMP | Routing Table Maintenance Protocol. This is Apple's distance-vector protocol. |
| SPF | Shortest Path First. This link-state routing protocol uses a set of user-defined parameters to find the best route between two points. |

# 7.5 Performance Considerations

Regardless of the type of router and its protocol support and routing algorithm, the processing required for its operation is considerably more than that required for a bridge. This means that you can expect the packet processing capability of routers to be considerably less than that of bridges.

High-capacity bridges marketed during 1993 can be expected to provide a forwarding rate between 10,000 and 20,000 packets per second. In comparison, most routers have a forwarding capacity rated under 5,000 packets per second. Although this may appear to indicate a poor level of performance in comparison to bridges, note that only when functioning as a local bridge will a high-capacity bridge actually use its full capacity. Otherwise, when used to interconnect remote networks via a wide area transmission facility, a remote bridge will be able to use only a fraction of its packet-processing capability for the forwarding of packets over a relatively slow-speed WAN transmission facility. In comparison, when routers are connected to a T2 or E1 line or to a Frame Relay service, they may be able to use their full packet forwarding capability. To see this, refer to Table 7.2, which indicates the maximum packets-per-second transfer capability of a router connected to five types of transmission lines, based on five packet sizes. Note that a T1 line operating at 1.544 Mbps supports a maximum transfer of 3015 sixty-four–byte packets per second. In actuality, since the wide area network transmission facility results in the use of a WAN protocol to wrap LAN packets, the actual PPS rate obtainable is normally 15 to 20 percent less than that indicated in Table 7.2. Thus, the forward rate of most routers greatly exceeds the capacity of a single WAN connection. This means that only a requirement for the use of multiple router ports should make the forwarding rate of the router into a key equipment acquisition issue. Otherwise, the communication, transport, and routing protocols supported are more important criteria for determining whether a vendor's product can support the requirements of an organization.

**Table 7.2**   Maximum packet transfer rates (packets per second)

**Wide Area Network Transmission Facility**

| Packet Size (bytes) | 56 Kbps | 128 Kbps | 256 Kbps | 512 Kbps | 1.544 Mbps |
|---|---|---|---|---|---|
| 64 | 109 | 250 | 500 | 1000 | 3015 |
| 128 | 54 | 125 | 250 | 500 | 1508 |
| 500 | 14 | 32 | 64 | 128 | 386 |
| 1000 | 7 | 16 | 32 | 64 | 193 |
| 1518 | 5 | 10 | 20 | 40 | 127 |

# CHAPTER **8**

# Gateway
# Methods

In Chapter 5, we discussed the basic operation of gateways and the ways in which they enable networks with different protocols to communicate. In that chapter, we discussed how a gateway operates through the highest layer of the OSI Reference Model, the application layer, and how gateways essentially perform protocol conversion. We also briefly described several methods by which an Ethernet network could be connected to an IBM mainframe computer system. Although those methods involved different types of gateways, our primary focus of attention until now was simply on concepts and the use of different types of hardware, without considering the relationship of network architecture to gateway operations.

Since the protocol conversion performed by a gateway is directly related to such architectures as IBM's SNA and Digital Equipment's DECnet, we must obtain a basic understanding of the architecture developed to support access to conventional mainframe computers. This will enable us to obtain an appreciation for the different access methods supported by gateways, along with their functions and applications. These are the focus of this chapter. We will first discuss SNA and IBM's 3270 Information Display System to obtain an understanding of the basic functions of hardware and software used to establish a wide area networking capability, providing local and remote terminal users with access to IBM mainframe computers in an SNA environment. This information will provide the foundation for discussing the use of gateways to exchange information between local area networks and mainframes connected to the dominant computer company network architecture. The latter, with plug-compatible computers, represents approximately 70 percent of all large computer installations.

# 8.1 Network Architecture

To satisfy customers' requirements for remote computing capability, mainframe computer manufacturers developed a variety of network architectures. Such architectures defined the relationship of a particular vendor's hardware and software products that is necessary to permit communications to flow through a network to the manufacturer's mainframe computer.

IBM's System Network Architecture (SNA) is a very complex and sophisticated network architecture that defines the rules, procedures, and structure of communications from the input/output statements of an application program to the screen display on a user's personal computer or terminal. SNA consists of protocols, formats, and operational sequences governing the flow of information within a data-communications network. Such a network may link IBM mainframe computers, minicomputers, terminal controllers, communications controllers, personal computers, and terminals.

Since approximately 70 percent of the mainframe computer market belongs to IBM and plug-compatible systems manufactured by Amdehl and other vendors, SNA can be expected to remain a common connectivity platform for the foreseeable future. This means that a large majority of the connections of local area networks to mainframe computers will require the use of gateways that support SNA operations.

## SNA Concepts

An SNA network consists of one or more domains, where *domain* refers to all of the logical and physical components that are connected to and controlled by one common point in the network. This common point of control is called the *system services control point* or *SSCP*. The SSCP can be considered the highest location in an SNA network whose structure is based on a rigidly defined hierarchy of devices. Within an SNA network, there are three types of network-addressable units: SSCPs, physical units, and logical units.

### The SSCP

The SSCP resides in the communications access method operating in an IBM mainframe computer. For example, it may be a virtual telecommunications access method (VTAM) operating in a System/360, System/370, 4300 series or 308X, 309X or an Enterprise series computer. It may also be in the system control program of an IBM mini-computer, such as a System/3X or AS/400. The SSCP contains the network's address tables, routing tables, and translation tables, which it uses to establish connections between nodes in the network and to control the flow of information in an SNA network.

Figure 8.1 illustrates single and multiple domain SNA networks. Each network domain includes one or more nodes; an SNA network node consists of a unique grouping of networking components. Examples of SNA nodes include cluster controllers (also referred to as control units), communications controllers, and terminal devices. The address of each device in the network is unique.

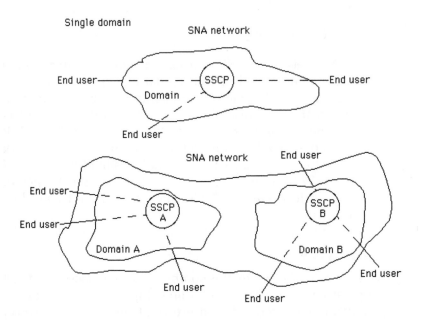

**Figure 8.1**   *Single and multiple domain SNA networks.*

### The PU

Each node in an SNA network contains a *physical unit (PU)* that controls the node's other resources. The PU is not a physical device, as its name suggests, but rather a set of SNA components that provide services for controlling terminals, controllers, processors, and data links in the network. In programmable devices, such as mainframe computers and communications controllers, the PU is normally implemented in software. In less intelligent devices, such as older cluster controllers and display terminals, the PU is typically implemented in ROM. In an SNA network, each PU operates under the control of an SSCP. The PU functions as an entry point between the network and one or more logical units.

### The LU

The third type of network-addressable unit in an SNA network is the *logical unit*, known by its abbreviation as the *LU*. The LU is the interface or point of access between the end-user and an SNA network. Through the LU, an end-user gains access to network resources and transmits and receives data over the network. Each PU can have one or more LUs; each LU has a distinct address.

## SNA Network Structure

The structure of an SNA network is a hierarchy in which each device controls a specific part of the network and operates under the control of a device at the next higher level. The highest level in an SNA network is a host or mainframe computer, which executes a software module known as a *communications access method*. At the next lower level are one or more communications controllers—IBM's term for a front-end processor. Each communications controller executes a Network Control Program (NCP) that defines the operation of devices connected to the controllers, along with their PUs and LUs, operating rate, data code, and other communications-related functions such as the maximum packet size that can be transmitted. Connected to communications controllers are cluster controllers, IBM's term for a control unit. These cluster controllers are the third level in an SNA network.

The cluster controllers support the attachment of terminals and printers, which are the lowest level of an SNA hierarchy. Figure 8.2 illustrates the SNA hierarchy and the Network Addressable Units (NAUs) associated with each hardware component used to construct an SNA network. Note that NAUs include lines connecting mainframes to communications controllers and cluster controllers, and cluster controllers to terminals and printers. In addition, NAUs also define application programs that reside in the mainframe. NAUs provide the mechanism for terminals to access specific programs via a routing through explicitly identified hardware and transmission facilities.

An SNA network is a relatively static network in which the addition and removal of terminal devices requires specific entries in address tables. Changing address table entries requires the creation and modification of macro instruction in the communications controller's Network Control Program (NCP) and in the mainframe computer's VTAM. Since NCP and VTAM program changes require a recompilation of each program, and this temporarily places the network in never-never land while the resulting compiled programs are loaded, such program changes are typically accomplished on weekends or very early in the morning during weekdays. In addition, many organizations batch NCP and VTAM changes and then perform those changes only once a week or perhaps once a month, further reducing the ability of SNA networks to be adjusted to dynamic working environments.

**Figure 8.2** SNA hierarchical network structure. The structure of an SNA network is built upon a hierarchy of equipment, with mainframes connected to communications controllers and communications controllers connected to cluster controllers.

As an example of the communications capability of SNA, consider an end-user with an IBM PC and an SDLC communications adapter who establishes a connection to an IBM mainframe computer. The IBM PC is a PU, and its display and printer are separate LUs. After communication is established, the PC user can direct a file to his or her printer by establishing an LU-to-LU session between the mainframe and printer, while using the PC as an interactive terminal running an application program for a second LU-to-LU session.

## Types of PUs

Table 8.1 provides a list of the six types of physical units in an SNA network and their corresponding SNA node types. In addition, this table contains representative examples of hardware devices that can operate as a specific type of PU. As indicated in Table 8.1, the different types of PUs, with the exception of PU 2.1, form a hierarchy of hardware classifications. At the lowest level, PU Type 1 is a single terminal. PU Type 2 is a cluster controller, used to connect many SNA devices into a common communications circuit. PU Type 4 is a communications controller, providing communications support for up to several hundred line terminations, where individual lines can be connected in turn to cluster controllers. At the top of the hardware hierarchy, PU Type 5 is a mainframe computer.

PU2.1 is a special type of node that supports IBM's Advanced Peer-to-Peer Networking (APPN). Unlike SNA, which is based on a hierarchical, master–slave control

**Table 8.1**   SNA PU summary

| PU type | Node type | Representative hardware |
| --- | --- | --- |
| PU Type 5 | Mainframe | S/370, 43XX, 308X |
| PU Type 4 | Communications controller | 3705, 3725, 3745 |
| PU Type 3 | Not currently defined | N/A |
| PU Type 2.1 | APPN | Any computer |
| PU Type 2 | Cluster controller | 3174, 3274, 3276 |
| PU Type 1 | Terminal | 3180, PC with SNA adapter |

structure, APPN permits cooperative program-to-program communications in which each computer on the network is considered as just another peer node. A session can thus be established between two type 2.1 nodes without requiring a data flow through an SSCP.

## Multiple Domains

Figure 8.3 illustrates a two-domain SNA network. By establishing a physical connection between the communications controller in each domain and coding appropriate software for operation on each controller, cross-domain data flow becomes possible. When cross-domain data flow is established, terminal devices connected to one mainframe can access applications operating on the other mainframe.

SNA was originally implemented as a networking architecture: users established sessions with application programs operating on a mainframe computer within the network. Once a session was established, a network control program (NCP) operating on an IBM communications controller, which in turn was connected to the IBM mainframe, controlled the information flow between the user and the applications program. With the growth in personal computing, many users no longer require access to a mainframe to obtain connectivity to another personal computer. Therefore, IBM modified SNA to permit peer-to-peer communications capability, so that two devices on the network with appropriate hardware and software can communicate with one another without requiring access through a mainframe computer. To this end, IBM introduced a PU2.1 node in 1987. When this node is used with LU6.2 (described later in this chapter), communication between two PU2.1 nodes without mainframe intervention becomes possible.

The PU2.1 node—in conjunction with LU6.2 and new releases of VTAM and associated communications prod-

**Figure 8.3**    Two-domain SNA network.

ucts—represents the evolving networking concept known as Advanced Peer-to-Peer Networking (APPN). Although the PU2.1 type node was announced in 1987, many portions of APPN were still evolving or were being developed. For example, VTAM Version 4.1, which allows IBM mainframes to participate actively within APPN as peer-to-peer APPN nodes, was released during the latter part of 1992. Other products, such as 3174 microcode to support an APPN network node function for both coaxial cable–connected terminals and workstations on a Token-Ring network, were scheduled for availability during 1993. Since many organizations have a large base of SNA communications equipment, replacing or upgrading that base of equipment to support APPN can be expected to be an evolutionary process. This is especially true because of the current lack of APPN software applications. Since many organizations have invested a literal fortune in SNA applications, the expected availability of APPN applications over the next few years will not by itself cause a massive migration to APPN. Instead, we can expect organizations to obtain APPN-compliant equipment and then gradually migrate to APPN.

## SNA Layers

IBM's SNA is a layered protocol that provides seven layers of control for every message that flows through the network. Figure 8.4 shows the SNA layers and provides a comparison to the seven-layer OSI Reference Model.

Like the OSI physical layer, SNA's physical control layer is concerned with the electrical, mechanical, and procedural characteristics of the physical media and interfaces to the physical media. SNA's data link control layer is also quite similar to OSI's data link layer. Protocols defined by SNA include SDLC, System/370 channel, Token-Ring, and X.25; however, only SDLC is used on a communications link in which primary stations communicate with secondary sta-

**SNA**                **OSI Reference Model**

| SNA | OSI Reference Model |
|---|---|
| Transaction Services | Application |
| Presentation Services | Presentation |
| Data Flow Control | Session |
| Transmission Control | Transport |
| Path Control | Network |
| Data Link Control | Data Link |
| Physical Control | Physical |

**Figure 8.4** *SNA and the OSI Reference Model.*

tions. Some implementations of SNA using special software modules can also support the still widely-used IBM pre-SNA protocol, bisynchronous communications (BSC), as well as asynchronous communications.

Two of the major functions of the path control layer are routing and flow control. Since there can be many data links connected to a node, path control is responsible for ensuring that data is passed correctly through intermediate nodes as it flows from source to destination. At the beginning of an SNA session, the sending and receiving nodes, along with all nodes between those nodes, cooperate to select the most efficient route for the session. Since this route is established only for the duration of the session, it is known as a *virtual route*. To increase the efficiency of transmission in an SNA network, the path control layer at each node through which the virtual route is established has the ability to divide long messages into shorter segments for transmission by the data link layer. Similarly, path control may divide short messages into larger data blocks for transmission by the data link layer. This enables the efficiency of SNA's transmission facility to be independent of the length of messages flowing on the network.

The SNA transmission control layer provides a reliable end-to-end connection service, similar to the OSI Reference Model Transport layer. Other transmission control layer functions include session level pacing and encryption and decryption. Pacing ensures that a transmitting device does not send more data than a receiving device can accept during a given period of time. Pacing is similar to the flow control of data in a network; however, unlike flow control, NAUs negotiate and control pacing. To accomplish this, the two NAUs at the session's end points negotiate the largest number of messages, known as a *pacing group*, that a sending NAU can transmit before receiving a pacing response from a receiving NAU. The pacing response enables the transmitting NAU to resume transmission. Session level pacing occurs in two stages along a session's route in an SNA network. One stage of pacing is between the mainframe NAU and the communications controller, and the second stage is between the communications controller and an attached terminal NAU.

The data flow control services layer handles the order of communications within a session for error control and flow control. The order of communications is set by the layer controlling the transmission mode. Transmission modes available include *full-duplex*, which permits each device to transmit at any time, *half-duplex flip-flop*, in which devices can only transmit alternately, and *half-duplex contention*, in which one device is considered a master device and the slave cannot transmit until the master completes its transmission.

The SNA presentation services layer is responsible for the translation of data from one format to another. This layer also performs the connection and disconnection of sessions, updates the network configuration, and performs network management functions. At this layer, the network addressable unit (NAU) services manager is responsible for formatting of data from an application to match the display or printer that is communicating with the application. Other functions performed at this layer include the compression and decompression of data to increase the efficiency of transmission on an SNA network.

The highest layer in SNA is the transaction services layer. This layer is responsible for application programs that implement distributed processing and management services, such as distributed data bases, document interchange, and the control of LU-to-LU session limits.

### SNA Developments

The most significant development to SNA is the addition of new LU and PU subtypes to support what is known as Advanced Peer-to-Peer Networking (APPN). Previously, LU types used to define an LU-to-LU session were restricted to application-to-device and program-to-program sessions. LU1-LU4 and LU7 are application-to-device sessions, as indicated in Table 8.2, whereas LU4 and LU6 are program-to-program sessions.

The addition of LU6.2, which operates in conjunction with PU2.1 to support LU6.2 connections, permits devices to transfer data to any other device that also supports this LU without first sending the data through a mainframe computer. The introduction of new software products to support LU6.2 permits a more dynamic flow of data through SNA networks, and many data links to mainframes that were previously heavily utilized can gain capacity.

Under APPN, multiple LU-to-LU sessions per LU6.2 become possible, since LU6.2 supports parallel sessions

**Table 8.2** *SNA LU session types*

| LU Type | Session Type |
|---------|--------------|
| LU1 | Host application and a remote batch terminal |
| LU2 | Host application and a 3270 display terminal |
| LU3 | Host application and a 3270 printer |
| LU4 | Host application and an SNA word processor, or two terminals connected by a mainframe |
| LU5 | Currently undefined |
| LU6 | Two applications programs typically residing on different mainframe computers |
| LU6.2 | Peer-to-peer |
| LU7 | Host application and a 5250 terminal |

with no restrictions on the session originator. In comparison, under SNA, peripheral nodes (such as LUs) in a control unit can participate in only one LU-to-LU session at any one time, and the host resident LU must function as the master. Other differences between SNA and APPN include the maximum number of LUs supported by a peripheral node and the manner in which resources and routes are defined.

Under SNA, the maximum number of LUs in a peripheral node is limited to 255. Under APPN, there is a theoretical limit of 64 K LUs per link; however, in operation there will probably be only one LU6.2 per node, since LU6.2 provides the ability to support multiple users. SNA is a relatively static networking environment in which tables must be coded manually to define resources and routes. Under APPN, most routes and resources are discovered by the equipment; this minimizes the necessity for extensive manual definitions.

# SNA Sessions

All communications in SNA occur within sessions between NAUs. A *session* can be defined as a logical connection established between two NAUs over a specific route for a specific period of time, where the connection and disconnection of a session are controlled by the SSCP. Currently, SNA defines four types of sessions: SSCP-to-PU, SSCP-to-LU, SSCP-to-SSCP, and LU-to-LU. The first two types of sessions are used to request or exchange diagnostic and status information. The third type of session enables SSCPs in the same or different domains to exchange information. The LU-to-LU session is the core type of SNA session, since all end-user communications take place over LU-to-LU sessions.

## LU-to-LU Sessions

In an LU-to-LU session, one logical unit, known as the *primary LU (PLU)*, becomes responsible for error recovery. The other LU, which normally has less processing power, becomes the *secondary LU (SLU)*.

An LU-to-LU session is initiated by the transmission of a message from the PLU to the SLU. That message is known as a *bind*, and contains information stored in the communications access method (VTAM) tables on the mainframe. It identifies the hardware devices by screen size, printer type, and so forth, as configured in the VTAM table. This information enables a session to occur with supported hardware. Otherwise, the SLU will reject the bind and the session will not start.

## Addressing

Previously, we discussed the concept of a domain consisting of an SSCP and the network resources it controls. Within a domain exists a set of smaller network units known as *subareas.* In SNA terminology, each host is a subarea, along with each communications controller and its peripheral nodes. The identification of an NAU in an SNA network consists of a subarea address and an element address within the subarea. The subarea is like an area code: it identifies a portion of the network. Figure 8.5 illustrates the relationship between a domain and three subareas residing in that particular domain.

In SNA, a subarea address is 8 bits in length, while the element address within a subarea is restricted to 15 bits. This limits the number of subareas within a domain to 256, and restricts the number of PUs and LUs within a subarea to 215.

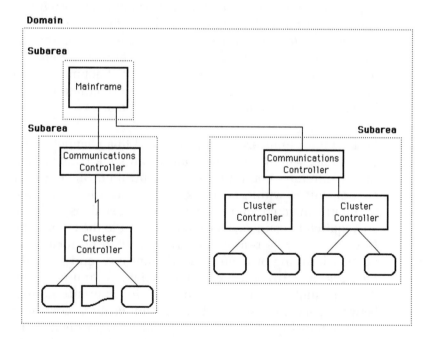

**Figure 8.5**  Relationship between a domain and its subareas. A subarea is a host or a communications controller and its peripheral nodes.

# 8.2 The 3270 Information Display System

The IBM 3270 Information Display System describes a collection of products, ranging from display stations with keyboards and printers that communicate with mainframe computers to several types of cluster controllers.

First introduced in 1971, the IBM 3270 Information Display System was designed to extend the processing power of the mainframe computer to locations remote from the computer room. Controllers, more commonly known as *control units*, were made available to economize on the number of lines required to link display stations to mainframe computers. Typically, a number of display stations are connected to a control unit on individual cables; the control unit, in turn, is connected to the mainframe via a single cable. Both local and remote control units are offered. The key differences between the two pertain to the method of attachment to the mainframe computer and the use of intermediate devices between the control unit and the mainframe.

Local control units are usually attached to a channel on the mainframe, whereas remote control units are connected to the mainframe's communications controller. Since a local control unit is within a limited distance of the mainframe, no intermediate communications devices, such as modems, are required to connect a local control unit to the mainframe. In comparison, a remote control unit can be located in another building or even in a different city, and normally requires the utilization of intermediate communications devices, such as a pair of modems, for communications between the control unit and the communications controller. The relationship of local and control units to display stations, mainframes, and a communications controller is illustrated in Figure 8.6. Note that this hardware relationship represents the hierarchy of equipment supported by SNA.

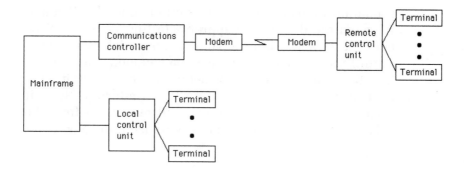

**Figure 8.6** Relationship of 3270 information display products.

## Data Flow

The control unit polls each connected display station to ascertain whether the station has data stored in its transmit buffer. If the station has data in its buffer, it will transmit that data to the control unit when it is polled. The control unit then formats the data with the display station's address, adds the control unit's address and other pertinent information, and transmits it in a synchronous data format to the communications controller or to the I/O channel on the mainframe, depending on the method used to connect the control unit to the mainframe.

Addressing information flowing to the mainframe begins with a terminal address. The control unit formats each data block received from a terminal device and adds its control unit identifier. If the control unit is connected to a communications controller, the latter device adds a line identifier address to the data block, indicating the port on the controller where the information was received. After operating on the data block, the mainframe responds by generating a screen of data that will be routed to a specific terminal. To ensure that the response is routed correctly, the mainframe includes the line, control unit, and terminal address. The communications controller strips off the line identifier and forwards the data to the appropriate line. Since an SNA network supports multidrop circuits, in which two or more control units can share the use of a common transmission line, the control unit address defines the control unit. That control unit removes the control unit address. Next, it examines the terminal identifier, and removes it from the data block once it knows the line to transmit the block.

## 3270 Protocols

IBM supports two different protocols to connect 3270 devices to a mainframe. The original protocol used with 3270 devices, still in limited use today, is the *byte-oriented bisynchronous protocol*, often referred to as *3270 bisyn* or *BSC*. In the late 1970s, when IBM introduced its Systems Network Architecture, it also introduced a bit-oriented protocol for data transmission known as *Synchronous Data Link Control*, or *SDLC*. Thus, communications between an IBM mainframe and the control units attached to the communications controller are either BSC or SDLC, depending on the type of control units obtained and the configuration of the communications controller. Today, almost all BSC control units have been replaced by more modern SDLC devices.

## Types of Control Units

Control units marketed by IBM support up to 8, 16, 32, or 64 attached devices, depending on the model. The IBM 3276 control unit supports up to 8 devices, while the IBM 3274 control unit can support 16 or 32 attached devices. Older control units, such as the 3271, 3272, and 3275, have essentially been replaced by the 3274 and 3276 and operate only bisynchronously. Certain models of the 3274 are "soft" devices that can be programmed with a diskette to operate either with the originally developed bisynchronous protocol or with the newer synchronous data link control (SDLC) protocol.

Devices to include display stations and printers are normally attached to each control unit with coaxial cable. Under this design philosophy, every display station must be connected to a control unit before it can access a mainframe application written for a 3270 type terminal. This method of connection prevented dial-up terminals from accessing 3270 type applications, and resulted in numerous third-party vendors marketing devices to permit lower-cost ASCII terminals to be attached to 3270 networks. In late 1986, IBM introduced a new controller known as the 3174 Subsystem Control Unit. This controller, which has now replaced older models, can be used to connect terminals via standard coaxial cable, shielded twisted-pair wire, or twisted-pair wire. Other key features of the controller include an optional protocol converter that can support up to 24 asynchronous ports and the ability to be attached to Token-Ring or Ethernet local area networks. The latter is accomplished through the use of a Token-Ring or Ethernet adapter card installed in a 3174 slot, converting the 3174 into an active participant on a Token-Ring or Ethernet network.

The 3174 can support 8, 16, 32, or 64 ports. A 64-port 3174 supports a maximum of 254 LUs, while a 32-port control unit supports a maximum of 128 LUs. All other 3174 control units normally provide an LU support capability equal to four times the number of ports on the device; however, there are some exceptions, and you should examine IBM equipment specifications to determine the LU support for different 3174 models. For example, the 64-port model varies slightly from this scheme, because LU0 and LU1 are reserved on that device and unavailable for general use.

When used with a Token-Ring adapter (TRA), the 3174 was originally limited to supporting up to 140 downstream PUs (DSPUs). In 1992, new microcode extended DSPU support to 250 for a local 3174. A DSPU can be considered a gateway PC; the software on each gateway determines the number of LUs supported on the Token-Ring. For example, Novell NetWare gateway software can be obtained to provide support for 16, 32, or 97 LUs. In this type of networking configuration, shown in Figure 8.7, the communications controller polls the control unit, the control unit polls individual PU gateways, and each gateway is responsible for polling the LUs it services. In this example, the gateway PC is a downstream PU that polls downstream LUs. Although Figure 8.7 shows the connection of a

**Figure 8.7** *Using a control unit TRA to interconnect a Token-Ring network. Through the installation of a TRA, both local and remote control units provide a connection capability to a Token-Ring network.*

3174 to a Token-Ring network, a similar connection can be established to a 10BASE-T Ethernet network. To do so, you would substitute an Ethernet adapter card for the TRA in the 3174 and cable the adapter to a 10BASE-T hub port.

Since SNA's architecture is a polling structure, it is wise to limit the number of LUs on a gateway. Otherwise, the polling time from the gateway PC to the LUs—different sessions on each LAN station or the screen and printer of a workstation—can result in excessive delays. A good rule of thumb is to add another downstream PU in the form of an additional gateway for every 32 stations on a local area network.

## Terminal Displays

IBM 3270 terminals fall into three display classes: monochrome, color, and gas plasma. Members of the monochrome display class include the 3278, 3178, 3180, 3191, and 3193 type terminals. The 3278 is a large, bulky terminal that covers a significant portion of one's desk. It was replaced by the 3178, 3180, 3191, and 3193 display stations, which are lighter, more compact, and less expensive versions of the 3278. The 3279 color display station was similarly replaced by the 3179 and the 3194, which are lower cost and more compact color display terminals. The last class of display stations, the gas plasma display, consists of the 3270 flat panel display.

The physical dimensions of a 3270 type screen may vary by class and model within the class. For example, the 3178 and 3278 Model 2 display stations have a screen size of 24 rows by 80 columns, the 3278 Model 3 has a screen size of 32 rows by 80 columns, and the 3278 Model 4 has a screen size of 43 rows by 80 columns.

**Table 8.3** IBM display stations

| Model Number | Display Type | Screen (inches) |
|---|---|---|
| 3178 | monochrome | 12 |
| 3179 | color | 14 |
| 3180 | monochrome | 15 |
| 3191 | monochrome | 12 |
| 3193 | monochrome | 15 |
| 3194 | color | 14 |

Table 8.3 lists a portion of the family of terminals marketed for use with the IBM 3270 information display system. Note that the 3170 and 3180 display stations can also be used with IBM System/3X minicomputers. In addition, the 3193 and 3194 terminals can support the display of up to four host sessions when connected to the 3174 controller.

Each 3270 screen consists of fields that are defined by the application program connected to the display station. Attributes sent by the application program further define the characteristics of each field, as indicated in Table 8.4. Any technique used to enable a personal computer to function as a 3270 display station requires the PC to obtain at least the field attributes listed in Table 8.4.

## 3270 Keyboard Functions

In comparison to the keyboard of most personal computers, a 3270 display station contains approximately 40 additional keys, which, when pressed, perform functions unique to the 3270 terminal environment. Table 8.5 contains a list of the more common of these new 3270 keys.

**Table 8.4**  3270 terminal field characteristics

| Field Characteristic | Result |
| --- | --- |
| Highlighted | Field is displayed at a brighter intensity than normal intensity field. |
| Nondisplay | Field does not display any data typed into it. |
| Protected | Field does not accept any input. |
| Unprotected | Field accepts any data typed into it. |
| Numeric-only | Field accepts only numbers as input. |
| Autoskip | Field sends the cursor to the next unprotected field after it is filled with data. |
| Underscoring | Field causes characters to be underlined. |
| Blinking | Field causes characters to blink. |

**Table 8.5**  Common 3270 keys differing from most personal computer keyboards

| Key(s) | Function |
| --- | --- |
| CLEAR | Erases screen except for characters in message area, repositioning cursor to row 1, column 1. |
| PA1 | Transmits a code to the application program that is interpreted as a break signal. In TSO or CMS, the PA1 key terminates the current command. |
| PA2 | Transmits a code to the application program that is often interpreted as a request to redisplay the screen, or to clear the screen and display additional information. |
| PFnn | The 24 program function keys on a 3270 terminal are defined by the application program in use. |

*(continued)*

**Table 8.5**  Common 3270 keys differing from most personal computer keyboards *(continued)*

| Key(s) | Function |
| --- | --- |
| TAB | Moves the cursor to the next unprotected field. |
| BACKTAB | Moves the cursor to the previous unprotected field. |
| RESET | Disables the insert mode. |
| ERASEEOF | Deletes everything from the cursor to the end of the input field. |
| NEWLINE | Advances the cursor to the first unprotected field on the new line. |
| FASTRIGHT | Moves the cursor to the right two characters at a time. |
| FASTLEFT | Moves the cursor to the left two characters at a time. |
| ERASE INPUT | Clears all the input fields on the screen. |
| HOME | Moves the cursor to the first unprotected field on the screen. |

Since most, if not all, of the 3270 keyboard functions may be required for the successful use of a 3270 application program, the codes generated from pressing keys on a personal computer keyboard must be converted into appropriate codes representing 3270 keyboard functions if a PC is to be used as a 3270 terminal. Due to the lesser number of keys on a personal computer keyboard, a common approach to most emulation techniques is to use two- or a three-key sequences on the PC keyboard to represent many of the keys unique to a 3270 keyboard.

### Emulation Considerations

In addition to converting keys on a personal computer keyboard to 3270 keyboard functions, 3270 emulation requires the PC's screen to function as a 3270 display screen. The 3270 display terminal operates by displaying an entire screen of data in one operation and then waiting for the operator to signal that he or she is ready to proceed with the next screen of information. This operation mode is known as full-screen operation. It is exactly the opposite of TTY emulation, where a terminal operates on a line-by-line basis. A key advantage of full-screen editing is the ability of the operator to move the cursor to any position on the screen to edit or change data.

To use a personal computer workstation located on a local area network as a 3270 display station, you must convert the transmission codes used to position the 3270 screen and effect field attributes to equivalent codes recognizable by the PC. This means that individual workstations on the local area network must operate a terminal emulation program. This program works in tandem with the application program and communications controller, through the 3174 control unit and gateway, to enable the workstation to be recognized as a supported 3270 type terminal. In addition to gateway software, each workstation on the local area network that requires access to the mainframe must operate a terminal emulation program.

# 8.3 Gateway Options

Now that we have a basic understanding of the architecture of SNA and the components and operations of the 3270 information display system, let us turn our attention to linking local area networks to IBM and IBM-compatible host computers. First, we will expand on our knowledge of how the 3174 control unit works, and how it differs as a gateway from a PC on a Token-Ring network connected to a 3174. Next, we will examine several recent enhancements to 3174 control units that extend this device's capability to function as a gateway supporting different organizational networking requirements.

## 3174 Control Unit

As shown in Figure 8.7, the IBM 3174 control unit provides a basic mechanism for connecting a Token-Ring or Ethernet network to an SNA network. Although Figure 8.7 shows a gateway PC, in reality the gateway is optional, and is used primarily for resource management and message switching. Without a gateway, all LAN station definitions and definition changes must be performed on the mainframe. If a new user is added to the LAN, new definitions must be added to VTAM on the mainframe. Normally, such changes require a new compilation to source code macro changes and are typically performed late at night or on weekends. New users may therefore experience a delay in obtaining access to a mainframe.

Such changes are performed more readily with a gateway PC, since mainframe sessions can be allocated to LU and PU "pools." The gateway then provides a mechanism to assign new users to the pool so they can obtain immediate access to the mainframe. Unfortunately, there is no free lunch. The gateway adds a degree of processing delay that may be noticeable when an extended process, such as a large file transfer, occurs.

### Enhancements

During 1992, IBM introduced several enhancements for their 3174 control unit that extend its capability for gateway operations. These enhancements include a multi-host support capability, extended support for up to 250 downstream physical units, Advanced Peer-to-Peer Networking (APPN) support, the ability of the 3174 to serve as an Ethernet gateway, and the introduction of a group polling feature.

**Multi-Host Support** The introduction of a concurrent communications adapter capable of supporting multiple SDLC, BSC, or X.25 protocols for the 3174 formed the basis for permitting the 3174 to serve as a multi-host gateway. Figure 8.8 illustrates the use of a 3174 as a multi-host Ethernet network gateway. In this example, the 3174 provides access to a local

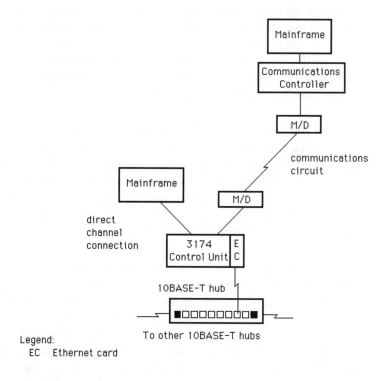

**Figure 8.8** Multi-host Token-Ring gateway. With a concurrent communications adapter, a 3174 control unit can connect LAN stations to multiple mainframe computers.

mainframe via a high-speed direct channel connection, and access to a remote mainframe via a communications circuit. The multi-host Ethernet gateway supports one direct channel and two communications circuit connections when implemented on a local control unit, and up to three communications circuit connections when implemented on a remote control unit. Regardless of the control unit used, all connections are restricted to IBM SNA mainframes.

**Extended PU Support**   The first 3174 introduced with a Token-Ring adapter supported a maximum of 140 downstream physical units. Newer 3174 control units are now capable of supporting up to 250 downstream physical units. However, not all 3174s are equal. For example, a low-cost 3174 Model 90R control unit, designed to provide a remote gateway connection to a communications controller at a data rate up to 64 Kbps, provides support for no more than 40 downstream physical units.

**Group Polling**   Understanding the performance enhancement obtainable by the support of group polling by a 3174 gateway requires a review of the method by which terminals and workstations access a host via a gateway control unit. Before group polling was available, the gateway would poll each PU on the LAN in response to polls generated by the communications controller.

To see the problem with this method of polling, picture a 3174 supporting both workstations and a group of conventional 3270 display terminals and printers via an Ethernet adapter. One PU would be assigned to the control unit to serve as a general address for the display terminals and printers that are cabled directly to the 3174. A second PU would be assigned to the Ethernet adapter. The communications controller would alternately poll each PU, and the control unit would alternately poll each group of LUs assigned to each PU.

Since a station on the Ethernet can transmit only in response to a poll, a relatively large amount of time can occur until the 3174 polls the appropriate LU with data to transmit. In the interim, the 3174 may be polling many PUs that have no data to send. Figure 8.9A shows how the Network Control Program (NCP) operating on an IBM communications controller would poll the two PUs associated with the 3174 control unit under our scenario.

Under group polling, PU addresses are assigned to each workstation downstream from the control unit, and are then referred to as *downstream physical units (DSPUs)*. The DSPUs are defined in the NCP, and the NCP issues a group poll to the control unit's PU address. For the example shown in Figure 8.9B, this would be to address PU B. When the group poll to PU B occurs, the 3174 responds by transmitting any LU data it has in storage. This enables the control unit to retrieve LU data from each DSPU and respond to the group poll by transmitting any LU data it has stored,

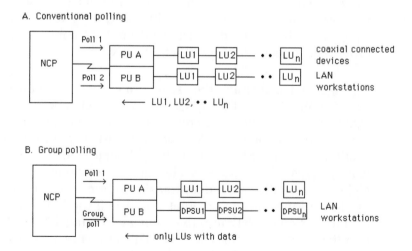

**Figure 8.9** *Conventional versus group polling.*

rather than having to wait for a specific LU poll. Group polling thus reduces the nonproductive polling cycles associated with conventional LU polling. This reduction causes an increase in the capacity of a communications line to support data transfer, and typically reduces LAN workstation response times by 10 to 20 percent.

**Ethernet Connectivity**    Until 1992, 3174 control units supported only the use of Token-Ring adapter cards, limiting direct connectivity of the 3174 to a Token-Ring network. Although IBM now provides an Ethernet adapter card for its 3174 control unit, there are alternative methods for using a 3174 to provide gateway support for Ethernet networks. These are worth examining, since we can then note some of the numerous vendor gateway construction options available for connecting different types of LANs into an SNA network.

In Figure 8.7, we saw how a Token-Ring network could be connected to an SNA network through a 3174 control unit Token-Ring adapter. A similar mixture of hardware and software can be used to connect an Ethernet/IEEE 802.3 network to an SNA network, as illustrated in Figure 8.8, in which an Ethernet card inserted into a 3174 control unit provides connectivity to an Ethernet LAN.

Figure 8.10 demonstrates the use of a gateway PC to connect an Ethernet 10BASE-T network to an SNA network. In this example, the gateway PC contains a Token-Ring adapter card for connection to a MAU and an Ethernet card for connection to a 10BASE-T wire hub. Although it may appear that the gateway functions as a bridge, it operates at a much higher level—although it does transfer information between the Token-Ring and the Ethernet network. If the Ethernet is operating Novell NetWare, the gateway PC translates LUs into IPX addresses and vice versa. This address conversion is based on configuring the gateway PC software when the gateway is installed. Since LU assignments are defined in the NCP in the communications controller, this means that the gateway installation process must occur in close coordination with NCP programmers, who encode the NCP to recognize the gateway as a downstream PU with LUs assigned to that PU. In addition, to enable stations on the Ethernet to gain full-screen access to mainframe applications, each station desiring such access must execute an appropriate terminal emulation program similar to that described for the previous Token-Ring network.

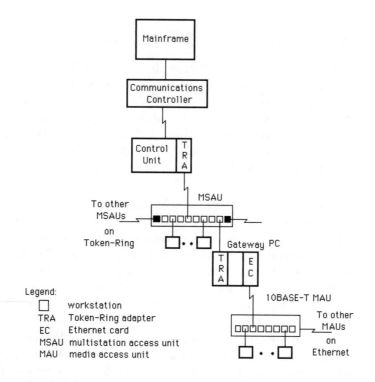

**Figure 8.10** *Using a control unit TRA to interconnect an Ethernet network. Through the installation of a Token-Ring adapter and an Ethernet card and appropriate software, the gateway PC provides a connection from a 10BASE-T network to the mainframe via a Token-Ring network.*

In the example illustrated in Figure 8.10, one vendor markets a gateway that can be configured to operate as one to eight separate PUs, with each PU capable of supporting up to 32 LUs. Since two LUs on one PU are reserved, that vendor's product provides the ability to support up to 254 LUs. This provides the servicing of up to 127 workstations that use separate LUs for screen and printer, or a lesser number of workstations that require the ability to execute multiple SNA sessions in the form of additional LUs.

## 3172 InterConnect Controller

A relatively recent addition to the family of IBM networking products is that vendor's 3172 InterConnect Controller. The 3172 can be viewed as a sophisticated local 3174 control unit gateway, because it provides access to a channel-attached host for workstations on Ethernet, Token-Ring, FDDI, and PC Network local area networks. The latter is a broadband LAN developed by Sitec for IBM during the mid-1980s.

Under the control of an InterConnect Control Program, LAN stations obtain access to a host subsystem operating TCP/IP. This enables the mainframe to provide TCP/IP functions to each connected LAN, including both static and RIP routing. In addition, the 3172 supports concurrent access to SNA and OSI subsystems. This controller can therefore support separate local area network connections via one common direct connection to the high-speed channel of a mainframe computer, such as an Enterprise system or an older S370/390. Other differences between the 3172 and a 3174 concern the number of Token-Ring network connections, the type of networks supported, and the number of DSPUs supported.

Table 8.6 compares the major features of a local 3174 to a 3172. In comparing the two devices, it becomes apparent that the 3172 is better suited for organizations that have a

**Table 8.6** Comparison of 3172 and 3174 general features

| Feature | 3172 | Local 3174 |
| --- | --- | --- |
| Parallel channel support | 2 | 1 |
| Token-Ring network support | 4* | 1 |
| Ethernet support | 4* | 1 |
| FDDI | 1* | 0 |
| PC network support | 4* | 0 |
| DSPU support | 1020** | 250 |

\* Maximum total of 4 LAN adapters.
\*\* Maximum of 255 per adapter.

number of LANs within a building where a mainframe is located. Since the 3172 supports a maximum of four LAN adapters, its use permits the replacement of four separate 3174 control units. In addition, by supporting four different types of local area networks, the 3172 provides a considerably greater level of networking gateway support than that obtainable with a 3174.

## Alternative Gateway Methods

The previous gateways used the services of a TRA or Ethernet card on a control unit, or an InterConnect Controller requiring the physical presence of a 3172 or a 3174 to connect to an SNA network. Several vendors, including IBM and third party vendors like Eicon Technology of Montreal, Canada, recognize that the additional cost of a control unit or InterConnect Controller can limit the effectiveness of that gateway method. They therefore market alternative solutions that enable different types of local area networks to access SNA networks over wide area network facilities. In the remainder of this section, we will examine several of these alternative solutions.

### SDLC Connectivity

An SDLC gateway consists of a pair of adapter cards installed in a personal computer and appropriate software to perform the required conversion from the local area network's packet format to an SNA data stream. One card is an SDLC adapter, which provides the framing for the bit-oriented protocol used by SNA. Most vendor SDLC gateways include SNA functions in ROM on the adapter card, which makes the card function as if it were a series of 3274 control units (multiple PUs), with each PU associated with a group of LUs. This second adapter is typically a Token-Ring or Ethernet adapter, used to connect the gateway to either a Token-Ring or Ethernet local area network.

Figure 8.11 shows the use of an SDLC gateway to obtain access to a communications controller via a wide area network or an extended distance cable. For the latter, the use of an SDLC gateway may permit the connection of a LAN to a communications controller via a lengthy cable within a building. This may be more attractive than using the gateway via a control unit LAN adapter whose cable distance is limited by LAN cabling restrictions.

Both RS-232 and V.35 connectors can be obtained with most SDLC adapters. Using an RS-232 connector limits the SDLC transmission rate to 19.2 Kbps, while using a V.35 connector enables digital transmission facilities at 56 or 64 Kbps to connect the gateway to the communications controller.

Some SDLC gateways are limited to support of one PU and 32 LUs. Other SDLC gateways expand considerably on that

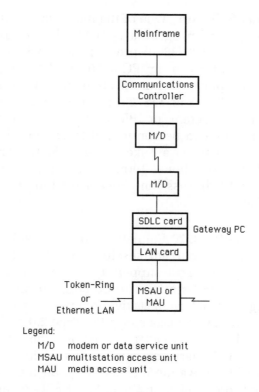

**Figure 8.11**  Using an SDLC gateway. An SDLC gateway provides access to an SNA network by providing communications between a LAN and a communications controller.

basic level of support. For example, an Eicon SNA gateway product that uses SDLC connectivity to a communications controller supports 32 PUs and up to 254 sessions. In addition, an Eicon gateway can be configured using up to four cards, and can then support a total of 128 PUs and 1,016 sessions. Of course, limiting the transmission to either 19.2 Kbps or 56/64 Kbps per card may severely restrict LAN performance during mainframe access.

**Gateway Software** One of the more commonly used gateway software programs is IBM's Personal Communications/3270 (PC/3270) program, which is a replacement for that vendor's earlier PC 3270 Emulation Program (EP). PC/3270 supports communications with LAN workstations using PC/3270 or OS/2 Extended Edition, PC 3270 Emulation Program, or IBM's 3270 Workstation Program. The gateway can be configured to communicate with an IBM SNA host via a Token-Ring or SDLC, or as an SNA Distributed Functional Terminal (DFT). Later in this chapter, we will discuss the concept behind DFT access to a mainframe.

Unlike the PC 3270 Emulation Program, which limits support to 32 concurrent sessions, a gateway using IBM's PC/3270 program can support up to 253 host sessions; it permits up to 256 stations to be configured per gateway, although only 64 can be active at any one time. The gateway appears to the host as a single PU Type 2.0 node with up to 253 attached LUs. To attached stations, the gateway appears as an SNA Primary communications device, emulating the PU and LU activation and deactivation functions that are required to establish and maintain SSCP-PU and SSCP-LU sessions between the host and the downstream workstations.

Another IBM software product worth mentioning is the OS/2 Extended Edition SNA Gateway (EE gateway). Although this program works very much like IBM's PC/3270 gateway, it adds LU pooling, which makes LU assignments considerably more efficient.

Under LU pooling, a group of LUs is allocated on a first-come-first-served basis. Since it is quite common for only a subset of users to require the simultaneous use of LU sessions—for example, by directing output to a printer—the pool of LUs can be smaller than when LUs are assigned on an individual basis. LU pooling can thus reduce the number of LUs required in the network and enable those resources, such as memory buffer areas, to be used more efficiently. This typically improves the response of a gateway to an LU request. In addition, to avoid any possible LU pool contention, OS/2 EE permits specific sessions to be dedicated and bypass LU pool contention. Another advantage of LU pooling is its ability to support more than 64 concurrently active stations: the OS/2 EE gateway places some or all of its available LUs into an LU pool and allocates those LUs when individual users request access to the mainframe.

**Gateway Configuration**    The configuration of an SDLC gateway is similar to that of most other gateways. That is, it requires the installer to make a large number of configuration decisions, and demands a prior knowledge of the SNA network to which the gateway will provide a connection. Some of the configuration parameters are related to the SDLC connection to a communications controller, while other configuration parameters govern the manner in which workstation users gain access to the SNA network through the gateway.

Examples of SDLC configuration parameters include defining the type of line connection (switched or non-switched), transmission mode (full- or half-duplex), circuit type (point-to-point or multipoint), clocking provider (modem/DSU or adapter card), the maximum information frame size, number of PUs and LUs, and the maximum window size for transmission. For an SDLC leased line connection, you would normally specify a non-switched, multipoint line. The maximum information frame size should be set to equal the MAXDATA macro definition, as defined in the Network Control Program (NCP), plus three bytes. The maximum window size is the number of frames that can be received before an acknowledgement is required; this, to a degree, governs the efficiency of the SDLC communications circuit. Conventional SDLC supports up to seven unacknowledged frames, while extended control field SDLC supports a maximum of 127 unacknowledged frames before requiring an acknowledgement. Normally, large window sizes are preferred for use on circuits that have a significant propagation delay, such as circuits established by a satellite transmission or a relatively long international circuit. Extending the window size reduces delays associated with acknowledgements that propagate in the reverse direction to transmission. This significantly increases the transmission efficiency of the line.

A second set of configuration parameters governs the manner in which the gateway functions as a control unit. Configuration parameters include the number of PUs and LUs and the manner in which LUs are allocated. Under dynamic LU allocation, the SNA gateway software maintains a list of all free LUs. When the gateway receives a request to function as an LU, one is assigned from the pool. In comparison, the direct allocation of LUs requires each station user to specify an LU number to be used. If the LU is not free, the user must then specify another LU.

## X.25 Connectivity

As previously mentioned in this chapter, SNA networks support the CCITT X.25 protocol. This support is not a standard part of an SNA network—it requires that an IBM software program known as NCP Packet Switching Interface (NPSI) be obtained and loaded as an NCP module in a communications controller. Through the use of NPSI, an IBM communications controller, such as the 3745, can be directly connected to a packet switching network. This, in turn, enables any terminal device capable of supporting the X.25 protocol to communicate with the communications controller via a packet network's transmission facilities.

To take advantage of NPSI and the use of a packet switching network as a data transport mechanism, several vendors introduced X.25 gateways. This type of gateway is also constructed through the use of adapter cards installed in the system unit of a personal computer. Typically, two or three adapter cards may be required, although the actual number is dependent on a vendor's use of ROM versus loadable software. One adapter card provides the connection to the local area network, and a second adapter card packages data into packets for transmission on the packet network. Either a third card or loadable software will make the gateway PC function as a downstream PU with LUs—in effect, as a control unit. Data from the local area network is converted into a 3270 format and encapsulated into an X.25 data stream by the gateway personal computer. That data is routed through the packet network to the IBM communications controller, where the NPSI port converts the datastream back into the 3270 format created by the gateway PC. Figure 8.12 shows the operation of an X.25 gateway.

One of the major advantages of an X.25 gateway is its ability, through of the use of packet switching, to support multiple logical connections inherently over a single physical connection. This means that one SNA X.25 gateway can be used to provide a connection to multiple IBM host computers connected to a packet network. Since each host computer requires a PU definition, this also means that there is a practical limit of 32 concurrent connections that are obtainable through the use of an X.25 gateway.

Figure 8.13 shows a single SNA X.25 gateway used to support multiple logical connections via a single physical link—in this example, to two SNA host computers. Software used for the support of multiple logical connections is referred to as *X.25 Qualified Logical Link Control (QLLC)*, and must operate on the gateway as well as on each IBM communications controller.

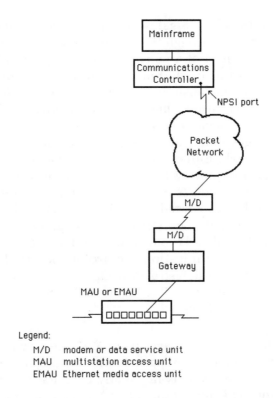

```
        Mainframe

     Communications
       Controller
                        NPSI port

          Packet
         Network

            M/D

            M/D

          Gateway

 MAU or EMAU

       000000000
```

Legend:

M/D   modem or data service unit
MAU   multistation access unit
EMAU  Ethernet media access unit

**Figure 8.12**   X.25 gateway operation. An X.25 gateway converts LAN packets into a 3270 data stream and encapsulates the data into X.25 packets for transmission through a packet network.

As with an SDLC gateway, the major constraints of an X.25 gateway are its operating rate, throughput, and PU and LU support. The operating rate of an X.25 card is limited to 64 Kbps; however, its throughput may be considerably less than that of an SDLC gateway operating at the same data rate. This is because the X.25 gateway not only packets data, adding additional overhead, but also has its data checked as it flows through the packet network. The additional delays due to the error checking performed at packet switches can add between 0.25 and 0.5 seconds to

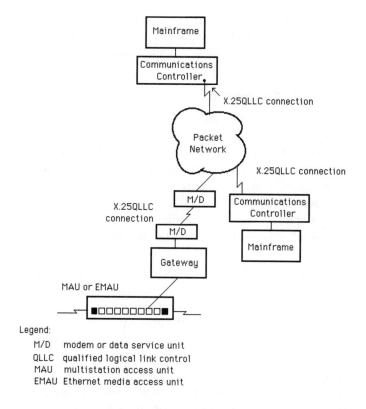

**Figure 8.13** *Supporting multiple logical connections.*

the response time of network users. However, one NPSI port can provide support for more than one X.25 gateway connected via a packet network to the mainframe location. In comparison, each SDLC gateway requires the use of a separate SDLC port on the communications controller. Therefore, the decision to use SDLC or X.25 gateways must consider the cost of using a public network versus building a network. There is also a trade-off between performance and hardware cost in the form of additional communications controller ports. Since an X.25 gateway encapsulates the functions of an SDLC gateway into X.25

packets, it should come as no surprise that their PU and LU support should be the same. This appears to be true for all vendor products examined by the author.

## The TIC Connection

Using a Token Interface Coupler (TIC) installed in a communications controller provides a gateway access method very similar to that of a control unit with a TRA. That is, the TIC is cabled to an MAU port, and one or more gateway PCs are also cabled to an MAU port. However, as the name of the TIC implies, it supports only the direct attachment of a Token-Ring network. At the time this book was written, there was no such hardware as an Ethernet interface coupler.

The primary differences between the use of a communications controller TIC and a control unit TRA are in the areas of connection method, cost, network interconnection distance, operating rate, and PU and LU support.

Although a TIC provides a direct connection for a Token-Ring network, it cannot be used similarly to provide connectivity for an Ethernet network. Instead, you would have to connect an Ethernet network via a Gateway PC to a Token-Ring MSAU, with the MSAU in turn cabled to a TIC.

A TIC can cost well over $10,000. In comparison, a TRA costs under $2,000. The use of a TIC restricts access to the LAN cabling distance, since the communications controller must be cabled to an MAU under lobe length distance restrictions. A local control unit, on the other hand, can be connected via coaxial cable to a communications controller. This enables the gateway distance to be extended. If a remote control unit is used, that device functions similarly to a remote communications controller, since both the TRA and the TIC cabling distances to an MAU are governed by lobe distance restrictions.

In a local environment, the communications controller and control unit are both channel-attached to a host computer, and their data transfer capabilities are similar. In a remote environment, the transmission rate of a control unit is restricted to a maximum of 56 Kbps. A remote communications controller can operate at T1/E1 data rates, providing over 20 times the data transfer capability of a control unit. Thus, the TIC can provide a higher level of throughput when used at a remote location.

The biggest difference between using a TRA or Ethernet card and using a TIC is in the area of PU and LU support. The NCP on a communications controller can support up to 9999 PUs for a TIC. Each gateway PC functioning as a PU will support a grouping of LUs based on the gateway software used. Another key difference between using a TRA or Ethernet card and using a TIC concerns the method of gateway communications.

When a control unit LAN adapter provides a connection to the Token-Ring or Ethernet network, the communications controller polls the control unit, the control unit polls each downstream PU, and each gateway polls its LUs. When a TIC is used, each downstream PU requests service from the TIC by using a dial-up service. This can considerably reduce the polls flowing on an attached local area network. As a result, the TIC can theoretically support up to 9999 PUs.

## 3278/9 Coaxial Connection

A rather outdated and limited function gateway is based on the use of a 3278/9 coaxial adapter card. Instead of emulating a 3X74 control unit like SDLC and X.25 gateways, the coaxial adapter permits a gateway PC to be connected to a port on a 3X74 control unit. That port can be configured as a distributed function terminal (DFT) port. When used in this manner, the DFT port provides access to five sessions, because it represents five LUs. Gateway software then divides the five SNA mainframe sessions among contending workstations on the local area network. This means that a coaxial adapter–based gateway is limited to providing a maximum of five simultaneous host sessions. As with the other gateways described in this section, a Token-Ring or Ethernet adapter card would be installed in the gateway to provide a connection to the local area network. Figure 8.14 shows the hardware used to provide a 3278/9 coaxial cable gateway.

Legend:

    DFT    distributed function terminal
    MSAU  multistation access unit
    EMAU Ethernet media access unit

**Figure 8.14** 3278/9 coaxial connectivity. Through the use of a 3278/9 coaxial adapter card, LAN card, and a DFT port on a control unit, up to five LAN workstations can access an SNA network simultaneously.

Although a coaxially connected gateway is limited in its session support, it operates at coaxial cable data transfer rates to the control unit. If a local control unit is used, the operating rate of a coaxially connected gateway can approach 2 Mbps. In comparison, SDLC and X.25 type gateways are limited to a 56 Kbps data transfer rate. Coaxially connected gateways can provide a high level of SNA access performance for small local area networks when such networks are at the mainframe location. In addition, this method eliminates the necessity of obtaining a TIC, TRA, or Ethernet card, and can be used with older 3274 control units that cannot support the installation of a LAN adapter. Thus, the coaxially connected gateway also represents the lowest cost gateway.

# CHAPTER 9

# Managing the Network

In this chapter, we will turn our attention to several products that enhance the management of local area networks. First, we will examine the use of *hubs*, which may enhance our ability to reconfigure network topology, test selected portions of a network, and obtain a variety of statistics concerning the operation of our network. Next, we will turn our attention to a product that can be used both to determine the current state of your network and initiate action that can prevent potential problems from occurring. To expand on our knowledge of network management provided by intelligent hubs, we will consider the use of several products for managing Ethernet networks. Although our discussion is limited by space constraints to only a few products, the concepts presented are applicable to the use of any network management tool. Thus, readers without access to a specific product mentioned in this chapter should be able to use a similar product in the manner described to manage their networks.

# 9.1 Intelligent Hubs

As we noted earlier, every Ethernet 10BASE-T network contains a minimum of one hub. The hub operates as a multiport repeater, receiving signals from any device connected to it and repeating the signal at its full strength.

As the number of stations on an Ethernet 10BASE-T network expands, a hub will eventually run out of ports. Expanding the network successfully requires the use of another hub, with one hub connected to another to form a bus structure. The process by which hubs are connected to one another is commonly referred to as *cascading*. Figure 9.1 shows the cascading of three hubs, each capable of supporting eight devices, resulting in the support of a total of 24 devices.

Although most hubs are capable of being rack mounted, most 10BASE-T hubs consist of an individual chassis. In addition, the installation of two or more hubs into a rack requires the cabling of one hub to another in a cascading manner to form a bus structure. To facilitate the installation of multiple hubs, vendors developed a device commonly referred to as a *concentrator*.

**Figure 9.1**   *Cascading hubs. The process by which hubs are connected to one another to form a bus is commonly referred to as* cascading.

## Concentrators and Hubs

An Ethernet 10BASE-T concentrator is a special type of hub: it has a built-in expansion capability that eliminates the need to install cascaded hubs as your network grows, if you desire that such growth be controlled from a centrally located wiring closet. A concentrator consists of a chassis to which you add module boards. Depending on the manufacturer, module boards may contain one or more ports. Some of the more common concentrators support up to 100 Ethernet 10BASE-T connections, with two additional connections reserved for special use. One connection is typically reserved to connect a personal computer or workstation running network management software, while the other reserved port connection allows diagnostic test equipment to be attached to the network without requiring a port serving an existing device. The backplane of the concentrator serves as a cascaded cable, and the insertion of module boards makes it relatively easy to expand the number of ports to accommodate a growing network.

A hub or conventional concentrator treats all network devices as equals. That is, each device is cabled to a port to obtain access to the network.

## Hub Cards

Hub cards provide an alternative architecture to standalone hubs and concentrators. First brought to market by Novell, hub cards are designed to turn a personal computer into a network hub. Using a Novell hub, you can integrate a hub function into a NetWare server, enabling the Novell software operating on the server to provide a network management capability. In comparison, standalone concentrators and other types of hubs that provide network management support typically require the use of a separate personal computer to initiate network management operations.

## Advantages of Use

In our introductory discussion of hubs, we alluded to a few of the advantages of their use. Now, let us focus in some detail on the advantages of using hubs by examining the capabilities of different hub configurations. In our discussion of the use of different hub configurations, we will actually refer to the use of intelligent hubs. Thus, we should first differentiate between intelligent and nonintelligent hubs.

## Intelligent vs. Nonintelligent Hubs

An intelligent hub is a hub with a built-in microprocessor designed to perform certain predefined functions. Those functions may include recognizing commands to turn ports on and off, obtaining statistics concerning the utilization level of different ports, displaying those statistics and the status of defined ports or groups of ports, permitting network traffic to be viewed from a control console, and facilitating diagnostic testing. In addition, certain types of intelligent hubs provide you with the ability to integrate different types of local area networks because they support the use of bridge and router modules. The modern intelligent hub is thus a building block for the construction of an enterprise network.

## Single Hub/Single LAN

A single hub used to support the connectivity requirements of users on a single LAN is one of the most common types of hub applications. Note that in using the term "hub," we are now excluding the conventional 10BASE-T hub from consideration. For the remainder of this chapter, we will restrict our use of the term "hub" to refer to an intelligent device with a built-in microprocessor capable of responding to predefined commands. For simplicity, we will refer to the intelligent hub as a hub; however, our discussion is also applicable to an intelligent concentrator.

The top portion of Figure 9.2 shows, from a physical perspective, the use of a 10-module hub to establish a four-station Ethernet 10BASE-T network. Here, the remaining six modules can be used to expand the network, provide spare connections, and connect test equipment or a network management console to the network. The lower portion of Figure 9.2 illustrates a logical view of the 10BASE-T network established through the use of the hub. So far, this is no different from the results obtained from a dumb hub, so you may be wondering what advantages there are to using intelligent hubs.

With most intelligent hubs, you can turn port traffic on and off with the simple click of a mouse, drag icons representing stations to reposition devices on a ring, or remove a

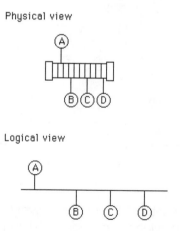

**Figure 9.2**  *Single hub/single LAN configuration.*

station from the ring for testing without disrupting traffic from stations remaining on the ring.

Figure 9.3 shows the physical and logical view of using an intelligent hub to isolate station D from the Ethernet 10BASE-T network and then test the adapter board in that station without disrupting traffic on the network. Note that in comparing Figure 9.3 with Figure 9.2, the use of an intelligent hub enables test equipment to be cabled to any available port module on the hub. Then, the intelligent hub enables the user to create a test logical bus–based network, which is used to connect test equipment to the station to be tested. This capability to separate one network into two or more logical segments derives from the ability of the backplane of the hub to transfer data at a rate significantly beyond that of a LAN. This enables the creation of two or more separate LANs within the hub by the multiplexing of separate LAN transmissions over time.

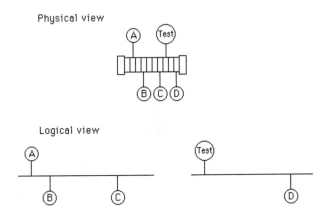

**Figure 9.3**  Ethernet 10BASE-T testing. Many intelligent hubs permit users to logically subdivide the network, enabling test equipment to be used without adversely affecting the operation of stations not being tested.

The ability of intelligent hubs to generate network statistics and segment a 10BASE-T network into multiple networks provides LAN administrators and network managers with a powerful performance measurement tool. When network utilization increases to the point where collisions becomes excessive, you will more than likely use an intelligent hub to segment an existing network. This provides you with the ability to balance traffic between workstations and from workstations to one or more servers.

## Multiple Hubs/Single LAN

Figure 9.4 shows how an intelligent hub can be used to segment a saturated Ethernet 10BASE-T network. The top

**Figure 9.4**  Multiple hub/multiple LAN configuration. A saturated Etnernet 10BASE-T can be segmented into two or more networks to increase performance.

portion of the illustration shows the physical view of the multiple hubs that may be necessary to obtain the required number of ports for constructing a large 10BASE-T network. In this example, it was assumed that each hub module is capable of supporting four ports. The interconnection of two 10-module hubs thus permits up to 80 devices to be connected to a single 10BASE-T network. For some hubs, the connection of one hub to another requires the use of a port on each hub, reducing the maximum number of devices that can be serviced by two 10-module hubs to 78.

The lower portion of Figure 9.4 illustrates the logical view of the network before and after the ring is segmented. In this example, it was assumed that as a result of a review of traffic statistics, we decided to segment the network so that 19 stations are located on one segment and 18 stations are located on the other segment. By adding a network interface card to the server, we can connnect that device to both networks. If the server supports bridging operations, internetwork connectivity between workstations on each network is obtained. Otherwise, if internetwork communication is required and the server cannot provide this capability, you can probably obtain a bridge module that can be inserted into a hub.

Two additional configurations available with intelligent hubs that warrant discussion are single hub/multiple LAN and multiple hub/multiple LAN configurations.

## Single Hub/Multiple LAN

With a sophisticated backplane design, most intelligent hubs support networks using different protocols, topologies, and types of wiring. When bridge and router modules are available for insertion into a hub chassis, you can not only support multiple LANs from a single hub, but also enable stations on one LAN to communicate with stations on another LAN, located even hundreds or thousands of miles from the hub.

The top portion of Figure 9.5 shows from a physical perspective the use of a single hub to support multiple LANs. The lower portion of the figure shows the logical view, in which Ethernet and Token-Ring networks are supported through a common hub. With a bridge module installed in the hub, you can obtain an inter-LAN communications capability. In addition, the filtering capability built into most intelligent hubs provides you with a mechanism to control the flow of information between LANs, as well as between any LAN segments you may wish to create. This

**Figure 9.5**  *Single hub/multiple LAN configuration.*

capability provides you with another mechanism to manage an enterprise network through the network management system of an intelligent hub.

### Multiple Hub/Single LAN

The fourth configuration obtainable through the use of intelligent hubs is an extension of the previously discussed single hub/single LAN configuration. That is, multiple hubs used to construct a single LAN can provide you with alternative network testing and control locations if you locate hubs in different areas within a building or throughout a college campus. For example, you could locate an intelligent hub in the wiring closet on each floor of a building and cable each hub together to form a building-wide network. In reality, as your network expands, you will probably subdivide your network, based on the number of stations located on each floor and use bridge modules inserted in the hub to connect each network.

## Network Management

One of the most important features of an intelligent hub is the ability of many vendor products to provide a network management capability. Obtaining an appreciation for the functionality of a hub's network management capability requires that we examine the operation of a product. In doing so, we can view some of the typical screens generated by a specific vendor product. In concluding this section, we will examine the Fibermux LightWatch network management system to demonstrate the management capabilities of many intelligent hubs.

### Fibermux LightWatch

The Fibermux LightWatch network management system is a window-based product that supports the point and click

**Figure 9.6** LightWatch network topology display obtained by selecting the Hierarchy option.

operations of a mouse. To illustrate its capability, let us assume our network consists of three hubs connected to one another in a triangular manner. By selecting the program's Hierarchy option, we can display our network topology as illustrated in Figure 9.6.

The Fibermux LightWatch network management system permits users to obtain a detailed physical view of each hub, including the modules installed. This is illustrated in Figure 9.7, which shows the physical view of hub A. Note that this view immediately tells an observer that two modules are unused—they are represented by blank panels in the hub. Thus, a simple point and click operation can provide a wealth of information about the modules and the capacity of each hub in our network.

**Figure 9.7** Viewing the physical layout of hub modules.

**Statistics and Alarms** One of the key features of LightWatch is its ability to generate and display a variety of statistics, both on a composite hub basis and for individual ports on each hub. In addition, LightWatch provides users with the ability to assign thresholds to different measurements and generate alarms when those thresholds are exceeded.

Figure 9.8 illustrates the port statistics display screen generated for hub A in our network. Figure 9.9 illustrates the alarm display screen for hub A. Note that the latter permits you to set the threshold values for six events, and to assign a major or minor alarm to a threshold event when a threshold value occurs or is exceeded. By carefully monitoring the statistics generated by LightWatch, and by setting appropriate thresholds, you can enhance the control of

**Figure 9.8**   LightWatch port statistics screen.

your network to the point where you can actually manage the network, instead of just responding to user complaints. Intelligent hubs provide you with the ability to be pro-active rather than reactive in controlling your network.

# 9.2 Network Management Tools

In our discussion of intelligent hubs in the first section of this chapter, we briefly examined the network management capability of a specific vendor product. Our primary focus of attention was on the use of a hub for network manage-ment, and our discussion was essentially limited to the sta-tistics and alarm generating capabilities of one product designed to work with a specific hub. In concluding this

**Figure 9.9**   LightWatch alarm screen.

chapter, we will expand on our knowledge of network management by briefly examining its main functional areas and the major activities associated with each area. This will form a foundation for our examination of two popular software products that perform most of the major activities associated with network management.

## Network Management Functions

There is a core set of five functions associated with network management. Those functions are configuration, performance, fault, accounting, and security management. Each functional area manages a set of activities.

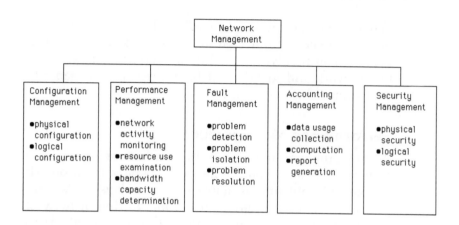

**Figure 9.10** Network management functional areas.

Figure 9.10 illustrates the functional areas commonly associated with network management and the set of activities managed by each area.

## Configuration Management

The process of configuration management covers both the hardware and software settings required to provide an efficient and effective data transportation highway. Thus, configuration management consists of managing the physical hardware—including cables, computers, and network adapters—along with the logical network configuration governed by the installation of the network operating system, the selection of a network protocol or stack of protocols, and the manner in which users can access server facilities. The latter concerns the setup of the network, including permissions and routings that enable users to access different servers. Although this may appear to involve security management, it is primarily focused on the setting and distribution of network passwords and the assignment of file permissions. Thus, logical configuration management permits a user to reach a network facility once he or she is connected to the network, while security management involves the ability of a user to gain access to the network and to different facilities made available by configuration management.

## Performance Management

Performance management involves those activities required to ensure that the network operates in an orderly manner without unreasonable service delays. This functional area is concerned with the monitoring of network activity to ensure there are no bottlenecks to adversely affect network performance.

Monitored network activity can include the flow of data between stations and between stations and servers; the use of bridges, routers, and gateways; and the utilization of each network segment with respect to its total capacity. By performing these tasks, you will obtain information that will enable you to adjust the use of network hardware and software, as well as to consider a variety of network segmentation options that can eliminate potential network bottlenecks before they occur.

## Fault Management

Networks have their less desirable moments in which components fail, software is configured incorrectly, and other problems occur. *Fault management* is the set of functions required to detect, isolate, and correct network problems.

A large number of hardware and software products are now marketed to provide a fault management capability for cables, hardware, and network software. The most common type of diagnostic device is a *time domain reflectometer*, which generates a pulse and uses its reflected time delay (or absence of a reflection) to isolate cable shorts and opens. LAN protocol analyzers allow you to test individual Ethernet adapters, and to monitor network performance and isolate certain types of network problems, such as jabbering. Both hardware-based LAN protocol analyzers and many software products provide a LAN frame decoding capability. This helps you determine whether the flow of frames and frame responses provides an insight into network problems. For instance, a station might be rejecting frames because of a lack of buffer space, which could easily be corrected by reconfiguring its software.

## Accounting Management

Accounting management is a set of activities that enables you to determine network usage, generate usage reports, and assign costs to individuals or groups of users by organization or by department. Normally, the network operating system provides a raw set of network usage statistics, and you will need one or more other software packages to generate appropriate reports and assign costs to usage. While cost assignment is commonly used in wide area networks and for electronic mail usage, it is not commonly used to distribute the cost of using local area networks. Instead, accounting management is normally employed to answer such questions as, "What would be the effect on the network if the engineering department added five new employees?" In this situation, accounting management data might provide you with network usage statistics for the engineering department, including total department usage as well as individual and average station usage data. Using these statistics in conjunction with performance monitoring, you could then determine the probable effect of the addition of new employees to the network.

## Security Management

As discussed in our overview of configuration management, security management involves primarily the assignment of network access passwords and access permissions to applications and file storage areas on the network. Other aspects of security management involve the physical placement of stations in areas where access to those stations is restricted, and the selection and control of specialized hardware and software security products. These products can range in scope from programs used to encipher and decipher electronic mail messages to network modems that can be programmed to perform a series of operations: prompt users for a code when they dial into the network, disconnect the user, and then dial a number predefined as associated with the user code.

Most network management products provide excellent coverage of a subset of the five core functional areas, but few products actually cover all functional areas. Most users will normally consider the use of two or more products to perform all five network management functions. In the remainder of this chapter, we will examine the use of software products marketed by Triticom of Eden Prairie, MN, and by Frye Computer Systems of Boston, MA. These products can be used to manage Ethernet networks.

## Triticom EtherVision

One of the more popular Ethernet monitors is a program marketed by Triticom of Eden Prairie, MN, under the trademark EtherVision. This program is designed to operate on a workstation, and must be used with a specific type of Ethernet/IEEE 802.3 adapter—a Novell NE/2, NE1000 or NE2000, a 3Com Etherlink II, a Western Digital EtherCard, or a Pure Data PDI8023, PDI 8023-16 or PDUC8023. At the time this book was written, EtherVision supported 14 adapter cards and Triticom was in the process of adding program support for additional vendor adapter cards. Only the workstation executing EtherVision requires a specific Ethernet/IEEE 802.3 adapter card; all other workstations, servers, and other devices on the network can use any vendor adapter card. EtherVision's rationale for requiring a specific vendor's adapter card is based on the necessity to write software that accesses MAC layer buffers in the adapter, so that the program can read frames transmitted on the network. These frames form the basis for numerous network-operation statistics generated by the program.

## Main Menu

The starting point for the use of EtherVision is the program's main menu. This menu contains a list of eight actions; these can be selected either by pressing the first letter of the listed options or by moving a highlight bar over an action and pressing the Enter key.

Options you can select from the main menu enable you to perform a variety of operations:

- monitor network traffic
- enable and disable a variety of alarms
- assign names, alarms, and filters to station addresses
- enable and disable network event logging
- test the cable connected to the workstation's adapter
- control the configuration options of the program
- generate different types of reports
- quit to DOS

By examining the use of several program options, we can obtain an appreciation for how EtherVision can assist you in managing your network.

## Traffic Monitoring

By selecting the Monitor Traffic option from the program's main menu, you can monitor either source or destination addresses on a real-time basis. Figure 9.11 shows the screen display when the monitoring of source addresses is selected. As indicated, the display consists of five distinct areas.

The top bar across the screen in Figure 9.11 shows both the date and time when monitoring began and the current time. The main area of the display lists the source addresses of stations identified on the network and the number of frames counted for each station. At the time this screen display was printed, EtherVision was in operation for 40 seconds and had identified 22 stations on the network. Although station addresses are shown in Figure 9.11 in hexadecimal format, by pressing the F2 key you can toggle the station address dis-

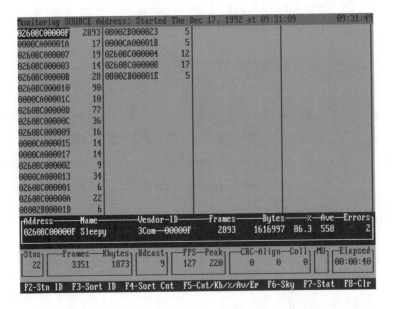

**Figure 9.11** EtherVision source address monitoring.

play to its logical name or the vendor-adapter address. The highlighted bar over the top source address indicates that information about that address is displayed in the third area on the screen display, which shows the hexadecimal address, logical name, and vendor-ID for the address highlighted. Note that in the first 40 seconds of monitoring, the station named "Sleepy" was anything but, accounting for 86.3 percent of all network traffic. If the network utilization continued to be relatively high for a long monitoring period and some users complained about poor response time, you would probably want to determine what the user with the logical name of Sleepy was doing. Perhaps a one-time download of a large file occurred and there is no cause for alarm.

The fourth area of the screen shown in Figure 9.11 provides summary information concerning all stations that have been identified. Here, we see 22 stations were identified, and together they transmitted 3351 frames and 1873 K of information. A total of nine frames were broadcast to all stations, and the frames per second (FPS) and peak frames per second activity were 127 and 220, respectively. During the monitoring period there were no CRC errors, frame alignment errors or collisions, nor were there any missed or unprocessed (MU) frames.

A missed or unprocessed frame typically results from data arriving too fast for the adapter to keep up with network traffic. This normally occurs when one or more stations on the network are active and request a file transfer. The network may be dedicated to carrying the traffic of only one or a few stations, and its traffic-carrying capacity results in the arrival of data at the station faster than its adapter can remove the data from the network.

The last area of the display shown in Figure 9.11 indicates the function keys and their assignments, and enables you to select different action options. For example, pressing the

F2 key changes the display of identified network adapters to logical names or a vendor-ID display format, while pressing the F8 key clears the display and resets all counters and the elapsed time to zero.

### Skyline Displays

To obtain detailed information about network utilization, you would press the F6 key from the traffic monitoring display. This provides you with the ability to view the program's skyline display of network utilization and the frames per second carried by the monitored network.

Figure 9.12 shows the EtherVision skyline display of network utilization, and Figure 9.13 shows the skyline display with respect to the frames-per-second rate of data flow

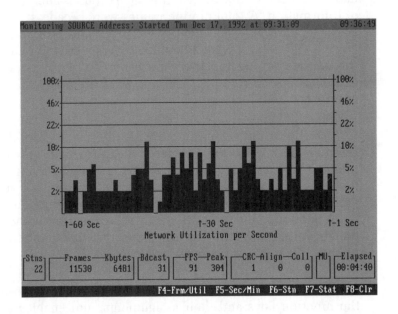

**Figure 9.12**   EtherVision Network Utilization skyline display.

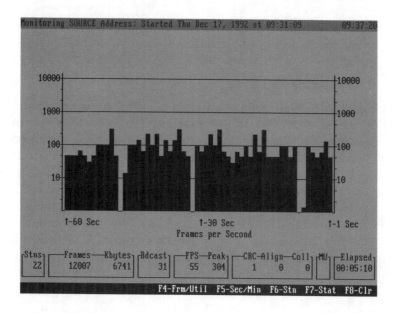

**Figure 9.13**  EtherVision Frames per Second skyline display.

on the network. In examining Figure 9.12, note that the display shows intervals for a 60-second monitoring period. By pressing the F5 key, you can change the monitoring period of the display to one hour—a more realistic period for examining network utilization. Since the network utilization in Figure 9.12 only slightly exceeded 10 percent, if this low level of utilization continued for a longer period of time it would indicate that you could expand your network through the addition of workstations before considering the use of bridges to subdivide the network.

The frames-per-second display shown in Figure 9.13 provides you with a general indication of traffic flow on your network. However, by itself this display does not provide you with meaningful information, because it does not indicate the average frame size nor the distribution of frames by their length. This information can be obtained by pressing the F7 key to generate the program's statistics screen.

## Statistics Display

Figure 9.14 illustrates the display of EtherVision's Statistics screen. Note that this screen provides you with summary information concerning frame counts, distribution of frame sizes, network utilization, and frame errors. Also note that in the Frame Counts window, the average computed frame size is displayed, while the Frames Per Second window displays the average and peak frames per second monitored on the network. By using this data, you can compute and verify the data in the Network Utilization window and compute the effect of adding additional workstations to the network. For example, the peak frames per second rate is 304 for 22 stations, or approximately 14 frames per second

**Figure 9.14** EtherVision Statistics display.

per workstation. Adding 10 workstations with similar operational characteristics to existing workstations can be expected to increase the network traffic flow by 140 frames per second. Since the average frame size is 561 bytes, 10 additional workstations can be expected to result in 561 bytes × 8 bits per byte × 140 frames per second, or less than 630,000 bps of network traffic.

## Alarms

The key to the effective management of a network is the ability to generate alarms when important predefined events occur. EtherVision provides network administrators with the ability to generate several key alarms, without which you would have to monitor several screens constantly. You can avoid this cumbersome process by using the program's Network Alarms/Options screen, illustrated in Figure 9.15.

**Figure 9.15**  EtherVision Network Alarms/Options screen.

The Network Alarms/Options screen illustrated in Figure 9.15 allows you to enable or disable five alarms and to set the threshold value for three alarms. When an alarm is enabled and the event occurs or an alarm threshold is exceeded, the alarm status will be displayed on the top line of any EtherVision screen you are using, as well as being written to the program's Network Event Log.

The network idle time alarm will be triggered when EtherVision senses no traffic for the specified period of time. Since NetWare file servers periodically transmit IPX frames to make servers aware of each other, a Novell-based Ethernet LAN will always have at least some traffic at periodic intervals. Thus, the occurrence of a network idle time alarm can inform you of a serious network problem, such as the failure of a server or a faulty adapter in the computer operating EtherVision.

The network utilization alarm allows you to determine whether your network is approaching or has reached a level of saturation that warrants its subdivision. Normally, a utilization level that periodically exceeds 50 percent on an Ethernet/IEEE 802.3 network indicates a level of use that warrants the subdivision of the network and its connection via a bridge.

The frame error alarm goes off when it reaches a specified number of frame errors. Since the error rate on a LAN is typically 1 in a billion bits, or $1 \times 10^{-9}$, you can use this alarm to determine whether your network has an acceptable error level. To do so, you would view the Statistics screen when a frame error alarm occurs to determine the number of bits that have been transmitted during the time it took until the frame error alarm was generated. With this information, you could determine whether your LAN's bit error rate (BER) is at an acceptable level. For example, assume the total number of frames in the frame count window in the Statistics display was 100,000,000 when the frame error count reached 100 and generated an alarm. Also assume, for simplicity, that the average frame size in the Statistics display was 1000 bytes. An average of 100,000,000/100, or 1,000,000 frames, flowed on the network for each frame error. Since we assumed that each frame has an average length of 1000 bytes, 1,000,000 frames × 1000 bytes per frame × 8 bits per byte, or 8,000,000,000 bits, are transmitted per frame error. This is equivalent to a BER of 1/8,000,000,000, or $1.25 \times 10^{-8}$, which is about what we would expect from a LAN that performs well, and that has properly connected cables routed a safe distance from sources of electromagnetic interference.

The alarm count interval can be used to generate an alarm when enabled and set to a specific time period. Then, if the number of frame errors specified by the frame error alarm occurs within the specified alarm period, an alarm frame count interval alarm will go off.

The intruder detection alarm operates by triggering an alarm when a new station enters the network that was not defined to the program by the assignment of a logical name. When we examine the Station Options screen, we will see how logical names are assigned to each station address. The last alarm shown in Figure 9.15 is Source Addr = Broadcast Alarm. Since all source addresses must be unique, this alarm occurs when a source address with its broadcast bit set is detected.

## Station Options Display

Through EtherVision's Station Options display screen you obtain the ability to assign names, filters, and alarms to specific hardware adapter addresses. Figure 9.16 illustrates the display of the program's Station Options screen.

**Figure 9.16**    EtherVision Station Options display.

In examining Figure 9.16, note that the highlighted bar is positioned over the top address, which was previously assigned the logical name "Sleepy." In this example, we are in the process of changing the station's name to "Dumbo." By moving the highlight bar over different station addresses and/or pressing appropriate function keys, you can control the assignment of names, alarms, and filters to stations. For example, F2 permits you to add or change a name, F3 prompts you to delete the name currently selected by the highlight bar, and so on. When assigning names, you can specify a filter (Ftr) for each station. Then, during monitoring, only those stations marked for filtering will be displayed on the program's monitoring screen. For a large network, filtering enables you to examine groups of stations, such as the accounting department's workstations. In addition to station filtering, you can use the Station Options display to set an idle alarm from 1 to

9,999, an error alarm of 1 to 9,999, and a usage alarm based on a percentage of network activity for each station. Thus, you can use the Station Options display to isolate a problem condition on a specific station or group of stations.

### Network Event Logging Display

Figure 9.17 illustrates EtherVision's Network Event Logging screen. From this screen, you can enable and disable the logging of events to the program's log file and select the logging of error frames and peak utilization data. In addition, from this screen you can view the event log.

Figure 9.18 displays a portion of the network event log, which can be scrolled through a window on your display. Since we previously enabled the logging of both frame errors and peak utilization, the contents of the log reflect

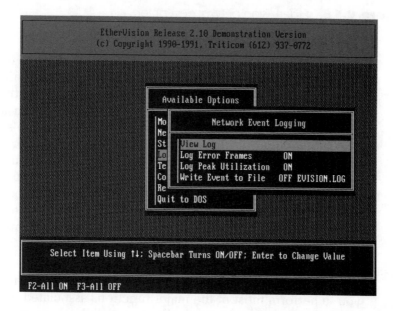

**Figure 9.17**  EtherVision Network Event Logging screen.

**Figure 9.18**  EtherVision network event log.

both types of activities. In examining Figure 9.18, note that "Frame Short" refers to any frame shorter than the minimum length of 64 bytes—a condition usually caused by a collision. Although collisions normally occur on an Ethernet/IEEE 802.3 network, a situation in which one station has a large number of collisions associated with its transmission may indicate a faulty adapter. Thus, from an examination of Figure 9.18 it appears that the adapter used on the station whose logical address is "Sleepy" may be in need of an awakening action, during which the adapter is tested, and if it continues to generate short frames, replaced.

As indicated by our short review of EtherVision, it permits you to perform most of the major functions associated with network management. Regardless of which management tool you use, you should always ensure that you have one available. The periodic use of an appropriate network management tool provides you with a detailed view of network activity, which can be invaluable in performing your network management functions.

## NetWare Management

While EtherVision provides you with a detailed view of your network's traffic and utilization of bandwidth, it overlooks one important component of your network. That component is your server. Since a large majority of Ethernet and IEEE 802.3 networks are based on Novell's NetWare operating system, we will focus our attention on NetWare management in this section, examining a software product from Frye Computer Systems of Boston, MA, as well as a built-in capability of Novell NetWare to provide a view of your network server. The first product provides detailed information about the operational characteristics of the file servers in your network, and the second product provides a more limited view of the server in some areas while providing additional information concerning certain server software characteristics.

### Frye Utilities for Networks

NetWare Management is more fully known as the Frye Utilities for Networks, which name probably served as the rationale for the selection of the executable program name of FUN. Running under DOS, or as a DOS session under Windows 3.X, Netware Management is easy to install; it fully supports Novell NetWare 2.1+ and 3.1+.

Once loaded, NetWare Management provides you with the ability to use 11 program modules, ranging in scope from detailed information about your file server to such trivial information as the version of NetWare you are using. The program includes a NetWare Loadable Module (NLM), which consists of hooks into NetWare that gather the appropriate information a NetWare file server computes. The FUN module then sends messages to the NetWare extracted parameters to provide you with a detailed insight into your Novell network.

Since the best way to illustrate the utility of a program is to take a look at some program module screens, let's do so.

**Server General Display** Figure 9.19 shows the General display screen of the program's server module. Note that the right side of the screen shows a graph of server utilization, defined as the fraction of CPU time for which the file server is doing productive work. Although this graph and several of the data elements and their values listed in the

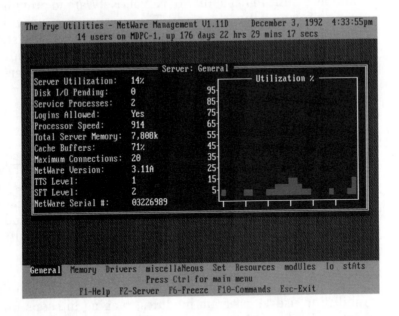

**Figure 9.19** Frye Utilities Server General display.

left part of the screen can be extremely valuable in isolating performance problems, utilization is unfortunately shown only for the past 30 seconds on the graph. In addition, the value of several of the listed performance parameters on the left portion of the screen is displayed almost in real time but is not accumulated over time. For example, Disk I/O Pending shows the number of disk operations that are currently in the server's queue. A large number indicates a high level of disk activity, and if the number stays relatively high for a long period of time, it tends to indicate that server performance could be improved by the replacement of your current hard disk with another that has a faster access time.

Because the program is unable to log utilization statistics over a long period of time, you will probably want to run this program periodically during the busiest hour of the day. For most organizations, the hour in which peak network usage occurs is typically the hour preceding lunch, or around 3 to 4 PM on a Tuesday or Thursday. Through the periodic monitoring of server and network utilization statistics, you will be able to determine whether an undesirable level of performance is due to the bandwidth constraints of network cabling and adapter cards or to the capability of the server. For example, monitoring of the network might indicate a network utilization level of 10 or 15 percent, but you might be receiving complaints from users concerning network performance. By using the Frye Utilities for NetWare, you might determine that the server utilization level is 60 to 70 percent, indicating that an improvement in overall network performance could be accomplished by either adding an additional server or obtaining a faster platform for server software to operate upon. Alternatively, you might want to increase RAM in the server if further investigation indicates that paging of modules and the time delay associated with paging are causing poor network response.

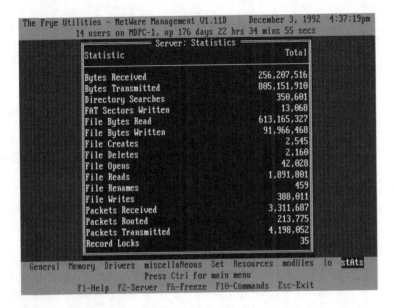

```
The Frye Utilities - NetWare Management V1.11D    December 3, 1992  4:37:19pm
           14 users on MDPC-1, up 176 days 22 hrs 34 mins 55 secs
                        ═ Server: Statistics ═
  Statistic                                       Total

  Bytes Received                               256,207,516
  Bytes Transmitted                            805,151,910
  Directory Searches                               350,601
  FAT Sectors Written                               13,068
  File Bytes Read                              613,165,327
  File Bytes Written                            91,966,468
  File Creates                                       2,545
  File Deletes                                       2,160
  File Opens                                        42,028
  File Reads                                     1,891,801
  File Renames                                         459
  File Writes                                      388,011
  Packets Received                               3,311,687
  Packets Routed                                   213,775
  Packets Transmitted                            4,198,052
  Record Locks                                          35

  General  Memory  Drivers  miscellaNeous  Set  Resources  modUles  Io  stAts
                          Press Ctrl for main menu
               F1-Help  F2-Server  F6-Freeze  F10-Commands  Esc-Exit
```

**Figure 9.20**   Frye Utilities Server Statistics display.

**Server Statistics Display**   Figure 9.20 illustrates the Frye Utilities Server Statistics display screen. At first glance this display may appear to represent no more than a simple accumulation of server statistics, and you may feel that, while interesting, such statistics are of limited value. However, the statistics displayed can be very valuable when combined with knowledge about your server's directory structure and other information. For example, the ratio of file reads to directory searches can indicate whether network users are familiar enough with your server's directory structure to make efficient use of the files on the server. A low ratio probably indicates that network users are having difficulty finding the files they need, in which case you may wish to consider rearranging or renaming directories, or publicizing your server's directory structure and the contents of each directory.

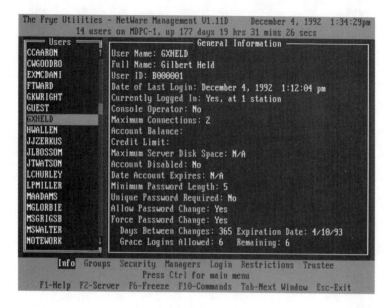

**Figure 9.21** Frye Utilities General Information screen of Users module.

**User Program Module** Figure 9.21 illustrates the General Information screen of the program's Users module. The left portion of the screen allows you to move the highlight bar over each network user name; the right portion of the screen displays information about the selected user name. By moving the highlight bar, you can easily view general information about each network user, and using the left and right arrow keys permits you to access the Groups, Security, and other Users module screens. While most of the displays generate interesting information, this information is normally known to the network administrator and is not earth-shattering by any means. Where Frye Computer's NetWare Management excels is in the comprehensive series of reports that it can generate and that you can direct to your screen, printer, or disk.

```
The Frye Utilities - NetWare Management V1.11D     December 3, 1992  5:12:55pm
              12 users on MDPC-1, up 176 days 23 hrs 10 mins 22 secs

┌────────────────────────────────────────────────────────────────────────┐
│ Select Report                                                  Report #  │
│                                                                          │
│ Weekly System Maintenance Report                              FUN121     │
│ Weekly System Maintenance Report - Annotated                  FUN122     │
│ System Exception Report                                       FUN123     │
│ System Exception Report - Annotated                           FUN124     │
│ Disk Utilization Summary - By Volume                          FUN131     │
│ Disk Utilization Summary - By User                            FUN132     │
│ Disk Utilization Summary - By Utilization                     FUN133     │
│ Disk Utilization Detail - By Directory                        FUN141     │
│ Node Statistics Report                                        FUN221     │
│ Node Statistics Report - Annotated                            FUN222     │
│ Node Statistics Exception Report                              FUN223     │
│ Node Statistics Exception Report - Annotated                  FUN224     │
│                                                                          │
│                                                                          │
│                                                                          │
└────────────────────────────────────────────────────────────────────────┘
                        Press Ctrl for main menu
           F1-Help  F2-Server  F6-Freeze  F10-Commands  Esc-Exit
```

**Figure 9.22**   Frye Utilities Select Report screen of Report module.

**Program Report Capability**   Figure 9.22 illustrates the Select Report display of the program's Reports module, and Figure 9.23 illustrates the Select Configuration Report display of the program's Configuration module. As you will note from the names of the reports listed in the two displays, you can generate a rather large number of reports to provide information about server resources, disk usage, workstation and server network statistics, and about the setup of your NetWare file server.

To illustrate the potential value of the program's report capability, we will select the Node Statistics Report from Figure 9.22, directing the report to our display.

Figure 9.24 displays one screen of the resulting Node Statistics Report, showing only a portion of the SPX statis-

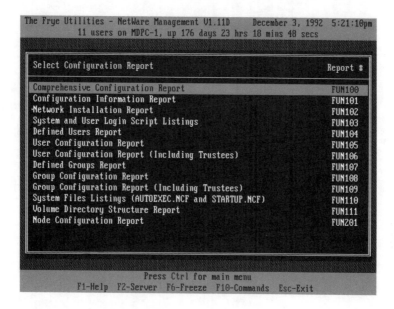

**Figure 9.23**   Frye Utilities Select Configuration Report screen of Configuration module.

tics and then all of the IPX statistics for one workstation. A large number of packets lost because of a lack of available Event Control Blocks (ECBs) normally indicates a potential network slowdown. More seriously, a number of malformed ECBs probably indicates an application that does not use direct IPX calls properly.

One of the best features of Frye Computer's NetWare Management is its manual's comprehensive reference section. If you have fought your way through Novell manuals, you'll find the Frye reference section refreshing: it defines and explains most NetWare terms in alphabetical order. In fact, it's probably quite worthwhile to read the manual's reference section, because it explains NetWare parameters and the effect of their settings on your network's performance.

```
The Frye Utilities - NetWare Management V1.11D    December 3, 1992  5:15:07pm
            12 users on MDPC-1, up 176 days 23 hrs 11 mins 30 secs

┌─────────────────────────────────────────────────────────────────────────┐
│12/03/92              NODE STATISTICS REPORT                     Page 1↑   │
│ 5:14:26pm              File Server MDPC-1                        FUN221    │
│                                                                           │
│                                  COUNT     % TOTAL     ERROR              │
│                               ──────────  ─────────   ───────             │
│Node Type:  Workstation                                                    │
│Node Address:  0000AAA1:10005A1C233F                                       │
│Time Since IPX Loaded:  3 days 5 hrs 24 mins 20.6 secs                     │
│Current LOGIN Name:  HPLASERJETII-209                                      │
│IPX Statistics:                                                            │
│  Packets Received              66,675                                     │
│  Packets Transmitted           57,019                                     │
│  Packets Lost (No ECBs)         4,899        7%       *****               │
│  Route Not Found Errors             0        0%                           │
│  Listen ECBs Posted            61,807                                     │
│  Malformed ECBs                     0        0%                           │
│  Peak/Maximum Open Sockets       9/20                                     │
│  Open Socket Failures               0                                     │
│SPX Statistics:                                                            │
│  Send Packet Requests             101                                   ↓ │
└─────────────────────────────────────────────────────────────────────────┘
      F1-Help  PgUp PgDn Home End Tab Shift-Tab ←↑↓→ Esc-Exit Report
```

**Figure 9.24**   A portion of the Node Statistics Report directed to the screen.

## The NetWare Monitor

One of the programs included in NetWare is the MONITOR, which operates on the server console or on a workstation with the NetWare RCONSOLE command. Although this program is no substitute for a comprehensive network management system, it does provide a significant amount of information that can facilitate the management of your network. Thus, in concluding this chapter we will focus our attention on the use of this NetWare program.

**NetWare Monitor Main Screen Display**   Figure 9.25 illustrates the main screen display resulting from loading the NetWare MONITOR program. The first line in the top window indicates how long the file server has been in operation. Note that in the left portion of the top window, server

**Figure 9.25**    NetWare Monitor main screen display.

utilization is shown numerically. Unlike the previously described Frye Computer NetWare utility program, which displays utilization over a small period of time, the MONITOR program indicates utilization on a real-time basis. Similarly, other information displayed by the MONITOR program is also displayed on a real-time basis.

The top window in Figure 9.25 displays information about fast computer memory (cache buffers) used to store information normally kept on disk, service processes, connections, and other operations. Service Processes encompass such tasks as a read or write. The higher this number, the busier the server—a large number normally indicates a high utilization level. The Connections in Use parameter simply refers to the number of workstations that are logged into the network; however, these users may be performing only local workstation functions, so this number does not provide an indication of network activity. The Open Files parameter indicates the number of files on the server that users have opened. Like the Connections in Use parameter, this information does not indicate a direct level of performance, since a user could open a file and then go to lunch.

The lower window shown in Figure 9.25 contains a menu of options you can select through the use of the MONITOR program. You can select an option by moving the highlight bar over an option and pressing the Return key. For example, pressing the Return key when the highlight bar is over Disk Information results in a screen display similar to the one illustrated in Figure 9.26.

**Figure 9.26**   Server Memory Statistics display.

**Server Memory Statistics Display**    The top window shown in Figure 9.26 displays specific information about the use of your server's memory. The lower window provides specific information about a variety of NetWare resources. In this example, we moved the highlight bar over REMOTE.NUM: AES Events. It was assumed that we wanted to obtain information on a NetWare Loadable Module (NLM) named "REMOTE." When you press the Enter key, the lower portion of your display changes, as shown in Figure 9.27. In examining the contents of the lower window labeled "Resource Information," note that it informs us that a NetWare asynchronous event scheduler (AES) event resulted in one remote console being in use. This tells us that one workstation is functioning as a remote console. If you are the Network Administrator, this information might be of considerable value, because the Remote Console user has very similar capabilities to the

**Figure 9.27**    Obtaining information as a resource.

NetWare Supervisor with respect to the functions and network control he or she can perform. By selecting different resources, you can display other information about NetWare resources on a real-time basis. Understanding the top window in boths Figure 9.26 and 9.27, labeled "Server Memory Statistics," requires a degree of knowledge concerning NetWare terminology and operations. For example, the Alloc Memory Pool (allocate memory pool), which currently represents just 2 percent of server memory, may appear small. However, NetWare uses this memory area for storing small objects for short periods of time, and expands it automatically from the total server memory as needed. The cache buffers indicate the amount of server memory currently used as disk cache buffers. Although the percentage will vary, if it falls below 25 percent of server memory, it will significantly degrade server performance or even cause the server to crash. Thus, this parameter should be monitored as an indicator of whether server memory requires expansion. In this example, it obviously does not require expansion.

The movable memory area is used for large, dynamically allocated objects. Objects placed in this memory area can be moved to provide larger amounts of contiguous memory for tables, such as File Allocation buffers that expand dynamically. In comparison, nonmovable memory is an area used for loading NLMs into memory and allocating large memory buffers that do not change in size. Since server resources like the MONITOR are initiated by loading an NLM, nonmovable memory may require expansion if too many NLMs require simultaneous operation. For example, Frye's NetWare Management program represents another NLM which, when loaded, uses nonmovable server memory.

**LAN Driver Information**   Perhaps one of the more valuable groups of data obtainable from the Available Options menu is under the LAN Information option. This option displays a window labeled "LAN Driver Information," which lists the LAN drivers active on your server, such as Ethernet or Token-Ring drivers. Next, selecting an appropriate driver displays a new window containing a series of LAN driver statistics, from which you can obtain specific information about the operation of one or more LANs connected to a Novell NetWare server. To illustrate the wealth of information, let us assume that you are using Novell's 3C503 Ethernet LAN driver. Table 9.1 lists 10 of the 27 statistics you can obtain from Novell's 3C503 LAN driver.

The Reset Count increments each time a hard transmit error, bad network error, or a hardware receive mismatch occurs and the network board is reset to a known state. A large Reset Count may indicate an adapter card problem.

The Carrier Sense Lost Count increments when the transmitter on the card loses the carrier. This condition occurs when the cable connection to the network is lost. If this count periodically increases, it may indicate a loose cable.

**Table 9.1**  Novell 3C503 LAN driver statistics

- Reset Count
- Carrier Sense Lost Count
- Enqueued Sends Count
- Excess Collisions Count
- Receiver Missed Packet Count
- Total Collisions Count
- Transmit Timeout Count
- Underrun Error Count
- Number of Ethernet 802.2 Packets Received
- Number of Ethernet 802.3 Packets Received

The Enqueued Sends Count increments each time the driver cannot transmit a packet and is thus forced to place the packet in a queue until the transmitter is available. A large count indicates network congestion.

When a collision occurs on a network board or in the cabling, the Excess Collisions Count is incremented. A large number of collisions may indicate that network traffic is too heavy to be efficiently carried, or that nodes are spaced too far from one another. The latter condition expands the length of the collision window, and may indicate a need to recable a portion of the network.

When a packet is addressed to a network board that cannot accept it because of a full receive buffer, the Receiver Missed Packet Count is incremented. Some adapter cards include the ability to select different size receive buffer areas. If the Receiver Missed Packet Count is high, you may wish to consider expanding the receive buffer area on your adapter card if that card has that capability.

The Total Collision Count increments in tandem with each network collision. When this count increases rapidly, it indicates a very high level of network activity. If the count increases rapidly only during short periods of time, it indicates that you may wish to consider splitting your network.

The Transmit Timeout Count is incremented each time the network card interrupts the file server with a "send bit" lost message. This indicates the occurrence of a hardware problem resulting from faulty cabling, a malfunctioned adapter card, or a missing terminator.

The Underrun Error Count can be considered the inverse of the Enqueued Sends Count. That is, the Underrun Error Count increments when the buffer on the adapter card is full, and the card cannot accept additional packets until the buffer is serviced and cleared.

The last two counts listed in Table 9.1 indicate the number of MAC and LLC packets. By comparing these two counters, you can determine the relationship between information and control frames flowing on the network.

## Summary

As indicated by our review of the operation and utilization of three management tools, the ability to determine the operational state of your network may require the use of more than one product. Vendor products, like people, do some things better than other things and may not do certain performance-related tasks at all. Since the health of a network depends on the capability of the wiring infrastructure and adapter cards to transfer information, as well as the ability of the server to process information requests, you will more than likely require the use of separate products to examine each network performance area. Otherwise, the examination of one area may provide you with misleading information about the actual level of performance of your network.

# CHAPTER **10**

# The Future
# of Ethernet

When a book is devoted to a well-defined technology, it is always important to discuss the future of that technology. This is especially true with respect to Ethernet, since many readers are employees of organizations that have invested or plan to invest tens to hundreds of thousands of dollars or more in acquiring network adapter cards and hubs, installing cabling, obtaining software, and teaching employees to use a network operating system. Thus, a logical question readers may have involves the safety of their current or planned investment in Ethernet technology. That is, what can you expect in the evolution of Ethernet technology, and will the introduction of new technology result in the obsolescence of your existing or planned Ethernet network? Although there is no simple answer to this multifaceted question, since the effect of technological advances is highly dependent on organizational communications requirements, we can examine trends in networking and Ethernet technology. This will provide us with a foundation of knowledge from which we can express some general observations about a previous or planned investment in an Ethernet network.

# 10.1 Ethernet Trends

In attempting to project the future of Ethernet, we should consider a variety of variables in addition to technological developments. Some of the major variables we must consider are the cost of technology, the performance it provides, and the potential to use existing technology in a more productive manner. The latter may minimize or reduce a requirement to migrate to new technology. In this section, we will focus our attention on the cost and performance of existing and evolving Ethernet technology, deferring an examination of new technology until the next section.

## Network Adapter Card Cost

Just a half-dozen years ago, the average price of an Ethernet adapter card was approximately $1,000, while the cost of a personal computer was between $3,000 and $4,000. Excluding the cost of cabling and a network operating system, an Ethernet adapter card represented an approximate 25 to 33 percent increase in the cost of a personal computer. By 1993 you could acquire an Intel 486-based personal computer with 4 M of RAM, SVGA support, and an SVGA monitor for approximately $2000. At the same time, the average cost of an Ethernet adapter card was under $100, so the additional cost to network a personal computer was only approximately 5 percent of an organization's hardware budget. Clearly, the cost of obtaining an Ethernet network communications capability was extremely nominal by mid-1993.

## Future Price Direction

Not only has the cost of Ethernet hardware significantly declined over the past few years, but advances in chip fabrication technology indicate that price declines are far from being over. In 1992 Zenith Data Systems introduced several notebook computers with a built-in Ethernet communications capability on the computer's motherboard. Additional computer manufacturers now provide a built-in Ethernet networking capability for their products, enabling portable computer users to simply plug a 10BASE-T jack into their computer's plug upon return to the office to obtain access to the corporate network.

According to several trade press articles, by 1995 the inclusion of an Ethernet chip set on nonportable personal computers will add less than $20 to the cost of the computer, and will make an Ethernet networking capability on personal computers as pervasive as the inclusion of a parallel port. In comparison, alternative network adapter cards, such as Token-Ring and Fiber Data Distribution Interchange (FDDI), are expected to range in cost from $300 to $400 for a 16 Mbps Token-Ring adapter to $600 to $750 for an FDDI adapter. Ethernet can thus be expected to continue to hold a significant cost advantage over competing local area network adapter cards. This should extend the use of Ethernet networks far into the foreseeable future.

## Network Performance Considerations

At the time this book was written, there was one set of Ethernet-based standards promulgated by the IEEE in which the maximum data rate was 10 Mbps. Although that maximum data rate is relatively slow in comparison to the 100-Mbps FDDI operating rate, and to the proposed 100-Mbps "Fast Ethernet" discussed later in this chapter, a logical question readers may wish to ask themselves is whether they need a 100-Mbps local area network to satisfy their current and future data transmission requirements. Even if the answer is yes, this answer, as we will soon note, may not mean that your previous investment in Ethernet technology is obsolete.

## Supplementing an Existing Network

To demonstrate how more modern and higher operating rate local area network technology can be used to supplement existing Ethernet equipment, let us assume that your organization previously installed a series of Ethernet networks on floors within a building, using 10BASE-T bridges and wiring through floor risers to interconnect users on each "floor"-based network. Under this networking scenario, it is quite possible that the initiation of a file transfer operation by two or more network users accessing a server on a third network via a 10BASE-T bridge would adversely affect other internet transmission until the file transfer operations are completed.

To see this potential for internet congestion, consider Figure 10.1, in which three "floor" LANs are connected with three 10BASE-T bridges wired together, perhaps using the riser within the building. Let us assume that stations A and C initiate file transfers to the server $S_n$ located on network C. If each network operates at 10 Mbps, the traffic offered to the middle bridge is 20 Mbps. However, since each network operates at 10 Mbps, the best performance possible for the middle bridge is to route the file transfer data at 10 Mbps to the server. Now suppose that station D on network B attempts to access the server S on network C. Frames generated by that station must contend with frames generated by workstations A and C for service

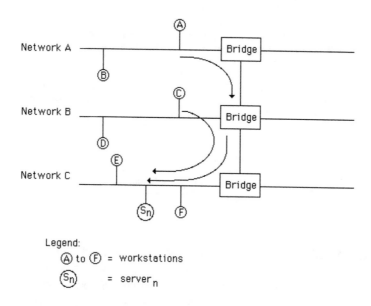

Legend:
Ⓐ to Ⓕ = workstations
Ⓢₙ = serverₙ

**Figure 10.1**    Potential for internetwork congestion. The initiation of file transfer operations from two or more workstations to a server on a third workstation can create network congestion.

by the bridge. It is thus quite possible for interactive queries, as well as file transfer operations across networks, to be adversely affected by existing file transfer operations.

**Using a Backbone Network**    Although one potential solution to internet congestion is to install new networks capable of supporting higher data transfer operations, doing so might require both new adapter cards and new network wiring. A far less expensive potential solution to internet congestion is to use a higher operating rate local area network to serve as a backbone net.

Figure 10.2 shows the use of an FDDI backbone network to interconnect the three previously installed Ethernet net-

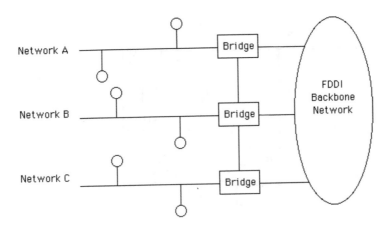

**Figure 10.2**   Using a high-speed backbone network. The use of a 100-Mbps FDDI network as a backbone to connect separate Ethernet LANs can remove a large degree of potential internet congestion while permitting the previous investment in Ethernet networks to be maintained.

works. Since the FDDI network operates at 100 Mbps, its use is equivalent to a high-speed interstate highway linking country roads together. That is, inter-LAN traffic is facilitated by a high-speed backbone LAN in the same manner that inter-road traffic is facilitated by an interstate highway. Once a frame is bridged onto the FDDI network, it flows at 100 Mbps, enabling more frames to be carried between linked local area networks per unit time than possible when a 10BASE-T or a Token-Ring network is used as a backbone network.

## Using Enhanced Adapter Cards

One of the key limits to the ability of a workstation to transfer large quantities of data is the type of network adapter card used in a workstation. A typical low-cost Ethernet adapter card may have a data transfer rate of only 200,000 to 400,000 bytes per second. Such adapters are capable of transmitting and receiving data at only approximately 10 to

20 percent of the transfer rate of a 10BASE-T network. While this transfer rate is usually more than sufficient for most client–server operations, it becomes a bottleneck for long file transfers and for devices such as bridges, routers, and gateways that may require a higher transfer rate capability. The selective use of enhanced Ethernet adapter cards may provide you with the ability to increase network performance and reduce or eliminate network bottlenecks.

Two types of Ethernet adapter cards you may wish to consider for workstations that have a large amount of file transfer operations or for bridges, routers, and gateways are bus mastering and parallel processing adapter cards.

**Bus Mastering Cards**　A bus mastering card is designed to perform I/O data transfers directly to and from the memory of the computer in which it is installed. To accomplish this, a bus mastering card includes circuitry known as a *direct memory access (DMA)*. The adapter card can initiate a DMA transfer, which permits data to be moved directly to or from memory, while the processor on the adapter card performs other operations. The net effect of bus mastering is to increase the transfer capability of the adapter card by 50 to 100 percent.

**Parallel-tasking Cards**　Standard Ethernet adapter cards perform networking operations in a fixed sequential manner. Although a bus mastering adapter permits memory access operations to be performed in parallel with some network operations, greater efficiencies are obtainable with the use of parallel-tasking Ethernet adapters. One such adapter is Etherlink III, manufactured by 3Com Corporation, which has the capability to transfer data at approximately 500,000 bytes per second.

To demonstrate the efficiency of parallel-tasking, the top portion of Figure 10.3 shows the operation of a pair of

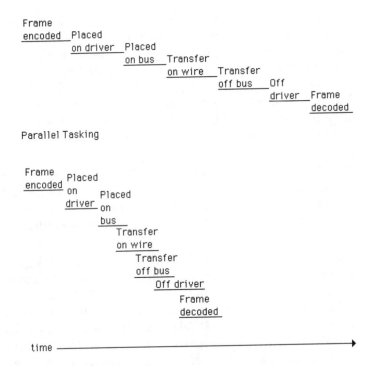

**Figure 10.3** Serial-tasking versus parallel-tasking Ethernet adapters. The use of parallel-tasking Ethernet adapter cards permits the overlapping of many operations, thus reducing the time needed to transfer information and increasing the data transfer capability of the adapter.

standard Ethernet adapters used to transmit and receive data. As indicated, each operation has to be completed before the next can be begun.

The lower portion of Figure 10.3 shows the tasks performed for the transmission of information between two parallel-tasking Ethernet adapter cards. As noted by the time chart, the performance of many tasks in parallel reduces the time required to transfer information, which enhances the transfer rate of the adapter card.

## Multimedia and Video Separation

Throughout 1993 you probably noted a considerable number of articles about the use of multimedia and video image applications on local area networks. What most of these articles had in common was the fact that the data transfer capability of Ethernet and Token-Ring networks could not support more than one or a few users simultaneously accessing the multimedia and video image applications that reside on a server, nor could it support the transfer of images between workstations. Thus, these articles typically went on to discuss the need for newer technology, such as FDDI II and the so-called "Fast" Ethernet, intended to operate at 100 Mbps to provide local area network users with the ability to network multimedia and video image transfer applications.

Before discussing "Fast" Ethernet, let's focus our attention on multimedia applications, the equipment required for multimedia, and the cost associated with migrating to a higher network operating rate. *Multimedia* is the integration of video—either still or full motion—with audio and text, designed primarily to facilitate the education and learning process of computer users. The primary application of multimedia in a corporate environment will probably be training.

**Hardware and Cost Considerations**   The upgrade of a personal computer to a multimedia-compatible computer typically involves the addition of a CD-ROM drive, a pair of speakers, and a sound board, as well as appropriate software. Although the placement of multimedia applications on a server through the attachment of a CD-ROM drive permits many network users to share both the use of a common CD-ROM drive and the application in the form of a CD-ROM disk, is doing so on a network cost-effective or technically practical?

You can acquire an internal CD-ROM drive for approximately $200, or an external drive for perhaps $50 to $100 more. Since a multimedia workstation still requires a sound card and a pair of speakers, placing the computer on a network saves money only in the use of a common CD-ROM player and CD-ROM disks. The license cost of permitting a number of users to access a common CD-ROM disk on a network may result in a savings of $50 to perhaps $100 per user over the cost of purchasing individual CD-ROM disks. However, the cost associated with purchasing a 100-Mbps adapter card, without considering the cost of new network cabling, is approximately $600 to $1,000. Unless there are numerous applications to be shared, the economics involved in supporting multimedia applications are such that it will usually be more economical to run such applications on multimedia-equipped computers than to share a common CD-ROM drive and set of applications on a network.

**Image Transfer Considerations**    A second area of technological evolution usually encountered in articles touting the need for higher speed local area networks is the requirement of many workstation users to transfer images. Computer-aided design engineers, real estate office workers, passport control officers, and personnel office workers are but a few examples of people who can be expected to gain from the ability to transfer images via a local area network. However, the frequency with which such workers transfer images and the effect of a few seconds' delay on the image display are two issues you may wish to consider before rushing out to replace an Ethernet network.

To see why the answers to the previously posed questions are important, let us consider a real estate office where the sales associates take several pictures of each home listing, and then have those pictures digitized and loaded onto the network server. At any particular time, a 20-agent office probably has a handful of agents and customers in the office. Thus, the frequency of image transfer from the server to an agent's desktop computer can be expected to follow an individual user pattern—unlike a training environment, where a number of network users access network resources simultaneously. Although the transfer of images on an Ethernet network places a heavy load on the network, in a real estate office environment this will probably not cause network bottlenecks like it would if the images were routed between networks.

Suppose that a group of four or five agents and their clients walked into the office at the same time and started examining the MLS listing and displaying pictures of property on their computer screens. Since the individual agents would be asking questions of their potential clients at their own pace, the simultaneous transfer of images could be expected to be low. Would a delay of a few seconds in displaying the picture of a home cause the loss of a potential client? We can probably state safely that for many working environments, Ethernet would be an acceptable network for the transfer of still images. Even if Ethernet were found to be lacking, instead of replacing the network adapter card on all stations on the network, you might wish to consider installing a new network to support only those workstations that require a video transfer capability. Then, you could bridge the two networks together and maintain your investment in your previously installed Ethernet network.

# 10.2 Fast Ethernet

*Fast Ethernet* is a term used to represent a proposed 100-Mbps extension to the IEEE 802.3 standard. Although fast Ethernet was among the hottest communications topics at trade shows and in trade literature during the first half of 1993, whether fast Ethernet can be considered a derivative of Ethernet remained to be seen.

At the time this book was written, work had begun by the IEEE 802.3 committee on a new standard to provide a 100-Mbps operating rate for Ethernet networks. Although this new network's data rate is equivalent to FDDI and to a new FDDI capability over copper wire (CDDI), fast Ethernet is designed to provide adapter cards that are approximately double the cost of 10-Mbps Ethernet adapter cards. Two additional design elements agreed to by vendors are the same star topology used in 10BASE-T networks and the same frame format used by the existing 802.3 standard. The latter will enable existing 10BASE-T and other types of Ethernet networks to be connected to a proposed fast Ethernet network via inexpensive converters that have memory buffers sufficient in size to handle operating rate differences between networks. Although there are vendor agreements about the topology and frame format for fast Ethernet, the same cannot be said about the proposed access method and type of wiring.

## Proposed Technology

After a series of IEEE 802.3 committee meetings, vendors were divided into two major camps with opposing technical views concerning the access method and type of wiring proposed for fast Ethernet.

### New Signaling Methods

LAN Media Corporation, 3Com Corporation, Grand Junction Networks, Synoptics, and several other vendors were backing the use of new signaling techniques that would permit the retention of the CSMA/CD MAC protocol. One signaling technique proposed by LAN Media Corporation and backed by 3Com, Synoptics, and Sun Microsystems involves the use of a coding scheme known as 8B6T. It is designed to operate on level 3 (voice-grade) and level 5 (data-grade) unshielded twisted-pair wiring, using a two-pair wiring scheme for data-grade wire and a four-pair wiring scheme for voice-grade wire. A second signaling technique, proposed by Grand Junction, is based on MLT-3 coding, in which three voltages are used to represent values of 0, +1, and −1. This encoding scheme requires the use of level 5 UTP two-pair wiring, and also permits the retention of the CSMA/CD protocol.

## The 100BASE-VG Proposal

The second fast Ethernet camp is based on a proposal from AT&T Microelectronics and Hewlett-Packard Company, backed by Banyan Systems, Novell, and Microsoft. Known as 100BASE-VG—a 100-Mbps transmission rate over unshielded twisted-pair voice-grade wire—this proposal involves the use of a new data access method known as Demand Priority Access. The 100BASE-VG proposal also differs from Ethernet, and from the other fast Ethernet proposals, in its proposed signaling method and wire use.

The joint AT&T Microelectronics Hewlett-Packard proposal for fast Ethernet is based on the use of all four pairs of wires in 10BASE-T wiring to transmit or receive, rather than one pair to transmit and one to receive. The use of four pairs of wires permits the use of quartet signaling, permitting each pair to operate at a 25-MHz signaling rate to produce a 100-Mbps network operating rate. Unlike 10BASE-T and other versions of Ethernet that use the CSMA/CD protocol, 100BASE-VG is a hub-based scheme in which a node transmits a packet over four wires to a hub. The hub acknowledges data and directs it to its appropriate destination. The hub responds to workstation-initiated transfer demands, hence the term "Demand Access Protocol."

The primary advantage of 100BASE-VG is the fact that because it uses four wires to split a 100-Mbps signal, it enables the attainment of a high data rate that can operate on voice-grade cable, and that is expected to meet FCC regulations. However, the use of a new access protocol, combined with a different signaling method and use of four wires, results in a considerable difference from Ethernet. This may result in conversion problems between Ethernet and fast Ethernet networks that may be expensive to resolve.

Although we can expect fast Ethernet to be a reality in the near future and to provide a 100-Mbps data transfer capability, we can question its applicability to our needs in the same manner in which we questioned the necessity for FDDI, CDDI, and other high-speed local area networks. That is, we have to ask whether we have a requirement for a 100-Mbps local area network, what the cost will be for establishing that type of network, and what alternatives we can explore—for instance, using fast Ethernet as a backbone network, or removing network users with high data transfer requirements onto a separate network—before deciding to acquire new equipment or perhaps install new wiring. Answering these questions will determine the applicability of new technology to your existing and planned Ethernet networks.

# Index